Creating Church Online

Online churches are Internet-based Christian communities, pursuing worship, discussion, friendship, support, proselytization and other key religious goals through computer-mediated communication. Hundreds of thousands of people are now involved with online congregations, generating new kinds of ritual, leadership and community and new networks of global influence.

Creating Church Online constructs a rich ethnographic account of the diverse cultures of online churches, from virtual worlds to video streams. This book also outlines the history of online churchgoing, from its origins in the 1980s to the present day, and traces the major themes of academic and Christian debate around this topic. Applying some of the leading current theories in the study of religion, media and culture to this data, Tim Hutchings proposes a new model of religious design in contexts of mediatization and draws attention to digital networks, transformative third spaces and terrains of existential vulnerability. *Creating Church Online* advances our understanding of the significance and impact of digital media in the religious and social lives of its users, in search of new theoretical frameworks for digital religion.

Tim Hutchings is a postdoctoral researcher in the Institute for Media Studies at Stockholm University, Sweden. He is a sociologist of digital religion, and his research has included studies of online churches, digital Bibles, evangelism and pilgrimage. His current work focuses on death, grief and memory in digital environments, as part of the Existential Terrains research program (et.ims.su.se) funded by the Knut and Alice Wallenberg Foundation, the Marcus and Amalia Wallenberg Foundation and Stockholm University. He is the editor of the *Journal of Religion, Media and Digital Culture* (jrmdc.com).

Routledge Research in Religion, Media and Culture

Edited by Jolyon Mitchell, David Morgan, and Stewart Hoover

Creating Church Online
Ritual, Community and New Media

Tim Hutchings

Routledge
Taylor & Francis Group

LONDON AND NEW YORK

First published 2017
by Routledge

2 Park Square, Milton Park, Abingdon, Oxfordshire OX14 4RN
52 Vanderbilt Avenue, New York, NY 10017

*Routledge is an imprint of the Taylor & Francis Group, an informa
business*

First issued in paperback 2019

Library of Congress Cataloging-in-Publication Data
A catalog record for this book has been requested

ISBN: 978-0-415-53693-6 (hbk)
ISBN: 978-0-367-33345-4 (pbk)

Typeset in Sabon
by Apex CoVantage, LLC

Contents

Acknowledgements

This book was made possible by the warm and generous welcome I received from the communities and leadership teams of four churches: Church of Fools (later renamed St Pixels), i-church, the Anglican Cathedral of Second Life and Church Online. I am grateful to all of them for their time and friendship, and in a few cases, for some really good arguments.

I began my research under the patient and incredibly helpful supervision of Dr Mathew Guest in the Department of Theology and Religion at Durham University (UK). My doctoral project was funded by the Arts and Humanities Research Council. My thesis was examined at viva by Professor Gordon Lynch and Dr Pete Phillips, and our conversations set me on the long journey that has ended (for the time being) with the volume in front of you.

I have discussed my work on digital religion at conferences around the world, but three societies have been particularly valuable for my thinking: the BSA Socrel Study Group, the Nordic Network on Media and Religion and the International Society for Media, Religion and Culture. The fingerprints of their methods and ideas are all over this book, if you know where to look.

I completed this project as a member of the department of Journalism, Media and Communication (JMK) at Stockholm University in Sweden, and I would like to thank my colleagues for their helpful conversation about many of the issues addressed here. My work on this book has formed part of my contribution to the project "Existential Terrains: Memory and Meaning in Cultures of Connectivity" (et.ims.su.se), led by Dr Amanda Lagerkvist and funded by the Knut and Alice Wallenberg Foundation, the Marcus and Amalia Wallenberg Foundation and Stockholm University.

Most of all, this book is dedicated to Rachel Hanemann, whose support is the key to everything I do, and to Florence. By the time you are old enough to read books, who knows what the world will look like?

Introduction
Welcome to the Online Church

Can a Dragon Lead a Church?

I first encountered the question of dragon religion in 2009, at a Christian media conference in the English city of Durham. Some of the leaders of a small group called the Anglican Cathedral of Second Life had encountered an unexpected challenge, in the form of a monstrous volunteer, and they put the matter to the assembled audience for discussion.

Second Life is a virtual world, launched in 2003 and designed for sociable and creative interaction. Visitors can talk to one another through type and audio chat. They can also build, buy or sell almost anything that can be imagined, from architecture and clothing to body parts and animated dance moves. Visitors navigate Second Life using an avatar, and this character can take any form. Many use this freedom to play with the categories of physical appearance, including species, gender, age, ethnicity and class, and some develop elaborate performances of roleplay.

At the Cathedral, a dragon was impressive, but hardly unusual. Other avatars in the congregation included plenty of imaginative creations, from mermaids to hippos. This dragon, however, wanted to start leading church services. With this elevation of status, species-swapping became a more serious theological and pastoral issue. The Cathedral's problem was two-fold: first, what aspects of the offline identity of a worship leader needed to be revealed to the online congregation? And second, who was qualified to make that decision?

This scenario raised questions that had long troubled Christian groups online. For example, where are the boundaries of acceptable conduct in a new world? As we shall see in this book, some practitioners of online church have long argued that new technologies demand moral, theological and ritual flexibility, while others consider such suggestions unacceptable. What is the relationship between transparency and authenticity, and where is the dividing line between roleplay and deception? Many online communities encourage anonymity or creative self-representation, but misrepresenting some aspects of offline identity, particularly gender, can be more controversial. In our discussion of the Cathedral's dragon problem, several participants quickly homed in on gender as the most important aspect of identity, arguing that congregation members had the right to know if their prayers were being led by a man or a woman. A congregation member might have more freedom, but at least some aspects of the identity of a person in a position of leadership had to be fixed and known. This was, eventually, the solution adopted by the Cathedral: all leaders must now submit their real names and photographs for inclusion on the church website, to ensure that congregants know exactly who they 'really' are.

For researchers in the field of religion, media and culture, the problem of dragon religion engages with some of our oldest debates. The anecdote shows that new communities are emerging in new worlds, with new leaders, new practices and new understandings of identity. Online churches have been studied extensively as laboratory spaces for the generation of new ritual forms. On the other hand, representatives from the Cathedral chose to ask for advice from a gathering of Christian academics, clergy and bishops— suggesting that established categories of authority and expertise might not have changed very much after all. Online churches combine new and old in ways that are not easy to understand.

To make sense of digital religion, we need to engage closely with the people who practice it. We need to spend time watching how communities, networks and practices take shape, flourish and fade away. Through this kind of long-term attention, we can begin to find out more about the factors that motivate participation. We can find out what participants themselves actually experience and what they value about their online activities. We can learn more about how participants build up the social and technologi- cal structures of a community, why particular architectures and practices are constructed, and how online activity relates to wider social networks. Online churches were discussed at length in academic research and Chris- tian theological commentary in the 1990s and 2000s, because they could be used as focal points for concerns about ritual, community and authority. This book will engage with those classic debates, but we will also move forward in our final chapters to engage with a new generation of academic theorising in the field of religion, media and culture.

When Is a Church Not a Church?

So what, exactly, are we looking at? In Christian discourse, the word 'church' can be used to refer to a building designed for Christian worship, the community that worships there, the denomination that that commu- nity belongs to or the sum total of all Christians who ever lived. This cur- rent study focuses on the first two kinds of 'church', considering particular Christian groups and the places where they gather.

The exact parameters of what kind of group can count as 'a church' vary according to theological tradition. In some theologies, church is something that happens wherever Christians meet together in the name of Christ. In other traditions, the criteria can also include performing particular rituals (sacraments), preaching the Christian message, obeying properly authorised leaders or operating as part of a specific organisational structure. Instead of trying to define what counts as a real church online, I have chosen to follow the self-definition of each community. For the purposes of this study, if a group calls itself a church, it is a church.

Self-described online churches tend to share a set of common features. For example, they develop some form of sustained and usually mutually supportive social interaction, which they refer to as 'community'. Online churches attract strong commitment from their members, who express a powerful sense of belonging and shared identity. A church can become a site of very strong friendships, and some of the participants I met during my research have now been friends for well over a decade. Online churches also pray together, usually (but not always) in real time. These prayer events generally develop into a form of church service, which combines open prayer with other practices like preaching, music, images and liturgy. These three features— community, belonging and prayer—were present in all of the online churches I have encountered, and these were the factors most often referred to when participants wanted to prove that their group really was a church.

Just because these features are present, however, does not mean that every member of a congregation participates in them or understands them in the same way. The meaning of 'community', for example, can vary widely, from a network of personal friendships to a movement based on shared goals and values. Prayer and worship events took place in all five groups described in this book, but many community members rarely attended. Some of the churches in this book did not originally expect live worship events to take place at all, and took months or even years to develop a successful format for them. Some participants may even disagree with the label of 'church', refusing to acknowledge their group as a 'real' congregation.

Christian readers hoping to find out if an online community can really be a church must answer that question for themselves, but this ethnographic study might still be of some use to their deliberations. If a church becomes real only when it performs specific rituals in a specific way, then online projects may be disqualified by definition. On the other hand, if the realness of a church depends on the quality of its preaching, the commitment of its community, the warmth of its relationships or the enthusiasm of its worship, then long-term participation—ethnography—is the only way to find out if a particular congregation counts. Theological considerations of the Internet have long been hampered by limited first-hand experience, and ethnographies like this one could provide some of the raw material needed to move discussion forward.

Welcome to the Church Online: Introducing the Volume

The Cathedral of Second Life is just one of the many thousands of congregations that can now be found online. Beginning in the mid-1980s, Christians have appropriated every form of new media to support worship, prayer, friendship, discussion, teaching and evangelism. Churches can be found high in the skies of virtual worlds, streaming video from local congregations, connecting through social network sites or debating ideas in forums and chatrooms. Some attract only the smallest handful of congregants, while others gather hundreds of thousands of people. Chapter 1 offers a brief survey of this complicated 30-year history, tracing the ever-changing landscape of online churches, identifying key turning points and describing some of the more significant, innovative and intriguing examples.

These churches have fascinated academics since the earliest days of research on digital religion. Some of the very first academic articles about religion and the Internet focused on online churches, as we shall see in Chapters 1 and 2, and interest continued to flourish through the 2000s. The 'online church' appealed as a case study because it promised all of the most dazzling possibilities of the Internet in their most concentrated form. Here, all in one place, we would find new rituals, new kinds of community, new styles of leadership and new challenges to old structures of authority. Ancient religion was merging with the latest technology to generate unexpected new connections and practices, and an online church might be the best place to see that convergence happen.

The idea of going to church online also appears frequently in Christian reports, articles and books published in the 1990s and early 2000s, but here the example is used in a very different way. For Christian authors, online church was a perfect demonstration of the most harrowing dangers of the Internet: the retreat from face-to-face communication to easy anonymity; the triumph of lazy consumption over embodied commitment; the rise of uncivil discourse; the death of true authority in a world where anyone could pretend to be anything. The local church, many feared, was going to be replaced by computer-mediated pseudo-communities.

The academic and Christian literature on the question of online churches is extensive, but it is also narrowly limited in scope. I will explore this literature in Chapter 2, categorising the major contributions according to five key themes: the relationship between online and offline churchgoing; the validity of online community; the form and efficacy of online ritual; the design of virtual architecture and sacred space; and the impact of digital media on religious authority.

This literature is also surprisingly brief in format, pursued through journal articles, book chapters, reports and brief case studies. To date, no one has published a book-length empirical study that explores exactly what goes on in these online churches. Why do people join them, and what do they do? How do they change over time, and why? What makes one church grow, while another fades away? How do different churches engage with or call upon larger Christian institutions for support, and what kinds of control do those institutions try to exert over their online projects? These are all questions that have remained unanswered, and largely unasked.

My work aims to tease out a more thorough and grounded understanding of what it can mean to be church online, using five in-depth ethnographic case studies. Ethnography requires long-term personal involvement in group life and repeated conversations with members, allowing the researcher to explore the perceptions and practices of a group in great depth and richness, and this flexible, contextual approach is particularly well-suited to the study of online religion. The ethnographer must become part of participants' relationships and activities, and this close involvement offers the chance to spend time learning what really matters to the members of a community. Through ethnography, we can learn to challenge our own assumptions through direct personal experience. Bringing ethnography to the Internet is not straightforward, of course, and the method of digital ethnography has itself become a major area of research. Chapter 3 will explain my own combination of methods in this study, while introducing the reader to some of the key methodological debates in the study of online communities.

Introducing the Case Studies

This book will analyse five online churches in the order in which they launched, beginning with the one created first. Chapter 4 considers Church of Fools, a small virtual world launched with funding from the Methodist Council of Great Britain in 2004. Church of Fools operated as a multiuser environment for only a few months, under financial pressure and intense attack from online trolls, but its virtual space was still open for private prayer until very recently. This chapter is based on interviews conducted between 2006–2009, some years after the virtual church closed, but participants still wanted to discuss their memories of their avatars, worship activities, games and—most of all—controversies.

Chapter 5 discusses i-church, which launched in 2004 as part of the Church of England. I-church is still active today, as part of the Diocese of Oxford, led by an ordained priest under the oversight of a group of trustees that includes an Anglican bishop. Like Church of Fools, i-church attracted international media attention and high numbers of participants and was forced to improvise new liturgies, community rules and leadership structures in response to unexpected moments of crisis. The vision for i-church shifted over time, and this chapter explores the ongoing relationship of negotiation between founding ideals and lived realities.

Church of Fools' virtual space was replaced in 2004 by a forum and chatroom. In 2006 this relaunched as a new website, St Pixels, which operated independently from any institutional oversight and funding. St Pixels is the subject of Chapter 6, which examines the diverse subcultures that emerged on the website itself and the regular offline gatherings that developed around it.

Chapter 7 moves to the virtual world of Second Life. Church of Fools and i-church were launched with direct financial sponsorship from Christian denominations, but the Anglican Cathedral of Second Life has tried to move in the opposite direction. The church began as a small group for Anglicans in Second Life, and built a Cathedral in 2006. The Cathedral decided to identify itself as Anglican, and then subsequently approached two bishops of the Anglican Communion seeking a more official form of authorization. The exact nature of this connection was discussed for many years, without any firm conclusion. In the meantime, the Cathedral developed its own architecture, liturgy, leadership style and community culture, serving a group of Second Life users who defined themselves as Anglicans or shared an interest in Anglican tradition and spirituality.

Chapter 4–7 form a cohesive group. These four churches are all connected to a major Protestant denomination (Methodist for Church of Fools, Anglican for the rest), through financial sponsorship, institutional oversight or aspiration. Their congregations are all theologically diverse, including liberal Christians alongside conservative evangelicals, and mixing practitioners accustomed to traditional liturgical worship with those accustomed to more informal and contemporary styles. In each congregation, most participants were British and American. Despite the very different media they use, these churches have also developed quite similar forms of online worship, and they were well aware of one other. In some cases, individual members transferred between these groups over time.

Chapter 8 looks at a completely different kind of online religion. Life. Church (known as LifeChurch.tv until 2015) is one of the very largest multisite evangelical churches in the United States, and it launched an Internet Campus in 2006 (followed by a Second Life campus in 2007). The Internet Campus, later renamed Church Online, brought the LifeChurch.tv experience to a global audience. The Internet Campus streamed video from LifeChurch.tv's physical locations alongside a chatroom, private prayer tools and social media activities, all under the supervision of an online pastor and his support team. This church shows a different and much more cohesive theology, greater investment in online evangelism work, a strongly hierarchical model of leadership and a very different style of online community. To avoid confusion, this book will use the name 'LifeChurch' instead of switching between LifeChurch.tv and Life.Church.

Each case study chapter takes a different approach, focusing on the particular themes, events and activities that most captured the distinctive qualities of that community. To compare these case studies, I will conclude each chapter with a brief summary using a seven-point framework. In each case, I briefly summarise the scale of the church; its style of community; the kinds of prayer, worship and spiritual experience described to me by participants; the level of commitment of community members to local churchgoing; the degree to which the church reproduced familiar elements of architecture, liturgy and structure; its system of internal control; and the church's sources of funding and external oversight.

Making Sense of Online Churches

These churches tell us something about online community, identity and ritual in religious contexts, but they also demonstrate a range of approaches to institutional authority. All five churches are connected in some way to an established religious institution, like a denomination, a diocese or a local church, and they extend the work of that institution online while benefitting (or at least hoping to benefit) from association with its brand. We can therefore use these churches to help understand the possible roles available to religious institutions in the digital landscape. These churches represent five different possibilities for the technologically mediated relationship between religious organisations and their audiences.

In Chapter 9, I reflect on the case studies to consider the process through which religious technologies take shape. The two most widely used ideas in this area are the religious-social shaping of technology or RSST (Campbell 2010) and the theory of mediatization (Hjarvard 2008), and each offers a different approach. In fact, the two ideas are directly opposed to one another. RSST emphasises the independent agency of a religious community, describing a process in which religious practitioners rebuild technologies to conform to their history, values and core practices. Mediatization emphasises the power of the media, describing a process in which all social institutions—including religion—are forced to adapt to the 'logic' of media in order to survive. Each of these theories tells us something about how online churches come to be, and I will propose a new model—'mediatized religious design', or MRD—that combines the strengths of both approaches.

In Chapter 10, we shift our attention from the work of designers to the experience of users. One of the most influential concepts in Internet studies since the late 1990s has been the 'network society' (Rainie and Wellman 2012), the idea that digital media function not as a separate cyberspace but as an integral part of society's infrastructure. Rather than studying online communities, we should therefore be studying the Internet as it operates in everyday life. This approach calls for efforts to map digital social networks and to understand the circulations of content and affect through those networks. Inspired by this approach, this chapter will begin by reimagining online churches in the light of 'networked religion', looking at the ways in which individual users integrate their online church involvement into their wider material, social and religious lives.

This networked approach is helpful, but overemphasising integration can also be misleading. Online activity is part of everyday life, of course, but these online churches also remind us of the importance of privacy, anonymity, boundaries and separateness. For many participants, the online church is valuable precisely because it is not integrated into their local religious and social practice. Separateness allows some participants to act more openly, more playfully and more experimentally than their family, friends and local church would allow.

Chapter 10 will end by exploring this theme of separateness in two ways. Members of the Center for Media, Religion and Culture at the University of Colorado, Boulder, have argued that the transformative potential of digital religion can be seen most clearly in 'third spaces' (Hoover and Echchaibi 2014), locations at the margins of traditional religion where participants find freedom to experiment with new ideas, practices and formations. At the Institute for Media Studies in Stockholm University, meanwhile, my current colleagues are pioneering an understanding of digital media as an 'existential terrain' (Lagerkvist 2016), a landscape in which participants are struggling, vulnerable and often suffering. The existential approach challenges media scholars to pay more attention to fear, pain, failure, and the strategies adopted as participants try to regain some feeling of security.

What Happened to the Future?

My research in the field of online churches began ten years ago, and that long scope allows for a historical overview of the trajectory of digital religion. In the *conclusion* to this book, I return to all five case studies to see how these churches have fared between 2010 and the present. These churches were launched between 2004 and 2007, and their founders expressed high hopes for their projects. Each was not just a new church but an experiment, planted at the frontier of ministry to discover the future shape of Christianity. Christian institutions needed to invest in online churches, they argued, in order to stay relevant, retain young members and attract new followers in a rapidly digitising society.

Christian institutions are still investing in online projects, but the form of that ministry has changed. Three of the five churches described in this book still exist, praying together online in a format that has altered very little since 2010; another survives as a Facebook group. Despite their longevity, however, the denomination-linked churches described in Chapters 4 to 7 have not attracted many imitators. In contrast, LifeChurch's Church Online has developed a model of video-based online worship that is now an integral part of the ministry of thousands of local churches in the US and worldwide. Protestant denominations are now following a similar path, encouraging local churches to livestream their services and build community through social media. I describe this as a shift from 'online church' to 'church online', replacing investment in self-contained online communities with projects that use digital media to extend the ministry of local congregations.

The history of technology is also the history of the future. Designers collaborate to imagine what society will become, and users invest in the products they expect to need tomorrow. The story of digital religion is full of attempts to discover a practice, network, tool or platform that consumers will respond to, to help an institution or an individual secure a place in the future. This book describes five dreams that could once have been the future, and shows what happened to those visions over time. By studying the futures of the past, we can find insights that help us make sense of the futures being offered to us today.

References

Campbell, H., 2010. *When Religion Meets New Media*. London: Routledge.

Hjarvard, S., 2008. The mediatization of religion: A theory of the media as agents of religious change. *Northern Lights: Film & Media Studies Yearbook* 6(1), pp. 9–26.

Hoover, S. and Echchaibi, N., 2014. *Media Theory and the "third spaces of digital religion"*. Boulder, CO: The Center for Media, Religion and Culture. [pdf] Available at: <https://thirdspacesblog.files.wordpress.com/2014/05/third-spaces-and-media-theory-essay-2-0.pdf> [Accessed 28 August 2016]

Lagerkvist, A., 2016. Existential media: Toward a theory of digital thrownness. *New Media & Society*, pp. 1–15. [pdf] Available at: <http://nms.sagepub.com/content/early/2016/06/10/1461444816649921.full.pdf> [Accessed 28 August 2016]

Rainie, L. and Wellman, B., 2012. *Networked: The New Social Operating System*. Cambridge: MIT Press.

1   A Brief History of Cyberchurch

To understand the context of the five churches discussed in this book, we need a grasp of the history of online experiments that preceded them. I offer here a brief timeline of some of the major milestones in the development of online churches, and I will also include a few references to the first published attempts to evaluate their significance.

In this chapter, I will focus only on the origins of online churches, beginning in the 1980s and following the story up to 2010. My task here is to give the reader a sense of the kinds of groups and debates that were emerging in the early years of online churches, to help highlight what was new (and not new) about the particular examples we will focus on. As we shall see, the churches I have selected for attention all emerged within a few years in the mid-2000s, and they represented major developments in online churchmanship, particularly in their ambition and scale and in their relationship to established religious organisations. We will return to this story in the conclusion to this book, to survey the landscape of online churches today and reflect on what has changed between 2010 and 2016.

The history of online activity is not easy to track, of course, and many early sites and communities have disappeared without leaving a trace. I rely here on references to churches found in published literature, but very few of the authors I will be quoting were trying to undertake a comprehensive survey of all the different churches available when they were writing. This narrative will hopefully be useful, but it is sure to be incomplete.

The Church of England document *Cybernauts Awake!* refers to the earliest online church I have discovered, launched in 1985. The founders 'claimed that for the first time people could worship in spirit and in truth', free from the distractions of others who might—in their own words—be 'fat, short, beautiful or ugly. People are pared down to pure spirit' (Church of England Board for Social Responsibility 1999, Chapter 5). *Cybernauts* doesn't name this church or explain what participants actually did, unfortunately, and I have found no other reference to it.

Another trace was recorded by the pioneering digital theologian David Lochhead. In 1986 the owners of the Unison service hosting the Presbyterian discussion network Presbynet asked if they could organise an event online in response to the Challenger space shuttle disaster. Presbynet planned 'a memorial liturgy with prayers, scripture, meditation and a section in which readers could add their own prayers' (Lochhead 1997: 52), followed by a time of open discussion. According to Lochhead, this event 'demonstrated the power of the computer medium to unite a community in a time of crisis beyond the limits of geography or denomination'—but it was also one of the first demonstrations of the potential of online ritual as religious expression.

Another early landmark was reported by game designers Chip Morning-star and F. Randall Farmer (1991). A game called 'Habitat' ran from 1986 to 1988 and was the first graphical multiplayer world, offering a simple 2D interface. Characters could steal from or kill one another. On dying, the victim would re-appear empty-handed in their 'home' space and any objects dropped could be collected by others. Participants hotly debated questions of identity, violence, death and discipline, and this dispute led to a small milestone for online religion:

> One of the outstanding proponents of the anti-violence point of view was motivated to open the first Habitat church, the Order of the Holy Walnut (in real life he was a Greek Orthodox priest). His canons forbid his disciples to carry weapons, steal, or participate in violence of any kind. His church became quite popular and he became a very highly respected member of the Habitat community.
>
> (Morningstar and Farmer 1991)

It is unclear what this church did, if anything; it may simply have been an organisation sharing an ethical code of nonviolence. Nonetheless, the Holy Walnut was the first self-declared 'church' founded in a graphically represented environment. The satirical humour evident in the name would become a recurrent feature of online churchmanship and of course, a wide-spread theme in digital cultures.

In a 1989 review of the use of bulletin board software (BBS) in the New York education system, Anneliese Sessa mentions a BBS called 'Cyber Church', and her account also focuses on the community's response to death and disaster. After the California earthquake of 1989, 'a priest from St Mary's Church . . . gave detailed reports of the damages and loss of life he encountered', and Sessa reports that 'his descriptive technique of writing drew pictures in my mind that made me feel like I was there with him' (Sessa 1989: 5).

The potential uses of the Internet expanded dramatically with the invention of the World Wide Web in 1990. Websites could offer graphics, text and hyperlinks, and online communities—including online churches—began to develop from the early email discussion lists and local BBSs into more complex and sophisticated forms. The first church to be created on a website may have been the First Church of Cyberspace, launched in 1994.[1] Charles Henderson, a Presbyterian minister in New Jersey, sought to establish an online congregation through the use of discussion forums and an always-open chatroom in which services were held once a day. Members could also access images, music and a multimedia online Bible.

A website called Partenia (www.partneia.org) also launched in the mid-90s, promoting the social views of the controversial Roman Catholic bishop Jacques Gaillot. Gaillot was moved by the Vatican from the French see of Evreux to Partenia in Algeria, a diocese that vanished under the desert in the 5th century. Taking up residence among immigrants in Paris, he chose instead to interpret 'Partenia' as a symbol for all those excluded from society (Partenia.org n.d.). The site soon attracted a worldwide following, with forums, chatrooms and summaries of Gaillot's views available in seven languages. Partenia referred to itself as a 'virtual diocese', but did not seem to consider itself a 'virtual church'; nor did 'St Sam's', an Anglican 'cyberparish' email list founded in 1988 and documented by Heidi Campbell (2005: 96 ff).

Online ministries were also emerging in Asia at around the same time. Yoido Full Gospel Church in South Korea, for example, claims to be the largest Christian megachurch in the world, with more than 800,000 members and many hundreds of pastors. YFGC began using satellites and the Internet to broadcast live services in the mid-1990s, and a focus on expansion and evangelism seems to have been central to the church's digital philosophy from the beginning (Kim 2007). When Pastor David Yonggi Cho met Rick Warren of Saddleback Church in 2001 to discuss the future of Christian ministry, one critical account reported that the pair planned 'to utilize cyberspace to reach into the homes of countless millions with their own distinctive brands of Christianity', generating a new kind of global religious empire (Glover 2004: 85).

I was able to visit Yoido in the summer of 2016, and one of the church's many hundreds of staff pastors described online broadcasting to me as a powerful tool for reaching into countries where Christianity was absent or marginalised. This account frames the Internet as a complement to existing Christian ministry activities, extending missionary work into new areas without undermining the work of local churches. Not everyone has been convinced by this complementarian approach, as we shall see in Chapter 2. According to one report, David Yongghi Cho himself once said to his congregation, 'Don't come to church, just stay at home and get your teaching through the Internet' (Glover 2004: 86)—suggesting that online and offline religion might in some cases be competing for attention.

Published discussions of online churches began to proliferate in the mid-1990s, inside and beyond academia, and these began to debate exactly how revolutionary the new medium might become. In an article calling for new models of Christian adult education, for example, John Lai foresaw major changes for the whole Christian church. Lai suggested that 'the emergence of what might be called the *virtual church* or *cyberchurch*' was going to 'require a reexamination of the organizational context of learning' (Lai 1995: 11). The cyberchurch would encourage new kinds of relations between Christians around the world, facilitating 'the emergence of more network-like church organisations vis a vis more traditional hierarchies', and 'the capacity of certain groups and individuals to exert normative control over others will be inhibited'.

In December 1996, *TIME Magazine* published a cover story by Joshua Cooper Ramo titled 'Finding God on the Web'. *TIME* shared some of these transformative expectations. The article describes religious websites, cha-trooms and newsgroups from around the world, suggests that computer communication could bring different groups together and quotes Jacques Gaillot, who 'marvels at the freedom he enjoys loosed from the hierarchy of the church' (Ramo 1996: 3). According to Gaillot, 'on the Internet there is no question of someone imposing rules on the way people communicate . . . The Net has no center from which will can be applied.' The authors reach striking, provocative and rather poetic conclusions: 'we stand at the start of a new movement in this delicate dance of technology and faith', they suggest, 'the marriage of God and the global computer networks' (Ramo 1996: 6). The consequences of this dance may be far-reaching: 'is it possible that God in a networked age will look, somehow, different? . . . Interconnected, we may begin to find God in places we never imagined' (Ramo 1996: 7).

The German-language journal *Praktische Theologie* (*Practical Theology*) published a special issue on the significance of the Internet for Christian churches in 1990 and again in 1996. The 1996 issue includes an interview with Germany's first '*Online-Pfarrerin*' (online pastor),[2] Melanie Graffam-Minkus, appointed by the Bavarian state church in October that year, and her perspective is much less radical than that of Lai or Ramo. Graffam-Minkus offered advice by email, responding to around five messages per day, and considered her work rather straightforward. 'It is a matter of meeting people where they are every day', she explained to interviewer Eva Lettenmeier, 'and for many digital communication is already an essential part of their daily lives' (Lettenmeier 1996: 277). The work might seem normal to a pastor, but users were surprised to find her online, and that surprise encouraged some people to contact her. Graffam-Minkus reported that many 'rather unchurched people' sent her emails, looking for 'a cute or serious conversation, understanding or advice, answers to theological and religious questions.' For many of her correspondents, their emails repre-sented 'the first contact with a pastor for a long time.'

In this interview, Graffam-Minkus is very clear about the limitations of what she is doing online. 'The computer cannot replace human contact', she insists, and she sees herself as an initial contact, sending correspondents to their local pastors if she can. The final exchange of the interview is of par-ticular relevance for this book:

> Question: Would your dream be a real 'Internet community' services with worship, Bible study groups, baptisms, weddings . . . ?
>
> Answer: No, I cannot imagine it is right for people to want to get married in tracksuits in front of the computer. Too much

of what makes the community of believers would be lost.
Feelings, impressions, gestures. . . . The sensory dimension
plays an important role in the life and work of the Church,
and for good reason. How can the fragrant scent of candles
be sensed through the computer? (Lettenmeier 1996: 277)

Another German online church launched two years later, in 1998: St Bonifatius, in the virtual environment of funcity. St Bonifatius is an ecumenical
community sponsored by three Catholic dioceses in northern Germany, and
offers a chatroom, email contact with a large team of chaplains and (since
2008) an online monastery occupied by more than a dozen monks and nuns
from different religious orders (Bonifatiuswerk 2010).

Ralph Schroeder, Noel Heather and Raymond M. Lee published one of
the first sociological case studies of an online Christian church in 1998, and
their analysis also emphasises continuity. Their article examines discourse
in 'E-Church' (a pseudonym), a small charismatic group. E-Church held a
weekly prayer meeting in a 3D environment that included a church building, and the authors emphasise consistency in its rituals rather than innovation. 'The "genre" of a real-world prayer meeting was constantly invoked'
(Schroeder, Heather and Lee 1998) through the use of standard forms of
language, with a high degree of liturgical patterning. Group prayers were
led by a woman, but the authors see this as a normal practice among house
groups rather than a transformation of authority. One area in which a
change is noted is in the pattern of conversation: 'the novel combination of
notional anonymity and intimacy which the virtual reality world fosters led
in this case to a surprisingly open airing of major personal problems.'

The UK's first online church launched in 1999 and remains online
today, although the website was last updated in 2009. 'WebChurch: The
WorldWide Virtual Church from Scotland' (webchurch.org) offers articles,
sermons and other resources and encourages visitors to email the pastor
with questions and prayer requests. The church promises that any prayers
received will be passed on to volunteers and remembered for a week.

In the US, some more theologically ambitious initiatives were emerging.
'Alpha Church' (www.alphachurch.org) was founded in 1998 by Patricia
Walker, a Methodist minister who—according to her own website—left
the church (or 'transferred to non-denominational status') to lead the project (Alpha Church, n.d.a). Alpha Church still offers sermons and worship
services today, with daily updates in the form of blog posts, images and
recorded resources to be read, streamed or downloaded by the visitor. The
visitor can email the pastor to ask for prayer, and donations are encouraged.
According to the site's own explanation of the history of Alpha, the church
was established with a particular focus on the needs of disabled Christians: 'two paraplegic young men gave us feedback as to what appealed to
them spiritually, visually, and logistically'. Before long 'we discovered that
the Internet was an excellent way to draw in people who could not get to
"regular" church', particularly 'those who were computer savvy' (Alpha

Church, n.d.a). Unlike Melanie Graffam-Minkus, Alpha Church encourages its members to consider the Internet as a sufficient alternative to face-to-face churchgoing.

Alpha Church invites visitors to share holy communion, which involves reading or watching recorded resources while eating and drinking something—not necessarily bread or wine—at the computer screen. Rev Walker encourages the worshipper to create an appropriate environment for these practices, suggesting (in an earlier version of her communion page, no longer available online) that we 'may light a candle nearby to represent the light of Christ', turn down our computer speakers 'to a medium level' and 'read aloud with the responses'. Spiritual efficacy is promised for these rituals: 'during the Communion-Eucharist service the elements will be blessed/sanctified and you will eat and drink them' (Alpha Church n.d.b).

Online communion can also be found at Grace Incarnate Ministries, the website of US Methodist pastor Rev Greg Neal. Neal launched his online ministry in 1998 to share his sermons and articles and offer prayer, and his website is still available online (revneal.org). According to Neal, he had no intention of offering online communion when he first posted a video of a service in 1999:

> Almost immediately I began receiving emails from people who told me that, while viewing the communion video, they had joined the congregation in the responses and had prayed as the music played and the people were receiving communion. One person who shared this with me even asked if it would be okay if she got bread and wine and partook of communion while watching the video.
>
> I was horrified by the concept [but] there wasn't any way for me to get the consecrated elements to her, she had never attended my church nor was she part of any church anywhere.
>
> (Neal 2013: 2)

The next year, however, his views were 'radically changed' by an experience of disability. Housebound, 'I felt I was starving for the sacrament' (Neal 2013: 2). Neal already knew that 30 percent of the listeners to his online sermons didn't attend a local church, and he began wondering if the 'means of grace' in the sacrament of communion could be conveyed over the Internet. Neal began encouraging visitors to partake in communion through his website in 2003, inviting them to eat and drink something while reading instructions and watching recorded videos. This experiment received mixed feedback: positive reactions 'encouraged me to accept that something real was going on' (Neal 2013: 4), but other responses were 'disturbing in the extreme' (Neal 2013: 3), including threats to report him to his bishop.

Some of the examples we have discussed were created by individual entrepreneurs, operating without institutional approval. Others (like WebChurch in Scotland and Graffam-Minkus's work in Germany) were designed to reconnect a struggling denomination with wider society. We turn now to a quite different initiative, launched in 1999: The Church of the Larger Fellowship, operated by the Unitarian Universalists. Both the Unitarians and the Universalists already had a long history of church-by-media projects. In the 19th century, for example, scattered Unitarian Christians across the United States developed 'Post Office Missions' and used letters, pamphlets, books and travelling ministers to connect and share their liberal theological views. According to the official history of the CLF, practitioners had begun thinking of these mail exchanges as a 'church' by at least 1904 (CLF n.d.). In the 1940s, this operation developed into 'The Church of the Larger Fellowship', a more formal mail network designed to serve the military overseas, and a Universalist version followed in 1947. The Unitarians and Universalists combined in the 1960s and merged their mail organisations, forming a new expanded program offering a correspondence course, a lending library of taped sermons and eventually a free telephone line to the pastor.

In this early period of mediated church, the denominations had to address some of the concerns we encountered above. In the 1940s, for example, the Unitarians were using the mail service 'to provide a spiritual home for isolated Unitarians and their families' (CLF n.d.), but also felt it was necessary to ensure that these media networks could not threaten local community participation. The mail network had to promise 'to transfer the allegiance of its members to local Unitarian churches whenever and wherever possible'. The key point, for the Unitarians, was that such transfers were not always possible: the faith was too widespread for local communities to thrive, forcing many to rely on the mail.

When Rev Jane Rzepka was appointed as senior minister in 1999, the CLF 'stepped up to the new millenium'. These long-running initiatives provided the perfect foundation for a move to the Internet. ' "Church by mail" became "church online" ' (CLF n.d.), and online communities, forums and web resources were launched. CLF remains active online today and now invites members to take part in an online community called 'Quest for Meaning', join online study courses, watch a live weekly talk show or participate in online worship through video and live chat. For members aged 18 to 35, a Church of the Younger Fellowship is available on Facebook. The CLF's history document ends with a flourish, connecting their contemporary online activities firmly back to Unitarian and Universalist tradition:

> The CLF of the 21st century is proud of its place as a refuge and a transitional community for isolated liberals wherever they are, and however they find us. The CLF is there for people seeking the light of religious freedom in parts of the world unfriendly to the concept. It is, by its heritage and its vision, a 'church without walls,' a church in every sense of the word.
>
> (CLF, n.d.)

The CLF—in its different mediated incarnations—shares more in common with the liberalism of Partenia than with the other churches I have described so far in this chapter. Where Grace Incarnate Ministries or Alpha Church spoke of reaching out to those who were prevented by illness from attending their local church, Partenia and the CLF were created to offer a gathering space for a like-minded minority who had no local church to turn to. In one of the very few academic studies of the CLF, a team of computer-human interaction researchers interviewed a CLF user called David, 'a teen with fundamentalist parents in a conservative state', and report that he 'sees his daily online exchanges as a refuge' (Hlubinka et al. 2002: 612).

These brief vignettes have outlined some of the online church experiments that emerged during the 1980s and '90s. No complete survey of the time exists, but these examples were certainly not alone. Patrick Dixon includes nine churches in the bibliography of his book *Cyberchurch* (Dixon 1997: 182), of which some (like Alpha Church) are still in operation today. Lutheran pastor Arne H. Fjeldstad conducted a more extensive study of online Christian activity for his DMin degree in 1997 and maintained a website to publicise and update his research for several years. By March 2000 he had found 34 active 'cyberchurches', not including four others that had already gone offline (Fjeldstad 2000).

These early online churches attracted fairly small numbers of participants and received a moderate degree of media coverage, academic interest and Christian theological debate. Evaluation of their significance relied heavily on speculation about what they might become in future. As we shall see in the next chapter, the well-known Christian pollster George Barna claimed in 1998 that 'millions' of Christians in the US were poised to 'drop out of the physical church in favor of the cyberchurch' (Barna 2001) within a few years, and he was not alone in his predictions.

That situation changed dramatically in 2004, when two new online churches were launched in the UK. Each was backed financially by a major Christian denomination. Church of Fools opened in May, with funding from the Methodist Council of Great Britain. I-church launched in August, as part of the Church of England's Oxford Diocese. These were not the first groups to receive support from an established Christian organisation, as we have seen, but they were by far the most high-profile experiments created at that time. I will discuss these two churches in more detail in later chapters of this book, so I will limit my comments here to a brief introduction.

Church of Fools was founded by the popular, somewhat anarchic Christian website Ship of Fools and was able to draw on considerable online experience and programming expertise. An earlier Ship of Fools project had sponsored the creation of a 3D virtual world, and this software was adapted to construct a church space in which avatars could walk, sit, perform gestures and communicate through text. The Methodist Church supported the project with a sizeable grant, but exerted no control over design or activity. The Anglican Bishop of London also helped fund the project and delivered the opening sermon.

Journalists from around the world were fascinated by the novelty of the experiment and its high-profile backers, and intense media coverage led to tens of thousands of daily visitors. Some of these visitors soon came with malicious intentions, seeking to hack the site's software and disrupt its services, and this irresistible story led to further media coverage and an even greater surge of visitors.

That 3D church closed after four months, but the community remained active, communicating through forums and chatrooms at a new website. In 2006, the church moved again to another new website, St Pixels, offering redesigned forums, a more advanced chatroom and a blog for every member. In 2012, St Pixels moved yet again to become a Facebook app, merging its community into Facebook's social network while retaining a blog and a space for services, and worship events continued online until the end of 2015.

I-church faced a very different range of opportunities, resources and problems. The church was an official part of the Diocese of Oxford and boasted its own salaried web pastor. The first pastor was appointed in June—only to resign in November, citing excessive time pressure. The diocese had drastically underestimated the appeal of its innovation and was stunned when people tried to register from six continents. Under a new pastor, appointed from within the membership, i-church closed its doors, stabilised its community and began a much slower rate of growth. By 2009 a third pastor had been appointed, with long experience in local and online ministry, a support team to help with site design and a close working relationship with the Oxford-based trustees. I-church remains in operation today, still led by the same pastor.

Meanwhile, another pioneering Christian project in 2004 passed almost unnoticed. The virtual world of Second Life, launched 2003, offers opportunities for socializing in a vast range of settings, from clothing boutiques to nightclubs, all constructed by players using a basic range of tools. This innovative system attracted intense media coverage, which in turn fuelled a rush of new visitors, including well-known companies, universities, politicians and pop stars. Publicity, high membership, free access and flexible design all made Second Life an obvious target for online religion, and churches soon started to appear.

Wagner James Au, Reuters' official Second Life journalist, blogged about churches in Second Life in April 2004—one month before the launch of Church of Fools and four months before i-church. A few weeks earlier, a short-lived Episcopalian church space had tried to give away virtual T-shirts bearing the slogan 'Jesus Had a Second Life Too' (Au 2004). When a user complained that 'she didn't care to see the promotion of religion in Second Life', the criticism 'unleashed a flurry of controversy, in the Second Life forum, on the bounds of theology, free expression, and community', and the new church quickly disappeared.

That early experiment was soon followed by others. Hearing about an in-world church event, Au visited a traditional-looking cathedral where he found 'something very much like an authentic Catholic mass already in progress. A man named OmegaX Zapata is at the altar, and he's dressed in priestly garments, and he's reciting the liturgy' (Au 2004). The consecration and sharing of bread and wine had been replaced by a question-and-answer session, but otherwise the service was as traditional as possible. Zapata's motives were partly educational: 'I wanted to bring more real-world things into SL', he explained, 'so people could experience them if they couldn't in real life'.

OmegaX Zapata, however, was not a priest, nor indeed a Catholic. The Vatican report *The Church and Internet* expressed concern that online resources might confuse the faithful by falsely representing themselves as Catholic (Pontifical Council for Social Communications 2002: para. 8), and Zapata came rather close to proving their point. 'The point of the church isn't to be just Catholic', Zapata told Au: 'it is to bring us together in praise of God'. At least one of his congregation agreed: 'I'm not Catholic [. . .] but I still believe in Christ, and it's the only church service on here, so I said what the heck, I'll go' (Au 2004).

Calculating the number of active churches in Second Life has always been difficult. The world offers search programs that can be used to locate groups, places or events, and searching for key terms like 'church', 'chapel', 'Christian' or 'Jesus' brings up extensive lists, but there is no guarantee that every place or event will be listed or that listings are accurate and up-to-date. Many places listed as 'churches' turn out on closer inspection to be shops, nightclubs, chapels for 'virtual weddings', art projects, historical reconstructions or mock-ups designed to add 'authenticity' to a themed village or mall. Other spaces seem to have been designed as churches but never attract a congregation; Douglas Estes found notices attached to empty buildings promising to hold a service if anyone contacted the owner to request one (Estes 2009: 147).

In some cases, Second Life churches have been designed as accurate replicas of specific physical buildings. In 2008, for example, the local paper of the English seaside town of Great Yarmouth announced the opening of a Second Life reconstruction of their parish church of St Nicholas, based on hundreds of photographs of the physical building. The project was designed to attract tourists to the town and raise money for the church, and the local vicar approved: 'I do not mind how virtual it is', he pointed out, 'so long as the money is real' (Great Yarmouth Mercury 2008). By 2011, according to a CNN blog post, the line between reconstruction, role-play and religious activity had become rather less clear-cut: the virtual church was still part of the virtual presence of Great Yarmouth and still raising money for the local church, but it was also now offering avatar weddings, events led by a Great Yarmouth man 'role-playing as a priest' and prayer services led by an automated vicar (JaneyBracken 2011).

Andree Robinson-Neal found 28 churches in October 2007 by searching for 'church', 'faith' and 'worship' (2008: 228). Other estimates are much higher. One Scandinavian Protestant in Second Life handed me his own list of Christian ministries in February 2008, running to some 52 sites, almost all evangelical. An Anglo-Catholic user composed a list of 36 in December 2008, looking only at Catholic, Orthodox and Anglican spaces, and circulated that list in Second Life (Burt 2010). 'Some of these places have actual worshipping congregations,' he wrote, but 'others are there for people to pop in from time to time to say a prayer, and still others seem to be simply impressive examples of art. This list is offered with the hope that people will go around and pray in these places.' Note again the complexity of clearly designating a site as 'church', when visitors, designers and owners may perceive and use a space quite differently.

My own Second Life inventory, collected during 2008 and 2009, contains 106 landmarks for places offering some kind of Christian worship or claiming to be a church—and this was not a complete list. In December 2011, Stefan Gelfgren and I attempted to conduct a more complete survey of Second Life churches, searching for places described as 'church', 'chapel' and 'cathedral' and visiting every result to decide if it should be included in our list. We anticipated a sharp decline in the number of churches, reflecting the decline of media interest in Second Life since 2009, but in fact, the number of churches has remained relatively stable since my earlier research. We identified 114 sims advertising some form of gathered worship, representing a wide range of traditions and ideologies (Gelfgren and Hutchings 2014).

Over time, religion in Second Life has become much more commonplace, considerably less controversial and perhaps, a little more conventional. We will encounter two different Second Life churches in later chapters of this book, each operating with the full support of an established Christian organisation.

Virtual world and text-based churches are diverse, numerous and visually creative, but they still tend to attract small congregations. Scale is a serious restriction for online communities, which must resolve problems of vision, design, technical support and funding if they intend to grow beyond a few dozen active participants. Since the mid-00s, a number of large American churches have tried to overcome this challenge by developing the model of the 'Internet campus'. Internet campuses combine high-quality video broadcasts of music and sermons with limited and closely monitored opportunities for response and extensive social media engagement. The result has been a transformation in the nature of community and the size of the audience, shifting online churches from a niche curiosity to something much closer to becoming a mainstream religious practice.

The Internet campus was first popularised by one of the very largest churches in America. LifeChurch.tv (now Life.Church) operates a 'multisite' system, broadcasting sermons by the senior pastor, Craig Groeschel, to 24 'campuses' in seven states. Each campus has its own local pastor, worship band and staff. The Internet Campus launched in 2006 to extend this basic idea online, broadcasting videos of music and sermons over the Internet through a website with opportunities for text chat, all under the supervision of a dedicated 'web pastor'. The use of electronic media to broadcast church services is of course nothing new, but the Internet Campus uses multiple media to generate a kind of community around these transmissions. Imitators were quick to follow, and The Leadership Network counted 48 churches with Internet campuses between October 2007 and November 2009 (Leadership Network 2007).

Internet campuses can attract truly vast audiences. Unlike a chatroom or virtual world church service, a video broadcast can be viewed by any number of people. LifeChurch claimed in 2010 to attract one hundred thousand viewers to its services every week, and Craig Groeschel has promised future congregations in the millions. LifeChurch will be the final case study considered in this book.

This chapter has briefly introduced some of the major milestones in the history of cyberchurches, from the 1980s to the late-2000s. As we have seen, 2004 proved to be a turning point, seeing the introduction of more popular, better-funded groups that attracted widespread media attention. Scholars were quick to notice this development, and our next chapter will consider academic efforts to make sense of the online church and its implications for digital religion.

Notes

1 The earliest entry in the *Internet Archive* shows the website as it was on 13–10–99: http://web.archive.org/web/19991013120229/http://godweb.org/.
ss, Charles a06). prs be mointored nal look more closely at the future of digital religion, to see where spaces for reflection
2 All quotations from *Praktische Theologie* are translations from the original German. I created an initial translation using Google Translate, and then asked German-speaking friends and colleagues to suggest improvements.

References

Alpha Church, n.d.a. About your pastor. [online] Available at: <http://www.alphachurch.org/yourpastor.htm> [Accessed 28 August 2016]
Alpha Church n.d.b. Holy communion at Alpha Church. [online] Available at: <http://www.alphachurch.org/holycommunion/holycommunion.htm> [Accessed 28 August 2016]
Au, W., 2004. Where two or more are gathered... *New World Notes*, 19 April. [blog] Available at: < http://secondlife.blogs.com/nwn/2004/04/where_two_or_mo.html> [Accessed 28 August 2016]
Barna Group, 2001. More Americans are seeking net-based faith experiences. *Barna Update*, 21 May. [online] Available at: <http://web.archive.org/web/20130121083241/http://www. barna.org/barna-update/article/5-barna-update/48-more-americans-are-seeking-net-based-faith-experiences> [Accessed 31 August 2016]
Bonifatiuswerk, 2010. *Sonderpreis beim Bonifatiuspreis im Jahr 2010: Preisträger Internetkirche St. Bonifatius / funcity. Bonifatiuswerk*, n.d. [online] Available at: <http://www.bonifatiuswerk.de/aktionen/bonifatiuspreis/preistraeger/2010/funcity/> [Accessed 07 January 2017]

Burke, D., 1999. *Cybernauts Awake! Ethical and Spiritual Implications of Computers, Information Technology and the Internet*. London: Church House Publishing. [online] Available at: <http://www.starcourse.org/cybernauts/> [Accessed 28 August 2016]

Burt, C., 2010. Catholic and Orthodox churches in second life. *CDBURT*. [online] Available at: <https://web.archive.org/web/20111223074429/http://home.comcast.net/~cdburt/site/?/page/Catholic_and_Orthodox_Churches_in_Second_Life/> [Accessed 28 August 2016]

Campbell, H., 2005. *Exploring Religious Community Online: We Are One in the Network*. Oxford: Peter Lang.

CLF, n.d. Our history. [online] Available at: <http://www.clfuu.org/about/our-history/> [Accessed 28 August 2016]

Dixon, P., 1997. *Cyberchurch: Christianity and the Internet*. Eastborne: Kingsway Publications.

Estes, D., 2009. *SimChurch: Being the Church in the Virtual World*. Grand Rapids: Zondervan.

Fjeldstad, A., 2000. Cyberchurches. [online] Available at: <http://web.archive.org/web/20091022132737/http://geocities.com/researchtriangle/1541/cybchur.html> [Accessed 28 August 2016]

Gelfgren, S. and Hutchings, T., 2014. The virtual construction of the sacred: Representation and fantasy in the architecture of Second Life churches. *Nordic Journal of Religion and Society* 27(1), pp. 59–73.

Glover, P., 2004. *The Virtual Church and How to Avoid It: The Crisis of De-Formation and the Need for Re-Formation in the 21st Century Church*. Maitland: Xulon Press.

Great Yarmouth Mercury, 2008. Visit church in cyberspace. *Great Yarmouth Mercury*, 11 September. [online] Available at: < http://www.greatyarmouthmercury.co.uk/news/visit_church_in_cyberspace_1_495625> [Accessed 28 August 2016]

Hlubinka, M., Beaudin, J., Tapia, E. and An, J., 2002. AltarNation: Interface design for meditative communities. In: Terveen, L. and Wixon, D. eds., *CHI'02 Extended Abstracts on Human Factors in Computing Systems*. Minneapolis: ACM. pp. 612–613.

JaneyBracken, 2011. Amazing great Yarmouth in SL. *CNN iReport*, 15 February. [online] Available at: <http://ireport.cnn.com/docs/DOC-556030> [Accessed 28 August 2016]

Kim, K., 2007. Ethereal Christianity: Reading Korean mega-church websites. *Studies in World Christianity* 13(3), pp. 208–224.

Lai, J., 1995. Andragogy of the oppressed: Emancipatory education for Christian adults. *ERIC Document #ED396104*. [doc] Available at: <http://eric.ed.gov/?id=ED396104> [Accessed 28 August 2016]

Leadership Network, 2007. Churches with an Internet campus. *Digital@Leadership Network*, 31 October. [blog] Last updated 22 November 2009. Available at: <http://digital. leadnet.org/2007/10/churches-with-a.html> [Accessed 28 August 2016]

Lettenmeier, E., 1996. Interview mit der Online-Pfarrerin Melanie Graffam-Minkus. *Praktische Theologie* 31(4), pp. 277–278.

Lochhead, D., 1997. *Shifting Realities: Information Technology and the Church*. Geneva: WCC Publications.

Morningstar, C. and Farmer, R., 1990. The lessons of LucasFilms' habitat. In: Benedikt, M., ed. 1991. *Cyberspace: First Steps*. Cambridge: MIT Press. pp. 273–302.

[online] Available at: <http://www.fudco.com/chip/lessons.html> [Accessed 28 August 2016]

Neal, G., 2013. Holy communion over the Internet: Reflections on an experiment in sacramental practice. [online] Available at: <http://www.revneal.org/communionfaq.html> [Accessed 28 August 2016]

Partenia.org, n.d. Who is Jacques Gaillot? [online] Available at: <http://www.partenia.org/english/biographie_eng.htm> [Accessed 28 August 2016]

Pontifical Council for Social Communications, 2002. The church and Internet. [online] Available at: <http://www.vatican.va/roman_curia/pontifical_councils/pccs/documents/rc_pc_pccs_doc_20020228_church-Internet_en.html> [Accessed 28 August 2016]

Ramo, Joshua Cooper, 1996. Finding God on the Web. *TIME*, 16 December. [online] Available at: <http://www.time.com/time/magazine/article/0,9171,985700,00.html> [Accessed 28 August 2016]

Robinson-Neal, A., 2008. Enhancing the spiritual relationship: The impact of virtual worship on the real-world church experience. *Online: Heidelberg Journal of Religions on the Internet* 3(1), pp. 228–245. [online] Available at: <http://www.ub.uni-heidelberg.de/archiv/8296> [Accessed 28 August 2016]

Schroeder, R., Heather, N. and Lee, R., 1998. The sacred and the virtual: Religion in multi-user virtual reality. *Journal of Computer-Mediated Communication* 4(2). [online] Available at: <http://onlinelibrary.wiley.com/doi/10.1111/j.1083–6101.1998.tb00092. x/full>. [Accessed 28 August 2016]

Sessa, A., 1989. A review of MS-DOS bulletin board software suitable for long-distance learning. *#ERIC Document ED353977*. [pdf] Available at: <http://eric.ed.gov/?id=ED353977> [Accessed 28 August 2016]

2 Making Sense of Online Churches

Online churches have attracted a great deal of attention from Christian commentators and academics, beginning in the mid-90s and accelerating rapidly after the mid-00s. This discourse is not just a matter of ethnographic curiosity: even when online congregations were very small, they were already being used to represent something much greater than themselves. The online church has been treated by scholars primarily as an experimental laboratory, a test case in which we might expect to identify the first signs of new ideas and practices. For Christian writers—with a few notable exceptions—online church has tended to feature as an extreme, self-evidently dangerous case invoked to demonstrate the limits of acceptable online activity.

Despite the volume of literature on this subject, research has focused on a very small range of issues. Studies of online churches have consistently returned to four main topics: the relationship between online and offline churchgoing; the validity of online community; the form and efficacy of online ritual; and the design of virtual architecture and sacred space. We must also consider a fifth topic: the impact of digital media on religious authority, which has great relevance for online churches but has been discussed primarily within other areas of the study of digital religion. Throughout discussion of these topics, two questions have repeatedly been asked: are online and local churches rivals? And can we identify something really new happening online? This chapter will explore a selection of commentary on each of these five topics, in order to build a foundation for the case studies to come.

The Relationship between Online and Offline Activity

The first of these themes, the online-offline relationship, is the most important, because this relationship establishes the background assumptions that drive the other debates. In academic and Christian discussion, we can identity four different positions. The first three are specific to online churches: they might compete for membership with local churches; act as a supplementary resource alongside local participation; or attract new audiences to Christianity. The fourth approach is a broader claim about the Internet itself: could online activity become a kind of religion in its own right, replacing the functions of traditional religious institutions? Our assumptions here will determine the kinds of questions that seem most urgent and the significance we assign to them.

The first approach emphasises competition. Early Christian discussion assumed that online churches would rapidly become commonplace, rivalling local churches in appeal, and this argument motivated a great deal of theological debate over questions of validity and sufficiency. In 2002, for example, the Vatican report *The Church and Internet* acknowledged that the Internet may complement and enrich religious life, but declared that cyberspace cannot 'substitute' for real community, the sacraments, preaching or embodied experience (Pontifical Council for Social Communications 2002: 3). The task of the Catholic is to lead believers 'from cyberspace to true community' (Pontifical Council for Social Communications 2002: 4), which can only be found face-to-face.

In her recent review of Catholic teachings about media, Daniella Zsupan-Jerome highlighted this passage for particular approval. By focusing on the sacraments, she argues, *The Church and Internet* reminds us 'that we are flesh-and-blood, and that our most sacred symbols are made from the stuff of the earth' (Zsupan-Jerome 2016: 103). Online communication 'can diminish our sense of this', because 'our spirit becomes contained in the words and pixelated images rather than in our physical bodies.' Interacting through a screen involves 'a different kind of embodiment', something separate from and inferior to the 'invaluable mystery' of physicality.

Early studies of online religion suggested the Vatican had good reason to worry about the temptations of cyberspace. A Christian polling company, the Barna Group, published a sensational report in 1998 called 'The Cyberchurch is Coming'. Barna prophesied a mass exodus from the pews to the Internet:

> Fifteen years from now, you may tell your grandchildren that back in the old days, when people wanted a religious experience they attended a church for that purpose. Chances are good that your grandchildren will be shocked by such a revelation [. . .]
>
> By 2010 we will probably have 10% to 20% of the population relying primarily or exclusively upon the Internet for its religious input. Those people will never set foot on a church campus because their religious and spiritual needs will be met through other means.
>
> (Barna 1998)

Barna released a second report in 2001, repeating these striking predictions. 'Millions' of Americans, the authors wrote, 'are turning to the digital dimension to get them in touch with God and others who pursue faith matters . . . within this decade as many as 50 million individuals may rely solely upon the Internet to provide all of their faith-based experiences' (Barna 2001).

Some would be new believers, 'but millions of others will be people who drop out of the physical church in favor of the cyberchurch.' Brenda Brasher's *Give Me That Online Religion* went even further, suggesting that 'using a computer for online religious activity could become the dominant form of religion and religious experience in the next century' (Brasher 2001: 19).

These claims have not yet been fulfilled, and the actual evidence that lay behind them was always rather weak. In Barna's 1998 survey, just 4 percent of the 620 teenagers interviewed said they had ever used the Internet to find 'a religious or spiritual experience', the lowest of all the uses surveyed. The headline-grabbing 10 to 20 percent predictions were based instead on what these teens said about their expectations for the future: 'One out of six teens (16%) said that within the next five years they expect to use the Internet as a substitute for their current church-based religious experience', rising to one in three among African-Americans. In 2001, less than 1 percent of adults in the survey were actually trying to replace their local church online, but this second study assured readers that 'people are in the early stages of warming up to the idea of cyberfaith': two-thirds of respondents said they expected to use the Internet for religious purposes in future.

The second approach dismisses these fears of competition and emphasises complementarity. A series of more rigorous surveys by the Pew Internet and American Life Project have reported that online religious activity actually operates as a supplement to local engagement, rather than a substitute. In 2001, *CyberFaith* surveyed 500 'Religion Surfers' and reported that 'the Internet is a useful supplemental tool that enhances their already-deep commitment to their beliefs and their churches, synagogues, or mosques' (Larsen 2001). The 2004 report *Faith Online* claimed that two-thirds of American Internet users had done something online related to religion, but concluded that 'the online faithful seem more interested in augmenting their traditional faith practices and experiences by personally expressing their own faith and spirituality, as opposed to seeking something new or different in the online environment' (Clark, Hoover and Rainie 2004). Heidi Campbell draws the same conclusion in an ethnographic study of online Christian communities, arguing that for most members 'online community was a supplement to, not a substitute for, offline church involvement' (Campbell 2005: 161).

This debate between substitutionary and supplemental perspectives is still continuing. Douglas Estes has argued that online churches really are an alternative to local churches, claiming from his own personal experience that only a minority of those who participate in online churches also attend church offline (Estes 2009). Disability is often a theme in substitutionary accounts, suggesting that online churches are accessible to congregations who could not otherwise attend church at all. According to one of the Second Life users interviewed by Alicia Spencer-Hall, for example, 'I have discovered hundreds of people from around the world, that are shut-ins, disabled, have social phobias, that cannot attend a [local] church, so for them, this is their Church' (Spencer-Hall forthcoming).

Greg Neal of Grace Incarnate Ministries has argued for a more supplementary understanding of what takes place online. Neal insists that his online communions 'should *never* be thought of as an alternative to partaking the Sacrament within a localized Congregation', because the local church is 'immeasurably better' than an online network. According to Neal, the Internet can actually be an invitation to renewed engagement with local congregations:

> many [people] have written to thank me for bringing the Eucharist to them over the Internet in a way that has touched their lives and given them a new experience of the Real Presence of Jesus. In most cases they have indicated a renewed interest in attending church and, in more than once case, I have helped them to find a church in their local community to attend.
>
> (Neal 2006)

More recently, Todd Mullins has also argued for a supplementary position. Mullins, now the senior pastor of the Christ Fellowship multisite megachurch in Florida, explored the development and theology of that church's online campus for a DMin degree in 2011. One of Christ Fellowship's 'faulty assumptions', he admits, was 'believing that the congregation for church online would be exclusive to its own campus.' Eventually, the church realized that 'church online became a ministry tool for people from the physical church campuses as well . . . These people affiliate themselves with Christ Fellowship and not necessarily with Christ Fellowship's church online' (Mullins 2011: 140). In this case, it was apparently common for members who attended the local church campuses to participate online as well, treating the online church as an additional resource rather than an alternative.

In 2015, the Barna Group published a new report that returned to the question of online religious experience. *Cyber Church* (Barna 2015) surveyed 600 American Protestant pastors and compared results against a similar survey from 2000. Eighty-seven percent of pastors now agree that 'in general, it is theologically acceptable for a church to provide faith assistance or religious experiences to people through the Internet' (up from 78 percent in 2000). Just under half of pastors thought that the Internet would become the only source of 'faith experience' for 'some people' within ten years (47 percent, up from 27 percent). Ninety percent now agreed that it would be commonplace for the Internet to provide 'at least part' of people's 'faith experiences, activity or information' (up from 73 percent). Several of these questions are unhelpfully worded, combining very different kinds of online activity, but the survey can still indicate something of a general trend in attitudes among Protestant church leaders.

Roxanne Stone, a vice president at Barna Group, concludes that 'most pastors aren't ready for the Internet to be people's only means of spiritual growth or religious experience' (Barna 2015) and attributes this reluctance to the importance of physicality in Christian faith. 'Much of a pastor's role—and the role of a local church—is about presence', she explains, including presence as a community and in worship, and while the Internet can 'offer an important and accessible supplement to these physical activities [. . .] pastors are reluctant to say it can fully displace them or their work'.

Barna's statistics suggest a combination of the supplemental and substitutionary positions. These pastors agree that the general trend of religious Internet use will be to supplement local involvement, but almost half also believe that some people are going to find all of their faith experiences online. The survey didn't actually ask what pastors thought about these developments, so Stone's interpretation is highly speculative, but her demand for physicality does echo one of the most significant theological criticisms of the online church.

Online church supporters have often proposed a third approach. Rather than competing for the allegiances of local congregations, this third option insists that online churches are actually reaching entirely new audiences, extending the traditional Christian project of evangelism into previously inaccessible or uninterested communities. We will encounter this idea in each of the case studies in this book: the founders of Church of Fools, i-church, St Pixels, the Anglican Cathedral of Second Life and LifeChurch's Church Online all cited evangelism as a key goal and motivation.

As Heidi Campbell has observed, the discourse of 'e-vangelism' frames the Internet in two ways, both based on long histories of Christian thought and practice (2010: 138–139). In the first framing, the Internet is a tool. E-vangelists must be trained to use it effectively, deploying the correct techniques to maximise their persuasiveness. This idea will appear most clearly in our case study of LifeChurch, an evangelical Protestant organisation which has embraced the Internet as a means to communicate a Christian message to a larger audience. LifeChurch uses digital media to enable people around the world to access teaching, participate in worship and talk to and pray with Christian volunteers, and language of tools and training is common in church discourse.

In Campbell's second framing, the Internet is a mission field, with its own distinctive cultures. E-vangelists need to learn how to enter this new space and engage with the native population. This perception of the Internet as a mission field is widespread among online church supporters, and we will encounter examples in all of our five case studies. I-church pastor Pam Smith, for example, suggests that Christians involved in the launch of Church of Fools and i-church 'saw the Internet as a new territory—cyber space or virtual reality—and believed that Christians should establish a presence there, just as missionaries had always travelled to proclaim the gospel in new lands' (Smith 2015, Chapter 1).

This spatial understanding of the Internet as a mission field is highly attractive to Christians interested in online ministry, and it is worth reflecting further on the appeal of this idea. The metaphor of 'cyberspace' was popular in the 1990s and early 00s, and missionary discourses allowed Christians at that time to conceptualise their own activities in a way that was consistent with this wider cultural understanding. The spatial idea of the Internet is also compatible with established traditions of Christian ministry, like church-planting and missionary work, and it is helpfully flexible, open to denomination-specific adjustments. Among Anglicans, for example, a spatial understanding of the Internet also suggests the model of parish ministry, in which a church takes responsibility for the spiritual needs of everyone living in a specific neighbourhood.

For Christian groups committed to evangelism, the mission field metaphor also activates a powerful prescriptive discourse (Campbell 2010: 137), implying an intense, urgent and undeniable need for online ministry. Christian pastor and author Douglas Estes is a keen advocate for online evangelism, and his arguments offer a particularly clear example of the rhetorical power of this spatial approach. Estes claims that 'the Christian church is engaging far less than 1% of the 20 million people who are active' in virtual worlds, making gamers 'by far the largest unreached people group on planet Earth' (Estes 2009: 29). To overcome this situation, Estes calls for missionaries to start building new churches inside virtual worlds: 'it's possible that if a synthetic world cannot contain a real church, that world is unreachable; the cause of Christ is lost in that world' (Estes 2009: 38). Christians need to build churches in the space of the Internet in order to offer care to those who need it, demonstrate the advantages of their virtuous lifestyle and gradually learn how to share their message attractively.

The idea of the mission field also distorts understanding of Christian activity online. The model of a missionary travelling to a new land constructs the people in that new land as isolated, unaware of Christian teaching, and in some kind of spiritual need. Christians must send missionaries and build churches, because without them the new land cannot be 'reached'. Talking about the Internet as a mission field brings with it the same assumptions, encouraging the speaker to overlook the flow of people and ideas in and out of online spaces, to ignore existing Christian activities and to emphasise the wickedness of digital culture. We see some of the consequences of this construction in Estes' argument, quoted above. Some virtual world users are Christians, some of them engage in Christian activities in-world and many of them could potentially be contacted by Christians offline, but the urgent call of the mission field can only be activated if these details are ignored.

The rhetorical implications of the mission field may also lie behind one of the most curious features of the online church: its eternal newness. Researching the history of online churches is extremely difficult, because so many of them claim to be the first. In Scotland, for example, the *Herald* newspaper recently announced that the Very Reverend Albert Bogle 'has spearheaded a separate project taking the holy message to the spiritual superhighway with religious apps for the first online congregation', a group called Sanctuary

First (Donnelly 2016). Online churches have been in existence for more than 30 years, but the trope of the mission field requires writers to ignore this long history and reconstruct the Internet as an unreached world of spiritual darkness.

So far, we have considered the idea that online churches can replace local churches, supplement them or extend Christian ministry to new audiences through online evangelism. For some writers, however, a more interesting possibility is that the Internet itself could become a rival to conventional forms of religion. From this perspective, efforts to create churches online could be seen as co-opting this new digital rival to reinforce conventional religion, collaborating with digital media to create new kinds of religion or, perhaps, as failing to recognise the dangers inherent in consorting with the enemy.

According to Robert Geraci, virtual worlds are 'rearranging or replacing religious practice' (2014: 1), even for players who might not realise that their gaming experiences are religious. Rachel Wagner goes further, suggesting that religion has always been the same kind of thing as games and narratives (2012). According to William Sims Bainbridge, religious faith is just a restricted type of fantasy, required by certain historical and economic circumstances, and as it declines 'we shall come to see religion merely as an especially solemn art form' (2013: 3). Other social institutions have now begun to take over religion's historic functions, causing its significance to decline, and 'games will play a role in the further erosion of faith' (2013: 24) by inviting us into richer, more liberated worlds of fantasy. All of these arguments rely on a functionalist understanding of religion, in which religion is that which meets human needs for community, meaning and transcendent experience. *World of Warcraft* offers guilds, mythologies and moments of triumph and can therefore replace—and perhaps even be—religion.

In a much-discussed blog post, experimental psychologist Richard Beck has used a similar functionalist approach to propose that 'Facebook killed the Church' (Beck 2010). Social media replaces location-based sociality, he argues, and this is why levels of Christian identification are falling among young Americans. For his own generation, 'church *was* Facebook', because church-going provided a weekly opportunity to maintain social relationships. Today, 'you don't need to go to church to stay connected. You have an iPhone' (Beck 2010). In a lengthy response for *Religion Dispatches*, Elizabeth Drescher objects that 'if church were, indeed, a robustly social experience, Facebook would enrich and enhance that experience', and argues that the real problem faced by declining institutions is that they 'don't know how to be social' in a meaningful, accessible way (Drescher 2011a). This is, more or less, Beck's point: church-going was once necessary whether or not it was enjoyable, and now digital media have made other options are available.

This section has outlined four different arguments about the place of online churches in the relationship between conventional religion (specifically Christianity) and digital media. In early Christian commentary, online churches were seen as a substitute, shifting conventional forms of religious practice from local to online contexts. Later studies have tended to frame the Internet as a supplement, arguing that online churches and other religious resources are used in combination with local religious practice. In e-vangelism discourse, online church is framed as an extension of Christian ministry through new tools and into new mission fields, expanding the reach of the Christian message to new audiences. For some academic observers, the reverse seems more likely: digital connectivity and entertainment are fulfilling the functions of conventional churches, speeding their decline. We will return to this debate in Chapter 10, building on the examples of our case studies to develop a more useful understanding of the relationship between the digital and the everyday.

Community

These approaches to the relationship between online and local activity offer a helpful starting point for understanding what's at stake in debates about online churches. We now turn to consider another major theme in online church discussion, in which the arguments we have just considered play a crucial role: the validity of online community.

In the late 1990s, a group of Anglican computer enthusiasts formed The Society of Archbishop Justus[1] to encourage Anglican online activities. In the Society's report *The Church and the Internet* (not to be confused with the similarly titled Vatican report of 2002), Internet pioneer Brian Reid argues that the Internet 'can help the church with its mission as no technology since the printing press has been able to help', in part because it 'allows people to form communities without needing buildings' (1999: 19).

This easy acceptance of online community has been rather rare in Christian discussion. Reid defines a community as 'a group of people who talk to one another because they share common interests' (1999: 14), a straightforward approach that emphasises quality of communications. For many Christian commentators, there is much more at stake than shared interests: community is not just communication but embodied presence, face-to-face relationships, discipline and the physical service of each member to the group. This argument emphasises the irreplaceable value of embodiment, and we encounter it in different forms from representatives of a very wide range of denominations (for a more extensive survey, see Hutchings 2014). The argument from embodiment relies on the conviction that online community (and church) operates as a replacement for and a retreat from face-to-face relationships, and the word 'substitute' appears frequently in the quotations below.

Protestant futurologist Patrick Dixon voiced grave concerns over digital community in his book *Cyberchurch*, warning of 'a superficial Christianity without any human obligations' (1997: 93) that puts the user, rather than God, in control. It is too easy to escape from one another online, and so 'the Internet can never replace face-to-face human relationships—never be a substitute for fellowship and Christian community' (1997: 156). Dixon addressed the Christian New Media Conference in London in 2011, and I was able to ask him if he had changed his mind. Not at all, he said: 'the Christian faith is such a local thing' that online church could never be satisfactory. 'Your most powerful witness will not come online.'

The Vatican expressed similar reservations in *The Church and Internet*. The authors declared that 'the virtual reality of cyberspace cannot substitute for real interpersonal community', and their physical, embodied language suggests that it is the materiality and immediacy of face-to-face communication that they consider essential. In fact, 'even the religious experiences possible there by the grace of God are insufficient apart from real-world interaction with other persons of faith' (Pontifical Council for Social Communications 2002, para. 9).

Episcopal bishop Katharine Jefferts Schori offered some more detailed arguments in favour of local church participation during a radio interview in 2008, focusing again on the importance of physicality. According to Jefferts Schori:

> faith communities of all sorts need physical proximity of human beings in order to discover each other, in order to grow individually and as a community. . . It is hard to build a faith community in a deep sense on the Internet. We deal with caricatures; we deal with perceptions and positions rather than full human beings sitting in our presence. . . the incarnate piece is missing.
>
> (quoted in Campbell 2009)

In a speech in 2009, Anglican bishop and biblical scholar Tom Wright insisted that 'community involves looking people in the eye' (Wright 2009). Online churches retreat from the physical, suggesting a hostility to the flesh that resembles 'cyber-Gnosticism' and leading to a failure of pastoral care: 'it's not easy to convey love to [congregants'] bodies if they're not actually there.' Parallels between cyberutopianism, transhumanism and gnosis have often been explored (e.g., Aupers and Houtman 2005), but the cybergnostic label has found particular resonance and longevity as an accusation in Christian discourse.

John Piper, the well-known Baptist author and preacher, has been even more dismissive. Piper describes online church as 'sick', and compares it to the anti-body thinking of the Docetic heresy. 'We are created in bodies, not just in minds', he argues, and dispensing with 'the entire bodily dimension of togetherness' would be 'spiritually defective, would be contrary to Christ's understanding of the church, and would be hurtful to the soul' (Piper 2009).

In at least one case, an online church experiment appears to have agreed with this line of attack. NewSpring, a multisite megachurch in South Carolina, launched an interactive online campus on the LifeChurch model in

2009 and then closed it down in 2010. A new perception of the dangers of online disembodiment seems to have played a key part in this decision: NewSpring began to worry that participants were abandoning their local congregations.

We can gain some insight into NewSpring's thinking during this period through a series of blog posts written by its web pastor, Nick Charalambous. In 2009, Charalambous was bullish about the prospects for this new kind of ministry. 'Ubiquitous access to skilled, accessible and powerful preaching' online was 'transforming people's expectations of how a local church fits in the modern Christian life', he assured his readers. Competition was going to force every church to improve its ministry: 'only the excellent will survive' (Charalambous 2009b). At the same time, the web campus called on volunteers to remember that attending online 'should never be viewed as a legitimate way to "go to church" while avoiding the challenges or the commitments involved in faithful participation of a local church body' (Charalambous 2009a). Online attenders were supposed to be going to local churches as well.

Within a year, the contradiction between these two positions became acute. In 2010, Charalambous wrote a series of seven posts explaining the decision to close the campus, and his arguments focus on the danger of undermining the local:

> I see a disturbing trend of online church attenders, if they are not also connected to local churches, behaving like "super-consumers" chasing the best teaching or the best worship or the convenience of the web church every week. Few of these people are "churchless" in any true sense of the word. They've decided their local churches simply aren't good enough.
>
> (Charalambous 2010)

Charalambous feared that such market-oriented thinking might even infect those who did stay loyal to their local congregations. Physical church-goers 'might also, almost imperceptibly, begin to question their commitment, participation and submission to their local church' (Charalambous 2010), led astray by easy access to more exciting, less demanding experiences.

Unsurprisingly, these critiques of online community as disembodied, inadequate and unhealthy have been hotly disputed by supporters of online ministry. Social media consultant Meredith Gould, author of *The Social Media Gospel*, declares in the most straightforward and uncompromising terms that 'virtual community is real community' (2013: 27). Gould adds a crucial extra dimension to Reid's communication-focused definition of community, arguing that 'time and energy put into quality interaction' is the key (2013: 27). Critics are simply inexperienced: for a real understanding of online relationships, 'just ask anyone who has invested enough time in online conversations about faith, spirituality, religion and church to discover the ever-expanding universe of support available within and beyond denominations.'

Online church pioneer Mark Howe, one of the leaders of Church of Fools and St Pixels, has defended online community on similar grounds. Howe's argument also focuses on mutual supportiveness, using a specific anecdote as a demonstration. When a member of St Pixels ('T') died unexpectedly, the congregation organised an online memorial event, inviting his family to participate. According to Howe,

> the meeting was virtual, but those involved knew and cared about T. The earlier physical service happened in a consecrated chapel, but one with which T had no connection . . . Sometimes the words 'real' and 'virtual' fail to capture the way in which online church relates to real life—and death.
>
> (2007: 5)

Gould and Howe argue that online relationships can be supportive even without physicality, and it is that quality of supportiveness that defines them as community. In his attack on online church, John Piper insists that church congregations must be able to 'minister to each other and help each other to die well' (2009). According to these defenders, an online community can serve that function very well.

Among Christian supporters of online community and online churches, more theological defences are also common (for a summary, see Hutchings 2015). The Incarnation offers a valuable resource for some online church advocates, because God's decision to become a physical human being can be seen as analogous to the act of creating new, contextually appropriate communities in online environments. Turning to the Incarnation is striking rhetorical move, an attempt to reclaim and repurpose one of the more common arguments of critics like Katherine Jefferts Schori (Campbell 2009).

Other supporters have taken a different approach, drawing on the theology of the Trinity. This argument begins with the claim that God is essentially relational (as Father, Son and Spirit). Humans are made in the image of God, and this is why they are also relational. If relationality is part of the image of God, then all forms of community (including online community) can be seen as an outworking of a divinely given impulse to connect. Douglas Estes, for example, argues that the appeal of virtual community 'originates with the innate, God-given need and desire to relate to other people. It's Trinitarian; it's genetic' (Estes 2009: 59). By offering anonymity, removing the anxieties of physical appearance and generating new opportunities to meet, online environments 'free us to follow our *imago Dei* need for greater depths of relationship' (Estes 2009: 60).

One crucial dimension missing from this debate has been attention to the medium and structure of the communities under evaluation. An online community that uses a forum is not going to be the same as one that uses

Facebook, or a chatroom alongside a video feed, but both supporters and critics of online church have tended to avoid this level of detail. Critics complain that online church is dangerous, because it is disembodied and superficial; supporters promise that it is really community, because participants care about and support one another. This book will offer case studies of churches that describe themselves as communities and exist through different combinations of media, and we shall see that the kinds of relationships, belonging and boundaries developed in each church are significantly different. We will reconsider the question of community in Chapter 10, using network theories drawn from the field of Internet studies to propose a more constructive approach.

Ritual

We now move on to the third of our five themes, and the one which has perhaps attracted the most academic interest. Rituals have been a primary focus of study since the earliest publications in the field of digital religion, and researchers have repeatedly tried to find evidence that the design of online ritual represents some kind of innovation. Commentators have also been fascinated by questions of authenticity: can this kind of ritual be 'real', acceptable or desirable?

Some early observers doubted the potential of digital media to generate meaningful ritual experiences at all. Lorne Dawson considers the Internet 'ill-suited to the mediation of religious experience . . . because it is a too exclusively ocular, image-driven, textual, change-oriented, individualistic, detached and disembodied medium' (2005: 19). Stephen O'Leary also emphasises the importance of embodied participation: 'the participant in such [online] ritual remains too much of a spectator, separated from the virtual space by the box on the desk' (2005: 44). Something must be left out for a ritual to be enacted online, and for some participants these changes will always be too great for the ritual to be recognized as authentic. According to the Vatican 'there are no sacraments on the Internet', and cyberspace cannot substitute for 'the incarnational reality of the sacraments and liturgy or the immediate and direct proclamation of the Gospel' (Pontifical Council for Social Communications 2002, para. 9).

Academic studies have usually avoided questions of efficacy, but they have consistently reported that online rituals reproduce offline forms (see for example Hutchings 2010; Gelfgren and Hutchings 2014). Schroeder, Heather and Lee's pioneering study of 'E-Church', a small charismatic congregation meeting in an early virtual world, reported that language patterns and group structure reproduced standard elements of charismatic housegroup worship (1998). Ten years later, Nadja Miczek's comparative study of three virtual-world churches also observed a lack of ritual innovation. Miczek suggests that 'the continuance of ritual content and a great part of the structure guarantee that the ritual is recognised as a Christian service which visitors can follow' (Miczek 2008: 167). This argument is supported by Andreé Robinson-Neal, who has described her own experiences as a worshipper at Abundant Life Ministries in Second Life. According to Robinson-Neal, online ritual activity was still reassuringly familiar: worship in Second Life 'is only slightly different from worship at my local church' (Robinson-Neal 2008: 235), and this sense of familiarity was augmented by the presence of ordained ministers—an example of the continuity of offline and online structures of religious authority. Robinson-Neal trusted ALM because it fitted smoothly with her understanding of what a real church should be (Robinson-Neal 2008: 236).

Heidi Campbell uses empirical studies of online rituals as examples of 'convergent practice', a concept that she identifies as one of the key themes of research in the field of digital religion. Campbell recognises the high degree of continuity between online and offline ritual, but argues that even the most traditional practices must still 'be adapted to fit within the technological structures and constraints of the Internet' (2012: 76). If a prayer meeting is hosted within a virtual world, for example, participants must find new ways to express themselves, perform gestures, participate in music and so on—even if they also reproduce enough familiar elements to ensure that the event is still recognizable. As Stephen O'Leary argued in 1996, ritual 'adapts, mutates, and survives to prosper in a new communicative environment' (1996: 793).

Campbell argues that online networks can also encourage 'the blending of rituals and information from multiple sources', developing a 'self-directed form of spiritual engagement' (2012: 76). The Internet 'serves as a spiritual hub' from which participants can select both new and traditional resources and practices, and 'allows people to modify and perform religious ritual outside traditional contexts, so they can easily modify the customs and even meaning attached to them' (2012: 15). This flexibility is not new to the Internet, and has long been recognised by scholars as an important theme of lived religion and contemporary seeker spirituality, but the Internet makes convergent practices 'accessible and visible to the wider culture' (2012: 16).

In the case of online churches, some Christian commentators have argued that these kinds of convergent innovation do not go far enough. Douglas Estes, one of the very few Christian authors to have written a book-length defence of the concept of online church, argues that online ritual is still in a cautious exploratory stage, excessively reliant on the reassurance of familiarity. Without radical experimentation, he argues, 'they will never grasp the potential of being the church in the virtual world' (2009: 108). After all, Estes claims, there is nothing essentially physical about the Christian church—so any reluctance to change is quite unnecessary. This approach is the direct opposite of the critical voices we encountered in our discussion of community, for whom Christian life is essentially and irreplaceably embodied.

In the remainder of this section, I will focus on the rituals of baptism and communion. The idea of offering sacraments online is highly contentious and has been addressed by a number of Christian commentators and online church practitioners. Baptism and communion have attracted attention not because they are commonplace—very few churches have actually tried to perform these rituals online—but because they are theologically extremely important. As Estes explains, there is a great deal at stake here: 'if a virtual church is a real church, should it not celebrate the Lord's Supper in accordance with Christian tradition?' If it does not, Estes suggests, that 'raises questions about its validity as a church' (2009: 117). The richness of this long-running debate allows us to move beyond questions of spiritual experience and liturgical familiarity, to see how and why rituals might be reimagined in an online context.

In many Christian traditions, only real churches led by real priests or pastors can conduct the ritual of communion. In some cases, it is the act of sharing communion that defines a group as a real church. Communion is therefore connected intimately with authenticity, and also with authority—specifically, the authority to decide what is a church and who is a minister. Only one of the church case studies in this book (LifeChurch's Church Online) actually performed an online communion during my research, but the topic was certainly raised in all of them, and it remains one of the most heated topics in Christian discussions of online churches.

As we shall see, supporters of online communion disagree about the exact form this ritual should take. I will identify three different positions: rituals performed using physical elements; rituals performed using virtual elements; and rituals that replace the physical elements with something native to the online environment that can convey the same meaning.

First, some online churches and ministries have encouraged visitors to consume bread and wine, or similar equivalents, while watching, reading or listening to online media. This is the most common approach, currently offered by a number of large American churches through their online campuses. LifeChurch invited online worshippers to join in with a communion event about once per year during my research, instructing participants to bring their own bread and wine or juice (Steward 2009). This approach uses digital media to connect separate physical spaces in which the worship leader and the congregation members use physical gestures and objects to perform their parts of the ritual, not always at the same time (see Chapter 1).

Some churches have taken the same physical-elements approach to baptism. In 2008, Flamingo Road Church in Florida organised its first online baptism, inviting the candidate ('several hundred miles away') to be immersed in her bathtub by friends and family while the pastor prayed with them over a webcam. A video of this event was uploaded to YouTube, where it has received just over 8,000 views to date (FRCInternet 2008).

The Methodist Church has forbidden this kind of online communion on two occasions, in 2010 and again in 2013. In both cases, these announcements were prompted by public announcements that an online communion using physical elements was about to take place, on Twitter in the UK

(Wynne-Jones 2010) and in an online campus-style video environment in the US (Bauerlein 2013). According to the Wall Street Journal, to participate in the US experiment:

> users can simply grab some grape juice and any bread or crackers they have in the house, and consume them after the pastor, in the sanctuary, blesses the juice and bread as representing the blood and body of Christ [. . .] "We believe that God is not bound by space and time," said the Rev. Andy Langford, Central's senior pastor. "We believe that when we bless the bread and the cup in one place, if there are others who are worshiping with us, God will bless that bread and cup wherever they are."
>
> (Bauerlein 2013)

This 2013 incident prompted the formation of an Online Communion Task Force, which generated an impressive archive of position papers[2] before declaring firmly that communion 'entails the actual tactile sharing of bread and wine in a service that involves people corporeally together in the same place' (Phillips 2013).

In the second kind of online ritual, avatars themselves are the ones to consume. Paul Fiddes, a Baptist professor of theology, wrote a brief statement for the Anglican Cathedral of Second Life in which he suggested that avatars in Second Life should receive communion in the form of virtual bread and wine:

> An avatar can receive the bread and wine of the Eucharist within the logic of the virtual world and it will still be a means of grace, since God is present in a virtual world in a way that is suitable for its inhabitants. We may expect that the grace received by the avatar will be shared in some way by the person behind the avatar, because the person in our everyday world has a complex relationship with his or her persona.
>
> (2009: 1)

Second Life pastor Neal Locke agrees with Fiddes. From a Lutheran perspective, Locke argues, the sacraments are the visible and audible signs of the distinctiveness of the church, so the senses of sight and hearing are more important than physical touch and taste. Locke suggests that 'churches in avatar-mediated virtual worlds can, through the avatars of ordained ministers, visibly break digital bread, audibly say the words of institution, and visibly pour out wine and water', and their congregants can hear, see and '*through their avatars* actively participate in the receiving of the elements' (2011: 62; emphasis original).

The Cathedral asked Anglican minister Bosco Peters to respond to Fiddes' proposal, and he was bluntly unimpressed: 'We cannot baptise an avatar in the virtual world—as there is no water there, nor is an avatar a person on whom we can confer baptism.' The water is essential: 'we cannot pour a jar of jelly-beans over someone and say they are baptised', and we can't use a picture of water on a computer screen either (Peters 2009).

The Cathedral was not convinced by Fiddes' proposal, either. The Cathedral published a new document about virtual world sacraments in 2012, written by Christopher Hill, the Anglican bishop of Guildford. Bishop Christopher expresses appreciation for Paul Fiddes' contribution while rather firmly disagreeing with him: 'no Christian Church that I am aware of from Baptist to Roman Catholic could countenance a virtual baptism as a real baptism' (Hill 2012: 7), he claims, or an avatar communion as real communion (Hill 2012: 11). The bishop suggests instead a hybrid event, in which one group gathers in a physical location with an ordained minister, while another group gathers online in a virtual location. By participating in the same event, with the appropriate attitude of faith and reverence, the online participants could be considered to receive a 'spiritual communion', a concept which is theologically valid and in accordance with High Anglican tradition but (crucially) not the same as physical communion. The online component of the event would involve no physical or virtual consuming of anything, to avoid any suggestion that the spiritual communion was the same as the physical one, and the difference should be regularly explained throughout the service (Hill 2012: 11). According to the bishop, he had already used this approach to lead a successful hybrid communion service for the Cathedral's Second Life community. We can consider this a modified version of the first of our three models of online ritual, using digital media to connect a congregation to a physical ritual space.

I am not aware of any virtual world churches that have actually tried to create versions of communion that an avatar can participate in, but a number of virtual communion sets (complete with altar, chalice, furnishings and animations) are currently for sale in Second Life. One version advertises a 'stout marble altar' with crucifix and furnishings, a chair in which the priest can strike 'a lovely modest praying pose' before the service, an altar rail with cushions on which the avatar congregation can kneel to pray, and 'a most beautiful communion pose' in which 'the priest avatar will bless each congregation member in a delightful animation' (Grantly n.d.). A chalice is present on the altar 'to add to the "clutter" effect', but the animation does not seem to extend to the sharing of virtual wafers or wine. The set is offered for sale by a Second Life user whose store ('Holey Moley') includes a wide range of church-based activities, ranging from christening sets for baptising virtual babies to funerals for the virtually deceased.[3]

In my own travels in Second Life, I did encounter one Christian church offering avatar baptism. A baptismal pool had been constructed near the church building, and animations had been created to allow one avatar to immerse another in the virtual water. When I asked the leader of the group to explain the theology behind this activity, she found my question rather puzzling. Some members of the group had asked for their avatars to be baptised, so the group decided to try it and see what happened; formal theological theorising had not seemed worthwhile. Group members had all been baptised by a local church anyway, she explained, so their avatar baptisms functioned as a public affirmation of faith and also an extension of the act of Christian dedication to the believer's new, in-world body.

A third possibility has not been so widely proposed or implemented, but offers an interesting alternative. British theologian Debbie Herring argues that online church is 'forever incomplete' (2008: 41) without communion, but she rejects both physical and avatar eating. Herring argues for a more innovative approach, encouraging online churches to abandon bread and wine altogether and find practices indigenous to online cultures that might carry the same significance (2008: 42, 45). If we understand the act of sharing food as a commitment to welcome a guest, or to spend time with friends and family, or to give pleasure to others, then we might argue that other activities already commonplace online could mean something similar—although I have not yet encountered any online groups who have tried to put this approach into practice.

This discussion calls our attention to the relationship between online and offline reality. An online ritual can incorporate physical gestures, objects and locations, or it can take place entirely within a virtual environment; it can attempt to reproduce traditional ritual form, or to convey what practitioners see as the core meaning of the ritual through new symbols and practices. Debates over online sacraments also highlight the complex and often tense negotiations between digital entrepreneurs, online communities and established structures of religious authority. The challenge of reimagining ritual practice for a new environment is one example of the social shaping of technology in religious communities, a process that will be explored in Chapter 9.

Architecture and Sacred Space

The themes of these arguments over ritual have been echoed in scholarly studies of the visual design of online churches. Online church architecture, like online ritual, represents a convergence between continuation and innovation, designed in this case in pursuit of the experience of authentic sacred space. As with ritual, a number of studies have demonstrated that online churches tend to carefully reproduce and recombine symbols and styles from the traditions of Christian architecture (Hutchings 2010, 2014; Gelfgren and Hutchings 2014). Innovation here is found more in the categories of people who set up these churches and the adaptations they must undertake to fit their visual traditions into new media environments, rather than in the actual forms that make up their designs. Online architecture does not arouse the passions or fears of online communion, but it does provide another opportunity to consider the merits of familiarity in digital religion.

For some researchers, digital architecture contributes to the generation of sacred space by marking boundaries between sacred and profane regions. Stephen Jacobs has identified this strategy in the website design of one online church, whose pastor sought to recreate the experience of attending a local church by designing a series of online rooms for visitors to navigate through. According to Jacobs, 'the act of signing in signifies a threshold . . . It connotes a crossing over into a designated zone of religious activity' (2007).

Chris Helland has challenged some of the assumptions of this kind of spatial argument about sacredness, drawing our attention back to the question of ritual. For Helland, sacred spaces in online environments are 'set apart' not because of their structured boundaries 'but rather because of the ritual activity that people are conducting' in them (Helland 2013: 34). It is the action that sacralises the boundary, not the other way around:

> Although there are magnificently recreated sacred architectural spaces in virtual reality worlds, they have no inherent "sacredness" until they become utilized for their original function, which is purposeful engagement with the sacred.
>
> (Helland 2013)

Helland still argues that boundaries are necessary in virtual worlds, but for a different reason. Offline, 'people have a general idea of how to behave at a sacred site', but online environments are still too new for users to have developed a cultural memory that 'orients them toward the sacredness of the events occurring': instead, 'the behaviour of many online avatars is anything but sacred or respectful' (Helland 2013). Simone Heidbrink, Nadja Miczek and Kerstin Radde-Antweiler have proposed a similar argument. Misbehaviour, they argue, occurs because 'the socio-cultural purpose of [online] environments is not clearly, universally defined': some visitors do not 'assess the ritual performances as serious events', because they see the church 'as a gaming place where they could play around in ways that would be prohibited in a real church by social and cultural boundaries' (2011).

Standards of behaviour can of course be enforced with rules, but they can also be encouraged through less confrontational means. Architectural familiarity can be understood as a way to communicate the cultural expectations that guide behaviour and encourage the perception of sacredness. According to Simon Jenkins, for example, the founders of Church of Fools wanted to appeal to people who never went to church offline. In order to attract this audience, they turned not to ritual but to architecture: 'we wanted a church which said "church" as soon as you saw it' (Jenkins 2008: 101), with the atmosphere of a real place of worship. Recreating traditional Anglican church architecture through computer graphics and sound effects allowed the church to combine clear branding and symbolic weight with a playful, experimental tone, immediately signalling to visitors that this space was special by drawing on pre-existing cultural memories.

Jim Barrett has analysed the religious architecture of Second Life through the very helpful concept of 'rhetorical holiness' (Barrett 2010). Symbols that are recognised as 'holy' are transferred from offline contexts into Second Life, as simulations and representations, and used to mark the values, functions and communication channels of online spaces. In the inclusive, theologically liberal church Koinonia, for example, space is marked as 'church' by its basic shape and use of vaulted timbers, a focus on the immanence of God is marked by a shrouded cross, and a rejection of clerical hierarchy is marked by the displacement of the pulpit in favour of a central gathering of armchairs. 'Reading these indicators of place', Barrett concludes, 'the focus of the structure is a multi-channel communication portal within the frame of the rhetorically holy' (2010: 21). Correct interpretation of this rhetoric, he points out, requires a degree of religious literacy—or in Helland's terms, cultural memory (Helland 2013: 34).

Stefan Gelfgren and I have attempted to chart the different styles of architecture popular in Second Life churches, and our analysis made use of the concept of 'skeuomorphism' (2014: 68). This concept was developed in the field of archaeology in the 19th century to describe the widespread practice of decorating a new material to reproduce the structural features of an old one, and it has been widely used (and critiqued) in recent discussions of digital design philosophy. By carefully etching the texture of a woven basket into the clay of a pot, or making the pages of an e-book turn over when you swipe them, the creator can signal that a new object is the same kind of thing as an old one. Familiar design helps users understand how and why an object should be deployed, and it also communicates value, for example by imitating a more prestigious material. The skeuomorph can also be used to comment on cultural change, humorously satirising older styles or nostalgically recalling their superior qualities. In the context of online churches, Gelfgren and I used the concept of the skeuomorph to give a historical context for the use of familiar design to convey expectations of behaviour and perceptions of value and to reinforce the distinctive identity of a community by reminding participants of their shared traditions (2014: 69).

Recognisable styles establish expectations of behaviour and attitude, but skeuomorphs can also be used to generate critical distance through parody (2014: 69). In a study of Church of Fools, Randy Kluver and Yanli Chen emphasise the fragility of the boundary between sacred and profane. The founders attempted to 'mimic the presence of worshipping in a church' through architecture and sound design, but also deliberately encouraged 'a provocative levity within the gravitas of the sacred space' (Kluver and Chen 2008: 136) through the satirical use of familiar styles and symbols. The church 'constantly undermined' its own sacredness through humour and foolishness (Kluver and Chen 2008: 135), until for some users it 'was too much fun to evoke a sense of spirituality' at all (Kluver and Chen 2008: 131). By destabilising received ideas of the sacred, Church of Fools offered critical commentary on older ecclesial cultures and demanded a commitment to questioning, unrest and eclectic individualism. For Kluver and Chen, this reflects a postmodern challenge to Eliade's ideas of the sacred as a source of order (Kluver and Chen 2008: 132, 137).

It is certainly true that even the most familiar-looking online church space does not evoke the same attitudes and understandings from all visitors. Familiar design can imply expectations of user behaviour, but users do not always recognise those invitations. However, disruption does not necessarily arise from a lack of cultural understanding, as Helland (2013) and Heidbrink, Miczek and Radde-Antweiler (2011) argued. In many cases, the culprits are interested in disrupting an event or environment precisely because they recognise its religious nature. As we shall see in Chapter 4, the prevalence of trouble-making activities in Church of Fools was at least partly motivated by open resistance to the visual rhetoric of sacredness. If participants didn't realise that they were supposed to behave respectfully in a church, there would have been no fun in doing otherwise. The challenge of anticipating and guiding the expectations of an audience will be considered further in Chapter 10.

Authority

This discussion of misbehaviour brings us to our final topic of discussion: authority. The fate of religious authority in digital culture has been a perennial concern for Christian and academic observers, and it brings together the themes of competition and innovation. Commentators have wondered if new voices are going to emerge online, and if those new voices will resist, undermine and compete with established religious leadership. Perhaps surprisingly, authority has not received much attention in the specific case of online churches, so in this case our survey must include attention to some wider arguments in the study of digital religion.

Early discussions of digital religion claimed that the Internet was unsuited to hierarchical systems, favouring a shift toward grassroots communication networks that might facilitate the rise of new, heterodox ideas and practices. According to journalist Jeff Zaleski, the Internet favours 'religions and spiritual teachings that tend toward anarchy and lack a complex hierarchy' (1997: 111). We have already mentioned *TIME Magazine's* 1996 cover story, 'Finding God on the Web', in which Jacques Gaillot 'marvels at the freedom he enjoys loosed from the hierarchy of the [Catholic] church' (Ramo 1996). In the Anglican report *The Church and the Internet*, Brian Reid observed that 'the Internet has a certain anti-authoritarian flavour to it' (1999: 8), that 'people feel safer' when communicating anonymously (1999: 13) and that intimacy, sharing secrets and 'cowardly acts' of abuse are all therefore easier. The assumption that the Internet is the enemy of established hierarchies remains prevalent today in popular writing and journalism, across fields ranging from education and business to politics.

This kind of argument has also been proposed in academic debate. Heidi Campbell identifies 'shifting authority' as one of the main themes of studies of digital religion, observing a 'struggle between traditional sources of religious authority and new authority figures appearing online' (2012: 74). Chris Helland's influential typology of 'religion online' and 'online religion', first introduced in 2000, is a good example. Helland distinguishes between two purposes for communication and identifies each with a different communication structure. 'Religion online' provides information about conventional religion through institution-controlled one-to-many communication, while 'online religion' shares religious experience through grassroots community interaction (Helland 2000). This was not just a typology but also a value judgement and a prediction: online religion was going to succeed, and religion online would ultimately fail. 'Hierarchies and networks are two very different systems', Helland argued later, 'and the Internet was really only designed for one of them' (Helland 2005). In a more recent version of his position, Helland reiterates that religious organizations accustomed to maintaining 'strict boundaries concerning their beliefs and practices' will not fare well online, where individuals have greater freedom to experiment (2013: 31). Pauline Cheong describes this kind of approach as 'the logic of disjuncture and displacement' (2013: 74), in which online activity inevitably erodes and replaces older forms of religious authority.

In practice, of course, the impact of digital media is much more complicated than Zaleski or Ramo expected. As Campbell points out, the Internet can also act as 'a sphere for the renegotiation and canonization of accepted sources of authority', because the most prominent voices online often choose to use their blogs or social media platforms to 'acclaim sources of power' rather than competing with them (Campbell 2012: 74). Established religious authorities are also seeking to bring online activity more directly under their own control. We have already seen this dynamic at work in our survey of online churches (Chapter 1), a landscape in which independent pastors compete alongside ministries funded by megachurches and denominations. Pauline Cheong describes this second approach as 'the logic of continuity and complementarity' (2013: 78), in which online activity is used to support and extend established structures of religious authority.

Examples of religious efforts to supervise digital media are not hard to find. In *The Church and Internet*, for example, the Catholic Church expressed concern about anti-Catholic 'hate sites' and called for industry self-regulation and state intervention to 'establish and enforce reasonable limits to what can be said' online (2002: 8). Among online church projects, the 'Internet campus' represents a more direct reassertion of authority, using digital media to promote the message of a pastor and closely monitoring chatroom responses. I-church demonstrates a different form of institutional response, in which an online community operates with considerable freedom while remaining under the oversight of representatives of a denomination. The Anglican Cathedral of Second Life has tried to build its own denominational connections to the Anglican Communion, a project that Heidi Campbell argues 'provides the Anglican Church a new opportunity to reflect on its traditional boundaries and forms of ministry', even raising the question of 'a Bishop of Second Life' (2010: 125). In practice, the consequences of that conversation have been much less dramatic, but Anglican bishops have remained in contact with the Cathedral and have at times proved theological and administrative guidance—like the instructions about online sacraments we considered above (Hill 2012).

Rather than controlling the Internet, some religious leaders have tried to build up their own personal presence online, 'weaving social media into their vocation' (Cheong 2013: 80). This work requires adaptation, learning new communication skills and in some cases developing new sites, tools and platforms to connect with online audiences. Pauline Cheong has referred to this process as a work of 'strategic arbitration', in which 'laity cooperation is elicited by retaining discretionary power among the leadership to determine informational and interpersonal outcomes such that they do not destabilise the organization' (2013: 81). In order to convincingly retain this power, 'authority practices are appropriated and remediated across different communication platforms' (2013). Leaders become talented online communicators in order to promote their brand, operate online ministries and share their teachings. By developing these new competencies, they can preserve their status as experts in religious knowledge. Religious leaders can be assisted in this work by their followers: bloggers and social media communicators can build new audiences, but they are often very loyal to established sources of religious authority.

The Catholic Church has frequently served as the test case for discussions of religious authority online, and debate in recent years has focused on the Vatican's use of social media. To conclude this section, I will use two examples—a criticism of Pope Benedict's Twitter account and a defence of Pope Francis's use of Instagram—to illustrate the logics of disruption and continuity (Cheong 2013).

Sociologist and commentator Elizabeth Drescher favours the logic of disruption. According to Drescher, a 'Digital Reformation' is underway across Christianity, driven by a new culture of digitally mediated, non-hierarchical conversation (Drescher 2011b). To survive, churches must adapt their leadership and communication styles to fit the new expectations of their followers. When Pope Benedict XVI joined Twitter in late 2012, assisted by representatives of the company, he quickly amassed millions of followers but chose not to follow anyone else. For Drescher, this represented a disastrous failure to understand the medium. The pope's approach to Twitter was not ministry but advertising (Drescher 2012), and so it was 'good news' that his project was doomed by the inevitable trajectory of technology. Social networking platforms are 'participatory and transgressive media', Drescher argues, and they 'inherently resist and subvert the kinds of message control to which broadcast projects launched in social networks pretend.' Drescher's position is an update of Zaleski's denunciation of the 'cyber-religion from a mountain-top' offered by the Vatican's beautiful but non-interactive website 15 years earlier (1997: 128): such projects ultimately cannot succeed, because their goals are incompatible with the basic drive of digital media.

When Pope Francis joined Instagram in 2016, Vatican spokesman Antonio Spadaro provided a theological defence that closely adheres to the logic of continuity and complementarity. Spadaro, a theologian with a longstanding interest in digital media, sees the Pope's online presence as a response to his followers' desire to be present with him. According to Spadaro, the truest representation of Pope Francis is actually a selfie shared on Instagram: it is 'precisely the images shot by the faithful [that] relate this Pope in all his pastoral and symbolic strength', because 'the Pope of the people' is captured most truly in the people's photography (Spadaro 2016). Such selfies do not 'diminish his authoritativeness at all', because they are made possible only by the Pope's choice to create moments of closeness in which his followers wish to participate.

According to Spadaro, faith is now 'expressed and shared' in photos, and in this 'flow of images' can be discerned 'the natural desire to see God'. Instagram allows the Pope to participate directly in this circulation of images. This is a rather different approach to online authority, in which the Pope's own communications and conversations are less important than the aura of holiness made visible and accessible by his image. We see here a clear example of the role of followers in the co-construction of authority, which—for Spadaro—can actually be enhanced by participatory networks. We will return to these discussions of authority in Chapter 9, and the role of religious institutions in the future of digital ministry will be considered in the conclusion to this book.

Conclusion

This chapter has identified four key topics in the discussion of online churches (competition, community, ritual, space) and drawn on wider discussions of digital religion to consider a fifth (authority). In each case, heated debates have continued from the 1990s to the present day. Commentators have seen online churches as a rival to local churches, a supplement to them or a way to reach entirely new audiences. Critics have complained that online churches cannot be valid expressions of Christian community, because they do not allow for embodied interaction. In reply, enthusiasts have pointed to the emotional investment of participants and the mutual supportiveness they experience. Observers have generally reported that online rituals and online architecture copy familiar styles, but some commentators have called for greater experimentation while others have emphasized the value and safety of conservatism. Finally, discussions of online authority have adopted two approaches, one anticipating change and disruption and the other emphasizing the power of established institutions to maintain their influence. Each of these debates requires closer theoretical analysis, and we will return to this task in the final chapters of this book. For now, we will focus on gaining a better empirical understanding of what actually happens in online churches, in order to establish which of these different views has the most to offer.

Notes

1　Justus was the fourth archbishop of Canterbury and lived in the 7th century. He was selected as patron of the society not because of any connection to technology but because he worked hard and avoided publicity—like a good communications officer.
2　For the full archive, see http://www.umc.org/what-we-believe/what-is-the-united-methodist-view-of-online-communion. Accessed 31 August 2016.
3　The store's definition of virtual death is quite broad: customers are invited to conduct funerals for friends who have left Second Life, those who have not logged on for some time or those who have recently changed their avatars.

References

Aupers, S. and Houtman, D., 2005. "Reality sucks": On alienation and cybergnosis. *Concilium: International Journal of Theology* (1), pp. 81–89.

Bainbridge, W., 2013. *EGods: Faith versus Fantasy in Computer Gaming*. Oxford: Oxford University Press.

Barna Group, 1998. The cyberchurch is coming. *Barna Update*, 20 April. [online] Available at: <http://web.archive.org/web/19991010051101/http://www.barna.org/PressCyber Church.htm> [Accessed 31 August 2016]

———, 2001. More Americans are seeking net-based faith experiences. *Barna Update*, 21 May. [online] Available at: <http://web.archive.org/web/20130121083241/http://www.barna.org/barna-update/article/5-barna-update/48-more-americans-are-seeking-net-based-faith-experiences> [Accessed 31 August 2016]

———, 2015. Cyber church: Pastors and the Internet. *Barna Research*, 11 February. [online] Available at: <http://www.barna.com/research/cyber-church-pastors-and-the-Internet/#.V8bi6GVltEI> [Accessed 31 August 2016]

Barrett, J., 2010. Religion in new places: Rhetoric of the holy in the online virtual environment of Second Life. *Working Papers in Teacher Education* 7, pp. 19–23.

Bauerlein, V., 2013. Church's online communion: Sacrament or sacrilege? *The Wall Street Journal*, 15 November. [online] Available at: <http://www.wsj.com/articles/SB1000 1424052702304868404579194423734251960> [Accessed 31 August 2016]

Beck, R., 2010. How Facebook killed the church. *Experimental Theology*, 5 March. [blog] Available at: <http://experimentaltheology.blogspot.se/2010/03/how-facebook-killed-church.html> [Accessed 31 August 2016]

Brasher, B., 2001. *Give Me That Online Religion*. San Francisco: Jossey-Bass.

Campbell, H., 2005. *Exploring Religious Community Online: We Are One in the Network*. Oxford: Peter Lang.

———, 2009. Can online community be incarnational? *When Religion Meets New Media*, 19 January. [blog] Available at: <http://religionmeetsnewmedia.blogspot.com/2009/01/ can-online-communty-be-incarnational.html> [Accessed 31 August 2016]

———, 2010. *When Religion Meets New Media*. London: Routledge.

———, 2012. Understanding the relationship between religion online and offline in a networked society. *Journal of the American Academy of Religion* 80(1), pp. 64–93.

Charalambous, N., 2009a. A Web campus: More than a podcast with bells and whistles. *Meditations (Web)Church*, 13 May. [blog] Available at: <https://ipiphanist.wordpress.com/2009/05/13/a-web-campus-more-than-a-podcast-with-bells-and-whistles/> [Accessed 31 August 2016]

———, 2009b. The rise of net campuses: Are local churches on the ropes? *Meditations (Web)Church*, 3 June. [blog] Available at: <https://ipiphanist.wordpress.com/2009/06/ 03/the-rise-of-net-campuses-are-local-churches-on-the-ropes/> [Accessed 31 August 2016]

———, 2010. Web church challenges, part 3: Is it dangerous? *Meditations (Web) Church*, 14 March. [blog] Available at: <https://ipiphanist.wordpress.com/2010/03/ 14/web-church-challenges-part-2-is-it-dangerous/> [Accessed 31 August 2016]

Cheong, P., 2013. Authority. In: Campbell, H., ed. *Digital Religion: Understanding Religious Practice in New Media Worlds*. London: Routledge. pp. 72–87.

Clark, L., Hoover, S. and Rainie, L., 2004. Faith online. *Pew Internet and American Life Project*, 7 April. [online] Available at: <http://web.archive.org/web/ 20090322033942/http://pewInternet.org/Reports/2004/Faith-Online.aspx> [Accessed 31 August 2016]

Dawson, L., 2005. The mediation of religious experience in cyberspace. In: Højsgaard, M. and Warburg, W., eds. *Religion and Cyberspace*. London: Routledge. pp. 15–37.

Dixon, P., 1997. *Cyberchurch: Christianity and the Internet*. Eastborne: Kingsway Publications.

Donnelly, B., 2016. Kirk to consider online baptisms. *Herald of Scotland*, 17 May. [online] Available at: <http://www.heraldscotland.com/news/14496669.Kirk__ to_introduce_online_baptism__in_bid_to_boost_membership/> [Accessed 31 August 2016]

Drescher, E., 2011a. Facebook doesn't kill churches, churches kill churches. *Religion Dispatches*, 24 March. [blog] Available at: <http://religiondispatches.org/facebook-doesnt-kill-churches-churches-kill-churches/> [Accessed 31 August 2016]

———, 2011b. *Tweet If You Heart Jesus: Practicing Church in the Digital Reformation*. New York: Morehouse Publishing.

———, 2012. Pope follows himself in Twitter echo chamber. *Religion Dispatches*, 10 December. [blog] Available at: < http://religiondispatches.org/pope-follows-himself-in-twitter-echo-chamber/> [Accessed 31 August 2016]

Estes, D., 2009. *SimChurch: Being the Church in the Virtual World*. Grand Rapids: Zondervan.

Fiddes, P., 2009. Sacraments in a virtual world. *Brownblog*, 22 June. [blog] Available at: <https://web.archive.org/web/20090627215729/http://brownblog. info/?p=886> [Accessed 31 August 2016]

FRCInternet, 2008. *Flamingo Road Church First Internet Baptism*, 22 March. [video online] Available at: <https://www.youtube.com/watch?v=qThUe1-RvXU> [Accessed 31 August 2016]

Gelfgren, S. and Hutchings, T., 2014. The virtual construction of the sacred: Representation and fantasy in the architecture of Second Life churches. *Nordic Journal of Religion and Society* 27(1), pp. 59–73.

Geraci, R., 2014. *Virtually Sacred: Myth and Meaning in World of Warcraft and Second Life*. Oxford: Oxford University Press.

Gould, M., 2013. *The Social Media Gospel: Sharing the Good News in New Ways*. Collegeville, MI: Liturgical Press.

Grantly, M., n.d. Holy communion set with multiple animations. [online] Available at: <https://marketplace.secondlife.com/p/Holy-Communion-Set-with-Multiple-Animations/1264110> [Accessed 31 August 2016]

Heidbrink, S., Miczek, N. and Radde-Antweiler, K., 2011. Contested rituals in virtual worlds. In: Grimes, R., Husken, U., Simon, U. and Venbrux, E., eds. *Ritual, Media and Conflict*. Oxford: Oxford University Press. pp. 165–187.

Helland, C., 2000. Online-religion/religion-online and virtual communitas. In: Hadden, J. and Cowan, D., eds. *Religion on the Internet: Research Prospects and Promises*. London: JAI Press. pp. 205–224.

———, 2005. Online religion as lived religion: Methodological issues in the study of religious participation on the Internet. *Online: Heidelberg Journal of Religions on the Internet* 1(1), pp. 1–16.

———, 2013. Ritual. In: Campbell, H., ed. *Digital Religion: Understanding Religious Practice in New Media Worlds*. London: Routledge. pp. 25–40.

Herring, D., 2008. Towards sacrament in cyberspace. *Epworth Review* 35(1), pp. 41–45.

Hill, C., 2012. *Second life and sacraments: Anglican observations and guidelines*. [pdf] Available at: <https://slangcath.files.wordpress.com/2012/09/second-life-and-sacrament-4.pdf> [Accessed 31 August 2016]

Howe, M., 2007. *Online Church? First Steps towards Virtual Incarnation*. Cambridge: Grove Books.

Hutchings, T., 2010. The politics of familiarity: Visual, liturgical and organisational conformity in the online church. *Online: Heidelberg Journal of Religions on the Internet* 4(1), pp. 63–86.

———, 2014. The dis/embodied church: Worship, new media and the body. In: Vincett, G. and Obinna, E., eds. *Christianity in the Modern World: Changes and Controversies*. Farnham: Ashgate. pp. 37–58.

———, 2015. Real virtual community. *Word & World* 35(2), pp. 151–161.

Jacobs, S., 2007. Virtually sacred: The performance of asynchronous cyber-rituals in online spaces. *Journal of Computer-Mediated Communication* 12(3), pp. 1103–1121.

Jenkins, S., 2008. Rituals and pixels: Experiments in an online church. *Online: Heidelberg Journal of Religions on the Internet* 3(1), pp. 95–115.

Kluver, R. and Chen, Y., 2008. The Church of Fools: Virtual ritual and material faith. *Online: Heidelberg Journal of Religions on the Internet* 3(1), pp. 116–143.

Larsen, E., 2001. Cyberfaith: How Americans pursue religion online. *Pew Internet and American Life Project*, 21 December. [online] Available at: <http://www.pewInternet.org/2001/12/23/cyberfaith-how-americans-pursue-religion-online/> [Accessed 31 August 2016]

Locke, N., 2011. Virtual world churches and the reformed confessions. *The Princeton Theological Review* 17(2), pp. 55–66.

Miczek, N., 2008. Online rituals in virtual worlds: Christian online services between dynamics and stability. *Online: Heidelberg Journal of Religions on the Internet* 3(1), pp. 144–173.

Mullins, T., 2011. Online church: A biblical community. *DMin. Liberty Baptist Theological Seminary*. [online] Available at: <http://digitalcommons.liberty.edu/cgi/viewcontent. cgi?article=1467&context=doctoral> [Accessed 31 August 2016]

Neal, G., 2006. Online Holy communion: Theological reflections regarding the Internet and the means of grace. *Grace Incarnate Ministries*. [online] Available at: <http://www.revneal.org/Writings/onlinecommunionremarks.html> [Accessed 31 August 2016]

50   *Making Sense of Online Churches*

O'Leary, S., 1996. Cyberspace as sacred space: Communicating religion on computer networks. *Journal of the American Academy of Religion* 64(4), pp. 781–808.

———, 2005. Utopian and dystopian possibilities of networked religion in the new millenium. In: Højsgaard, M. and Warburg, W., eds. *Religion and Cyberspace*. London: Routledge. pp. 38–49.

Peters, B., 2009. Virtual Eucharist? *Liturgy*, 28 June. [blog] Available at: <http://liturgy.co.nz /virtual-eucharist> [Accessed 31 August 2016]

Phillips, L., 2013. Online communion conversation. *UMC Media*. [pdf] Available at: <http://umcmedia.org/umcorg/2013/communion/online-communion-conversation.pdf> [Accessed 31 August 2016]

Piper, J., 2009. What are your thoughts about being part of an online church? *Desiring God*, 29 June. [blog] Available at: <http://www.desiringgod.org/interviews/what-are-your-thoughts-about-being-part-of-an-online-church> [Accessed 31 August 2016]

Pontifical Council for Social Communications, 2002. *The Church and Internet*. [online] Available at: <http://www.vatican.va/roman_curia/pontifical_councils/pccs/documents/rc_pc_pccs_doc_20020228_church-Internet_en.html> [Accessed 28 August 2016]

Ramo, Joshua Cooper, 1996. Finding God on the Web. *TIME*, 16 December. [online] Available at: <http://www.time.com/time/magazine/article/0,9171,985700,00.html> [Accessed 28 August 2016]

Reid, B., 1999. *The Church and the Internet*. St Albans: The Society of Archbishop Justus. [pdf] Available at: <http://justus.anglican.org/press/SoAJ-Internetrpt.pdf> [Accessed 31 August 2016]

Robinson-Neal, A., 2008. Enhancing the spiritual relationship: The impact of virtual worship on the real-world church experience. *Online: Heidelberg Journal of Religions on the Internet* 3(1), pp. 228–245. [online] Available at: <http://www.ub.uni-heidelberg.de/archiv/8296> [Accessed 28 August 2016]

Schroeder, R., Heather, N. and Lee, R., 1998. The sacred and the virtual: Religion in multi-user virtual reality. *Journal of Computer-Mediated Communication* 4(2). [online] Available at: <http://onlinelibrary.wiley.com/doi/10.1111/j.1083–6101.1998.tb00092. x/full>. [Accessed 28 August 2016]

Smith, P., 2015. *Online Mission and Ministry: A Theological and Practical Guide*. London: SPCK.

Spadaro, A., 2016. *Cybertheology: Thinking Christianity in the Era of the Internet*. Trans. Way, M. New York: Fordham University Press.

Spencer-Hall, A., forthcoming. *Medieval Saints and Modern Screens: Divine Visions as Cinematic Experience*. Amsterdam: Amsterdam University Press.

Steward, T., 2009. Remember with us: Communion. *Internet Campus Blog*, 18 February. [blog] Available at: <https://web.archive.org/web/20090223124340/http://Internet.lifechurch.tv/2009/02/remember-with-us-communion> [Accessed 31 August 2016]

Wagner, R., 2012. *Godwired: Religion, Ritual and Virtual Reality*. London: Routledge.

Wright, T., 2009. Discipleship in the digital space. In: CODEC, *Christianity in the Digital Space*, 13–15 July. Durham: St John's College. [video online, 9 parts] Available at: <https://www.youtube.com/user/digitalsymp> [Accessed 31 August 2016]

Wynne-Jones, J., 2010. Church minister to tweet Holy Communion to the faithful. *The Telegraph*, 24 July. [online] Available at: <http://www.telegraph.co.uk/technology/twitter/7908263/Church-minister-to-tweet-Holy-Communion-to-the-faithful.html> [Accessed 31 August 2016]

Zaleski, J., 1997. *The Soul of Cyberspace: How New Technology Is Changing Our Spiritual Lives*. New York: HarperCollins.

Zsupan-Jerome, D., 2016. *Connected toward Communion: The Church and Social Communication in the Digital Age*. Collegeville, MN: Liturgical Press.

3 Methodology
How to Study an Online Church

As we have seen, discussion of online churches has focused closely on a small range of themes—comparison with offline churches, study of new forms of ritual, architecture and community, and questions about their impact on religious authority. I have suggested that these debates really come down to two main issues, innovation and competition.

In many cases, particularly in Christian discussion, online churches play only a symbolic role in these debates. The author's real concern lies elsewhere, most often in an argument about the supposed tendency of the Internet to individualize and isolate its users. The Internet is all very well, the argument goes, but we mustn't forget about the 'real world'—or we might even end up going to church online!

To progress, we need a robust understanding of what actually happens in online churches and why people value them. Despite the wealth of articles and brief discussions of online church, we are still waiting for a book-length study describing their actual practices and practitioners. This volume tries to address that gap in our understanding, using a series of long-term online ethnographies.

Ethnography and the Internet

As Christine Hine has written, 'ethnography is prized as a method for getting to the heart of meaning and enabling us to understand, in the round and in depth, how people make sense of their lives' (2015: 1) The ethnographer commits time to his or her field site, getting directly involved in the practices of its inhabitants. Through long-term participation and close observation, the ethnographer builds up a personal knowledge of what inhabitants do and—eventually—hopes to learn to see the world as they see it. This long-term personal engagement gives the ethnographer time to develop new theories, and to check those theories in conversation with other inhabitants of the field site.

Ethnography is a slow, time-consuming method but promises the kind of data and insight we need to make sense of online churches. As we saw in Chapter 2, researchers have reported that online churches look and act a lot like offline churches. Critics have argued that they are superficial, appealing only because they allow participants to avoid the difficult aspects of 'real' community, while supporters have promised that they can help bring new audiences into Christian fellowship. To evaluate any of these claims, we need to find out why online churchgoers build and maintain (and sometimes leave) these spaces, and that means spending time with them.

Ethnographers have been working online since the earliest years of Internet research. According to Laura Robinson and Jeremy Schulz, the first, 'pioneering' wave of research emerged in the 1990s, when 'initial forays into the brave new virtually constituted world . . . represented online interaction and identity performances as qualitatively different from those taking place in the offline world', with particular attention to 'identity play and deception' (2009: 686). This was soon followed by a second 'legitimizing' wave, emphasizing the unity of online and offline practice and 'endorsing a vision of the cyberfield as part of a flow between online and offline realities' (2009: 686). Ethnographers in this second wave paid more careful attention to the methodology of online research, seeking to demonstrate that ethnographic methods and frameworks really could be viable online. Robinson and Schulz suggest that their own contemporaries were creating a new wave of 'multimodal' ethnography, seeking to engage with user-driven content, video and audio materials, and virtual worlds. These new ethnographers 'acknowledge that the Internet's constant evolution necessitates continual reassessment of fieldwork methods', which might include learning to create their own digital content or exploring new modes of publication (2009: 692).

Methodology writers continue to debate the degree of novelty and innovation involved in these adaptations of ethnography. According to Robert Kozinets, 'online access to vast amounts of archived social interactions alongside live access to the human beings posting it entirely changes the practice of ethnography and, in fact, all of the social sciences' (2015: 4). Kozinets claims that there are six major differences between traditional ethnography and 'netnography'—his word for ethnography that focuses on data collected over the Internet. Communication is *altered* to suit the requirements of specific media; we now have a quite different kind of *access* to distant friends and strangers; vast amounts of our online communication are *archived* and preserved; data is available for *analysis*; new debates arise around the *ethics* of privacy and publicness; and our interaction has been *colonized* by corporate interests (2015: 74–75).

For Christine Hine, any kind of ethnography of mediated communication faces a challenge, because we cannot be physically co-present with all participants at once. There will always be something we have missed. That experience of uncertainty is a very productive problem, however: confusion becomes part of the situation we are trying to explore, because the participants we study face the same challenge. The key strength of ethnography is its flexibility, its ability to adapt to new circumstances. Instead of coining a new term to emphasise the uniqueness of the Internet, we can allow methods to emerge and shift more gradually while recognizing their continuity with older frameworks. 'An ethnographer, even in the Internet age, continues to develop a distinctive form of knowledge by being, doing, learning, and practicing, and by a close association with those who do so in the course of their everyday lives' (Hine 2015: 21).

Hine describes today's Internet as 'embedded, embodied and everyday', or 'E³'. The Internet today is 'entwined in use with multiple forms of context and frames of meaning-making' (Hine 2015: 33), as one aspect of families, schools, workplaces and neighbourhoods. Through social media, our virtual identities are more likely to be extensions and expressions of our physical bodies, rather than opportunities for role-play (Hine 2015: 41). The Internet may even disappear altogether from awareness, becoming a mundane infrastructure that users fail to notice (Hine 2015: 46). For all these reasons, 'it is not helpful to assume in advance that there is something special about the digital' (Hine 2015: 29); we need to establish, instead, what the Internet means for particular people, at particular times, in particular circumstances.

I have chosen to focus in this book on five specific churches, all of which maintained a primary online site of interaction during the main period of my fieldwork. In each case, there was a clearly distinguished 'field site'—a website, or an island in a virtual world—that I could visit regularly. These sites included exchanges of text, audio, video and virtual constructions, and I was able to participate directly in most of the activities pursued there. These were not the kinds of invisible, everyday online practices Hine describes: participants in each church talked regularly about how digital communications impacted their spiritual and social lives.

Nonetheless, the ethnographic work shared here bears out many of the claims above. The opportunity to check back through archives of at least some forms of communication was crucial for much of my research, as Kozinets would expect, and we will see examples of altered communication, enhanced accessibility and a form of organizational colonization throughout the case study chapters to come. Any study of religion online must pay careful attention to the ways in which activity is 'embedded' in wider frameworks, structures and meanings, and to the user's expressions and experiences of embodiment—just as Hine argues.

Defining the Field Site

The idea of the 'field site' has been much discussed by ethnographers in recent decades and deserves attention here. In the mobile, networked world of contemporary society, it is rarely possible to draw clear boundaries around a single site of interaction. The ethnographer must be prepared to follow connections, move with participants and discover the shape of the field site over time. This flexibility is just as necessary online.

In each case, I initially joined the church through its primary interaction site, and then gradually became aware of a whole network of alternative channels of communication. Churchgoers emailed each other, exchanged phone calls, played games on Facebook and met up offline. Within a website, the different areas and media of communication developed their own cultures and boundaries; the participants in a debate forum might not enter the chatroom, and vice versa, while the regular attenders at worship might not be the same people I encountered at social gatherings.

Making sense of these multi-modal communities requires a multi-sited ethnography (Marcus 1995), a form of qualitative research devised to study cultural formations that are not bounded by a single field site. Rather than focusing exclusively on specific, restricted areas and applying a common set of pre-determined research methods to each, the researcher constructs the object of study itself by tracing out the relationships between different regions of activity. Relevant areas and connections are discovered by following people, ideas or objects as they circulate through networks.

As described by George Marcus, multi-sited ethnography traces associations and connections among research sites and uses these links to construct aspects of the global systems in which those sites are embedded (1995: 96). My own study was not quite that mobile or grand in scope, but the principles of multi-sited ethnography were still key to the conduct and analysis of each individual case study. Participants might focus their attention on one primary interaction space, such as one part of a church website or one location in a virtual world, but adequate understanding of their commitments and practices required exploration of the multiple, often unofficial connections they were also constructing through a wide range of other digital and electronic media.

Multi-sited ethnography encourages the researcher to adapt methods to make sense of each new context as it emerges, without expecting equivalent richness, consistency or reliability of data to emerge from every site of study. As Marcus explains, 'multi-sited ethnographies are invariably the product of knowledge bases of varying intensities and qualities' (1995: 100), and require 'different practices and opportunities' for each fieldwork location. In my own case studies, I have included face-to-face, chatroom, email and telephone interviews, observations, analysis of archives, studies of design and architecture, published survey data and other sources as appropriate for each setting.

This flexibility requires careful attention to the strengths and weaknesses of each source, particularly when engaging in comparative analysis, but adopting a single consistent approach to each study site would fail to recognise the distinctive challenges and opportunities offered by each medium, platform and social group. Before we move on to the case studies themselves, we must therefore consider the details of my approach, with some attention to the strengths and weaknesses of my strategic choices and my methods.

Selecting the Case Studies

I first joined an online church, Church of Fools, in 2005. I had read some of the extensive media coverage of this new kind of church and was curious to find out more. I was tentative at first, but was quickly drawn in by the chance to discuss, argue and debate through online forums. Later that year, I began a master's degree in theological research at Durham University. Online church was new, exciting and relatively unstudied and seemed to raise all kinds of intriguing theological and sociological questions. My new friends in Church of Fools (which would later become St Pixels) were supportive, and I embarked on an online ethnographic study of their conversations. When I looked for a suitable comparative study, I discovered i-church—launched at the same time, using similar media, but connected much more closely to an established Christian organisation.

I continued to study these groups for my doctoral research in the sociology of religion, also at Durham University, but quickly added two more examples. LifeChurch.tv launched its Internet Campus (later Church Online) in 2006, offering a very different kind of worship and community; this seemed too important a development to ignore. My attention was drawn to Second Life when the leader of a church there, the Anglican Cathedral, contacted the Association of Internet Researchers mailing list to request a community historian. My fifth case study only came into focus when I began to write: I had such a wealth of information from my study of the Church of Fools community that I divided that material into two chapters, the first focusing just on the 3D project launched in 2004.

This final combination of case studies has four major strengths. First, the five churches studied here were all high-profile; they attracted the most media attention during my initial period of research, and Church of Fools and the Cathedral in particular have attracted a considerable number of academic studies. Studying these five churches offers opportunities to engage with the work of other commentators and researchers. Second, this range of churches is diverse in their use of media. Websites, forums, chatrooms, blogs, video streaming, virtual worlds and social network sites all feature. By using this range of case studies, we can compare quite different forms of communication, presence, design and ritual. Third, each of these case studies has constructed a different hierarchy of authority, motivated by different Christian traditions and theological principles. Church of Fools was funded by a denomination, i-church is owned by a diocese, the Cathedral of Second Life was founded as an independent project that claimed an Anglican identity and LifeChurch.tv's Internet Campus was created to extend the voice and ministry of a single church. Comparing these groups enables us to examine and contrast different understandings of hierarchy, freedom and control. Fourth, these groups all maintained congregations over a period of years, but they differ markedly in size. Each can be seen as a leader in its field, but even the largest and most successful church in Second Life can only bring together a handful of people at once; the video broadcasts of Church Online have attracted thousands. By following these different groups over time, we see the potential of online church, observing activities and practices and cultures that attract committed participants over many years—but we can also see some of the limitations and frustrations of groups that have, in some cases, finally had to close down.

Methods: Participant Observation

Each project began with an initial period of observation and participation. I first approached one or more leaders of each group to secure their permission for my study to go ahead, assuming that a participant ethnography would be extremely difficult without their consent. I then presented my research to the congregation in the most appropriate way I could find, offering a chance for questions and objections.

My primary period of participant observation continued from 2006 to 2010. I took part in online discussions, attended worship and social events, explored online environments and attended as many face-to-face events as possible. I wrote extensive field notes throughout my research, copying down descriptions of scenes and interesting quotations from conversation. I also conducted a series of interviews, speaking to at least 25 members of each group. I spoke with a representative sample of participants, including leaders, core members and individuals with particular viewpoints I wanted to explore. I also asked for volunteers, so that my own perceptions of who or what mattered most in the community would not be the only factor guiding my data collection. In each case, churchgoers were very supportive of my research and eager to be interviewed. Indeed, finding a polite way to stop undertaking more interviews without hurting anyone's feelings proved somewhat difficult.

Alongside my ongoing participation in each group, I decided to include a one-month period of focused participant observation in 2008 or 2009, during which I would attempt to participate in as many events and activities as possible. My long-term membership allowed me to track changes over time and to build up a sense of the community, and my short-term intense involvement allowed me to explore all the different activities going on in the community at a particular moment.

Through participant observation, I gained direct experience of some of the strengths and weaknesses of these churches. I could feel for myself something of the power of online worship, the intimacy of online prayer, the warmth of online friendship, and the practices used to engage with or silence disagreement. Of course, as with any ethnography, I could not assume that my own personal perspective would be shared by others, so I tested my ideas in conversations, listened carefully for different perspectives, and tried to interview as wide a range of participants as possible. Nonetheless, I do believe that personal experience is of great value to the online researcher. When evaluating critiques or enthusiastic praise of online churches, it is invaluable to have a bedrock of lived awareness to fall back on.

Long-term involvement also helped build up familiarity and trust, and this rapport encouraged group members to share their experiences with me. In some cases, my long-term presence encouraged church leaders to invite me to take on a leadership role of my own, participating in strategy meetings, helping to draft guidelines or even joining the leadership team. Participation in leadership is problematic, of course, because the researcher risks creating his or her own object of study—but in this case, my involvement alongside a team of others generated extremely helpful insights into group management processes while actually enacting rather minimal change (somewhat to my disappointment at the time, it must be said).

Unsurprisingly, this kind of involvement came at a cost. Taking part in community life also embroiled me in some serious internal conflicts, ranging from heated debates over points of theology to even-more-heated debates over the management of whole churches. As we shall see in my chapter on i-church, participation in leadership discussions could at times lead to some quite complicated research disasters.

This book will be completed in 2016, some years after my primary period of participant observation. In the interim, the Internet has evolved, and online churches have evolved with it. Our attitude to digital media is not constant, as Hine has demonstrated, and digital religion is also ever-changing. To update my case study chapters, I returned to each group for a second, much briefer period of participant observation in 2015 or 2016. In each case, I attended services and spoke to participants, and I also paid close attention to any evidence of redesign in the church's web presence. The current state of each church will be discussed briefly in the conclusion to this book.

Methods: Interviewing

My interviews were conducted through a variety of media. The first took place face-to-face at a meeting of St Pixels members, but I soon wanted to talk to members I could not encounter so easily. No part of the online church space could be appropriated as an interview room, so I decided to experiment with telephone interviews instead. Volunteers came forward in much higher numbers than expected, and I eventually conducted more than 30 interviews, almost all by Skype. If interviewees declined to be contacted in this way, citing time pressure or privacy concerns, I spoke to them through an instant messenger program instead. I used this same mix of face-to-face conversations, telephone calls and occasional IM chats to interview members of i-church and LifeChurch.

I chose a different approach for research in Second Life. Visitors to the Anglican Cathedral and LifeChurch's in-world space preferred to communicate through text chat, not voice, even though voice conversations were an option at that time. I decided to respect this preference, conducting interviews in-world through text communication. I observed a much higher degree of boundedness in Second Life, a stronger sense that this was a separate world with its own rules and norms. Users constructed avatars that did not always resemble their physical bodies, and insistence on a telephone call would have broken that power of play and disguise. Insisting on out-of-world contact would therefore greatly limit the number and diversity of people I could speak to, by aligning my research with a particular philosophy of authenticity that I had no interest in promoting. On a practical level, I could be sure that all the members I spoke to were comfortable expressing themselves through typed chat, because that was their normal mode of interaction in-world. This was not true of any of the other churches studied, where members could participate in community life without visiting a chatroom.

The only interview medium I tried to avoid was email. Email conversations proved time-consuming, slow and uninformative. Writing a careful email can take as long as a phone call, and a response may not arrive for weeks. Most attempts at email interviews tailed off unfinished. Emails to busy church leaders rarely received a response unless I was already engaged in regular communication with the person I was emailing and had established some kind of rapport; I had to visit the i-church trustees and Life-Church pastor team in person for really useful conversation. Even email exchanges could be helpful at times, however, and some valuable accounts were collected.

Online interviewing has strengths and weaknesses, analysed by many previous ethnographers. Kozinets, for example, points out that 'synchronous, text-based, chat interviews often can offer a thin, rather rushed and superficial interaction' (2015: 60)—something I did experience in some of my IM interviews. Typed text conversations took more than twice as long on average as voice conversations, often lasting for several hours, and answers tended to be very brief. There was less scope for simply letting the interviewee talk about his or her experiences, unprompted, as I tried to do face-to-face and over the telephone. On the telephone, on the other hand, it is very difficult to signal politely that an answer is too long or has drifted from the point; all the opportunities that exist face-to-face for non-verbal guidance are lost, and the interviewer has no option except extreme patience or an audible interruption.

Not all studies of online religion have accepted the value of online interviewing. For Heidi Campbell's first ethnography, she selected a small number of email list participants in the UK and North America and visited them in person, staying in their homes, observing their Internet use, talking to their families and visiting their local church. Her intent, she explains, was 'not only to verify data collected online about members, but also to observe more fully how the Internet shaped their engagement with their offline community and local church' (Campbell 2005: 78). This embodied, geographically located approach has also been advocated in the work of Daniel Miller, whose studies in Trinidad (e.g., Miller 2011) have explored what the Internet means in very specific contexts. As Christine Hine explains, 'the Internet means quite different things to different people, and takes on multiple identities' (Hine 2015: 38); if we situate our study in a home, neighbour-hood or region, we can map some of those identities and resist lazy, homog-enizing rhetoric about 'cyberculture'.

For this study, such an approach did not seem appropriate. My primary focus was the culture emerging in particular online groups, and I gleaned information about the wider embeddedness of online activity from my observations and interviews. I trusted the people I spoke with to tell me the truth; not the whole truth, perhaps, but at least a large and informative part of it.

This question of trust requires some additional comment. Campbell repre-sents one extreme in her early work, insisting on face-to-face conversations with users, family and friends. The opposite extreme can also be found, par-ticularly in writings on Second Life: insistence that 'actual' realities should not be sought out and need not be known. Journalist Wagner James Au, for example, avoids 'real life' details about interviewees in his own writings about the virtual world (Au 2005). This protection of boundaries preserves the integrity of the world as a space with its own culture, important in its own right. Any conversations about 'real life' should be taken as role-play and used to understand the in-world persona of the speaker. Tom Boellstorff also accepts in-world activity and conversation as 'legitimate data about culture in a virtual world':

> if during my research I was talking to a woman, I was not concerned to determine if she was "really" a man in the actual world, or even if two different people were taking turns controlling "her". Most Second Life residents meeting this woman would not know the answers to such questions, so for my ethnographic purposes it was important that I not know either.
>
> (Boellstorff 2008: 61)

My own research project falls somewhere in between these two extremes. Online events and conversations that involve pseudonymity, role-play or the concealing of offline identities can give much insight into online culture if interpreted sensitively. Insisting on offline 'verification' would be both pointless and unhelpful, and could violate the carefully negotiated balance of privacy and self-disclosure cultivated by participants. On the other hand, this research did require interest in 'real life'. As Campbell and Hine have argued, online activity must not be perceived in isolation from local and physical activities, experiences and relationships—and this is particularly true of online religion, as we shall see. Very few people develop or prac-tice their religion exclusively through online communication. We can only understand what takes place online if we understand the local context of participants. Indeed, online churches integrate discussion of local life into their everyday online activity—one example of the 'embodiedness' of the Internet discussed by Hine.

In fact, each church placed a high value on honest communication, understood in a particular cultural context of acceptable and unacceptable forms of role-play and anonymity. If that context was properly understood, I believe (and just as importantly, participants in my case study churches believed) that conversation partners could be relied on to tell me the truth, or at least to tell me that they would rather not. When I met churchgoers face-to-face, they almost invariably turned out to be more or less as I had expected, and this closeness between online and face-to-face experiences was often remarked on at those meetings. Role-players in these communities were usually easy to spot, rarely became regular visitors and could at least sometimes be encouraged into sincere and heartfelt conversation. Actual intentional deception was rare and caused very great disruption and distress on the very few occasions I witnessed its discovery. I will discuss some examples of role-play and deception in the case study chapters ahead.

Research Ethics

Having discussed my methods of participant observation and interviewing, I must also briefly consider the ethics of online research. My ethical policy was based on flexible, case-by-case assessment rather than rigid rules (in line with the recommendations of the Association of Internet Researchers—see Markham and Buchanan 2012). Three principles were particularly important throughout: context, transparency and consent. I needed to ensure that my methods were appropriate for the group I was studying, that group members knew who I was and what I was doing, and that I asked for permission wherever necessary for quotes and interviews. Group ideas of 'public' and 'private' could vary significantly, and each church offered a different range of media that I could use to publicise my work and discuss appropriate methods, so adhering to these three core principles led to slightly different research strategies for each group. Two examples are given here to illustrate the kind of negotiation required.

In St Pixels, every member could write a blog. I used my own to introduce my work, advertise for interviewees, ask advice on method and regularly update readers about my progress. Community members who knew me well vouched for me in comments to my posts, expressed interest in taking part and in some cases acted on their own initiative to promote the project to others. Most of the website is public access, but these conversations made it clear that many regarded the website as a 'private' space and felt they were talking to trusted friends; indeed, some objected vehemently to being treated as 'guinea pigs' or 'rats in a maze' by prying researchers. I therefore promised to ask permission from the author of any post on the site that I wanted to quote; to do otherwise would have caused great distress, not to mention ruining any chance of further support for my research.

My approach to LifeChurch's Internet Campus (or Church Online) was quite different. LifeChurch services may be attended by hundreds or even thousands of participants who need not log in or in any way disclose their identity, and posts to the chatroom appear alongside the service broadcast for all the congregation to see. I therefore treated chatroom posts as public statements and quoted them without seeking permission. This an appropriate response to chatroom culture, which tends to be public and impersonal, and there was no other way to proceed—participation is much too fluid to strike up a conversation with each contributor, and there were no user profiles or blogs that could be used to introduce or discuss my research.

Other media were simpler to deal with. I treated all blogs and blog comments as public material available for quotation, except in the case of St Pixels. I treated website designs and virtual world constructions as public, along with any texts included in those designs. These decisions were based on consideration of audience, including the audience who could actually access the material and the audience the author seemed to have intended. In some cases, research design was also restricted by posted statements about the kinds of research a website would permit. St Pixels and i-church both adopted such statements some years after my research began, in response to increased interest from students.

I followed standard ethnographic procedure in interviews by giving out an information sheet about my research to each participant and requesting a typed signature on a consent form, although most considered this unnecessary and something of a nuisance. The format of the consent form required adjustment. In Second Life, I distributed forms using 'note cards', small text files that can be exchanged and edited in-world. Consent forms needed to be appropriate to online contexts in which real names were sometimes closely guarded and usernames serve as adequate identification, so I allowed participants to complete them under a username if they wished. I also asked for an email addresses, so I could contact respondents in future if they left the group.

I adopted a conservative attitude in uncertain situations. Several interviewees, for example, operated multiple avatars in Second Life, using them to engage in different activities and communicate with different groups of people. Others designed avatars of a different gender, age or race, or dressed in clothes associated with another religious tradition. I could have used these options myself, creating a range of avatars in order to test the reactions of other users; some of the participants I interviewed did exactly that, using alts to see if anyone treated them differently. I decided not to try this approach, primarily because it would have been highly controversial in the groups under study, causing distress, undermining trust in me as a researcher and jeopardizing my future work in that community. In any case, I could learn at least as much from conversations with a demographically diverse range of group members. Tom Boellstorff dismisses using an alternative avatar or 'alt' as 'ethically and methodologically inadequate' (2008: 80), and in this case I agreed.

One final issue must be mentioned: names. I have decided to include the real names of all the churches I studied: Church of Fools, i-church, St Pixels, the Anglican Cathedral of Second Life and the Internet Campus (Church Online). All five have received media attention, including interviews with leaders and members, photographs of websites and participants and coverage in newspapers, radio and television. All five are highly distinctive, so anyone with good knowledge of the field would have little trouble identifying them even from anonymised descriptions. Finally, in each case I am joining a tradition of published discussion of these specific groups; I need to identify what I'm describing so other researchers can see how my account may differ from their own.

I include real first and surnames when quoting a member's published work or someone who has been publicly identified as a leader. The pastor of a named church cannot realistically be made anonymous. In all other cases I used pseudonyms to refer to anyone I quoted and tried not to include information that might identify them. I selected a first name to refer to each interviewee, making no attempt to reflect nationality, ethnicity, class or generation, but preserving gender. Each individual has only one username, even if they appear in more than one chapter or church, so the reader can follow his or her progress across the online church landscape.

This chapter has briefly outlined the principles of Internet ethnography, described my own approach to participant observation and interviewing, and introduced some of the challenges of Internet research ethics. With that foundation, we are ready to meet our case studies.

References

Au, W., 2005. Taking new world notes: An embedded journalist's rough guide to reporting from inside the Internet's next evolution. *First Monday* Special Issue 5. [online] Available at: <http://firstmonday.org/ojs/index.php/fm/article/view/1562/1477> [Accessed 1 September 2016]

Boellstorff, T., 2008. *Coming of Age in Second Life: An Anthropologist Explores the Virtually Human.* Woodstock: Princeton University Press.

Campbell, H., 2005. *Exploring Religious Community Online: We Are One in the Network.* Oxford: Peter Lang.

Hine, C., 2015. *Ethnography for the Internet: Embedded, Embodied, and Everyday.* London: Bloomsbury.

Kozinets, R., 2015. *Netnography: Redefined.* Thousand Oaks: Sage.

Marcus, G., 1995. Ethnography in/of the world system: The emergence of multi-sited ethnography. *Annual Review of Anthropology* 24, pp. 95–117.

Markham, A. and Buchanan, E., 2012. *Ethical Decision-Making and Internet Research: Recommendations from the AoIR Ethics Committee.* Association of Internet Researchers. [pdf] Available at: <http://aoir.org/reports/ethics2.pdf> [Accessed 1 September 2016]

Miller, D., 2011. *Tales from Facebook.* Cambridge: Polity Press.

Robinson, L. and Schulz, J., 2009. New avenues for sociological inquiry: Evolving forms of ethnographic practice. *Sociology* 43(4), pp. 685–698.

4   Church of Fools

There ought to be a church on the net. It's like someone has created a new town and no one has thought to build a church there. It's almost scandalous.

—Simon Jenkins (Doney 2004)

The Church of Fools existed for a decade as an empty space, a miniature virtual world for curious visitors and solitary prayer. For four brief months in 2004, however, that small world bustled with activity. Its innovative 3D space offered the chance to meet, converse and worship through avatars, text and music and attracted many thousands of visitors each day. With the Church of Fools, online religion blossomed into an anarchic, argumentative sacred space that could attract as many congregants as a cathedral or megachurch. Church of Fools received unprecedented worldwide coverage in mainstream and Christian media, and also attracted almost uncontrollable waves of trouble-makers. The experiment was short-lived, as its designers had intended, but formed a community that remains active as I write today. The brief life of Church of Fools demonstrates something of the complexity of the relationship between institutions, ideas, practices and technologies and will help us start to look deeper into the appropriation of new media by religious groups.

By the time I joined Church of Fools, in 2005, its virtual environment had been replaced by a simple text forum and chatroom. I never saw the 3D Church in action, welcoming bishops to worship or besieged by griefers, but participants who were active in the community at that time have shared a wealth of memories, experiences and impressions with me through our conversations. This chapter is divided into seven sections, discussing the origins of the Church, its launch, the use of architecture and space, the avatar, worship, griefing and control. I draw on stories retold in my own interviews, observations from my own visits to the 3D space, and a range of published and unpublished research by some of the original members.

The Ship of Fools and the Ark

The story of Church of Fools begins with the *Ship*, a short-lived print magazine from the 1970s relaunched online in 1998. According to the editor and designer, Simon Jenkins, the 'Magazine of Christian Unrest' aims 'to help Christians be self-critical and honest about the failings of Christianity, as we believe honesty can only strengthen faith' (Ship of Fools n.d.). Regular features include satirical commentary on Christian life, caption competitions and humorous special features that attract occasional coverage from mainstream media (e.g., Beckford 2008).

The site also boasts extensive forums (forum.ship-of-fools.com), each with its own brief introduction. The 'Heaven' section is described as 'a merry chaos of creativity, comedy and random questions'. 'Purgatory' is 'our serious discussion space', where 'all views are welcome—orthodox, unorthodox, radical or just plain bizarre—so long as you can stand being challenged.' Behaviour is moderated, not theology. Even good behaviour is not always a requirement: 'Hell' is a space for 'a complaint, a rant or a personal argument', where 'normal rules of civility are abandoned'. Anyone looking for a fight with another site member can summon them to Hell for a blunt and public exchange of views.

On April 20, 2003, the *Ship* launched 'The Ark' (http://ark.saintsimeon.co.uk/). 'The Ark' was a unique virtual environment, designed by special-moves with funding from Jerusalem Productions and Premier Christian Radio. The website is still online in 2016, offering visitors the chance to enter the environment, watch clips, read stories and take a guided tour. Twelve biblical characters, from St Paul to Jezebel, were installed in Noah's Ark and animated by players around the world. Characters could perform gestures and communicate in typed text, with words appearing in speech bubbles that moved upward to disappear at the top of the screen. Each character maintained a homepage and journal. In keeping with the 'reality TV' theme of the endeavour, the audience voted for their least favourite characters to 'walk the plank'. The winner, after 40 days, was John the Baptist.

The Ark featured a swimming pool and helipad-style 'dove pad', a variety of rooms for sleeping, showering and socialising and a storage area for animals below deck. Characters were given tasks, including putting on a variety show, a performance of Romeo and Juliet and a soap opera, and struggled to save the Ark's one Tyrannosaurus from extinction when it fell ill. Characters were also invited to climb the mast to the 'crow's nest', where they could communicate directly with God to receive that week's news and challenges. God's words, of course, appeared at the top of the screen and moved downward.

The Ark also included a weekly Sunday service. This prompted considerable creativity, making use of the gestures and rooms provided to construct events combining humour, irreverence and some degree of sincere spirituality—in keeping with the ideals of Ship of Fools. In the third week, a specially designed chapel appeared in place of one of the living rooms, but services continued to include creative uses of space and action. The Ark's description of the first worship service is worth quoting at length:

> After a delayed start due to rowdy Bible characters, Sunday night's divine service including preaching, hair washing and a walk round the

ship. [. . .] Job prayed for the Ark's as yet unseen animals: "We are called to the sacred task of caring for your creation, including the critters below. May they have life and presence, unlike George W. Bush. Amen." [. . .] John led an "act of repentance" in the washroom, inviting everyone to wash their hair and sing, "Gonna wash those sins right out of my hair"—but this potentially moving moment left Martha [. . .] cold: "Touching . . . but impractical. I have great difficulties with symbolic gestures like this." [. . .] Still, when it came to the last part of the service—a prayer walk led by Esther—it was Martha who volunteered to pray: "let us learn from each other; let us learn about forgiveness."

(Ship of Fools 2003)

The opportunity to playfully rework religious practices, language and concepts was evaluated quite differently by different participants, but even those trying to interpret the worship seriously did not act in quite the same way as they might in a face-to-face ritual environment. Martha prays sincerely and she disagrees with signs of frivolity in the sermon, but she also interrupts throughout the event to offer her own commentary.

The Church of Fools

According to Simon Jenkins, the two key discoveries made during the Ark project were the contestants' 'emotional involvement in the game' and the success of the weekly worship events. These services included 'preaching, Bible readings, prayers and discussion' and 'planted an idea in our minds that this might be a way to realise the idea of online church. How would it be if we detached the chapel from The Ark and ran it week by week as a virtual church?' (Jenkins 2008: 98–99).

The Ship of Fools team identified three specific purposes that they felt a virtual church could fulfil:

1. We wanted to try translating church into the medium of the net. It was to be a genuine experiment, seeking visitor feedback, to find out if online church is a viable way to 'do church'.
2. We wanted to create moments of genuine depth and spirituality, helping people feel they were connecting with God, themselves and others.
3. We wanted to educate and inform people who would never darken the doors of a church about Christian worship and fellowship. We hoped to break down the barriers people have about going to church.

(Jenkins 2008: 100)

We see here an example of the 'eternal newness' of online churches, discussed in Chapter 2. Online churches had already been active for 20 years, but Jenkins frames the idea as a radical new experiment in evangelism.

Church of Fools was launched just over a year later, in May 2004. Like the Ark, this was to be a short-term, high-publicity project. Planned to run for three months until August, the project eventually closed on September 26. The homepage announced that the new church was 'an attempt to create holy ground on the net' and 'partly intended for people on the edges (and beyond) of faith',[1] echoing Jenkins' emphasis on proselytism. Well-known speakers were invited to address the congregation every week, with the first sermon delivered by the Bishop of London.

The bishop helped fund the project, but the most important donor was the Methodist Council of Great Britain. Neither the Methodist Council nor the Church of England asked to impose their denominational style on the new church, or to restrict what it could do. Online community was apparently deemed theologically unproblematic, compatible with the interests of each institution. Instead, these religious institutions used their financial strength to fund an experiment in community-building.

Jenkins has linked the experimental approach of Church of Fools with the ecclesiology of John Wesley, founder of Methodism. This connection is strategic, underlining the appropriateness of the decision of the Methodist Council to grant funding, but also frames this project as a continuation of the historic Christian mission to build churches in new social settings: 'Just as the Methodist church leader John Wesley took his preaching out of churches and into the fields and streets in the 18th century, we wanted to take church to where people are in the 21st century—on the Net' (Jenkins 2008: 100).

Jenkins expressed a similar idea in 2004 in an interview with the *Church Times*, an Anglican newspaper. Church of Fools did not intend to compete with offline churches, Jenkins insisted, but merely to answer an unmet need:

> An estimated 200,000 people are joining the Internet each week worldwide; so we'd better go where the people are. There ought to be a church on the net. It's like someone has created a new town and no one has thought to build a church there. It's almost scandalous.
>
> (Doney 2004)

By establishing a church online, the church-builders were setting up a presence amid the activity of contemporary life, 'going where the people are' and so bringing 'the people' into contact with a Christian community. As noted in Chapter 2, this kind of missionary language conflates a space where people spend time—a fair description of the Internet—with the much more problematic conception of 'cyberspace' as a separate 'world': Douglas Estes quotes Jenkins to support his highly questionable claim that virtual world users are 'the largest unreached people group on planet Earth' (Estes 2009: 29).

Initial media coverage of the Church of Fools focused on the evangelistic aspect of its vision. Giles Wilson, writing for the BBC, began his article by setting the church firmly into this frame: 'Churches are having to use their imagination to attract new members. The 3D virtual-reality Church of Fools is just one idea, but does it have any chance of building a congregation?' (Wilson 2004). The title of his piece—'In cyberspace, can anyone hear you pray?'—highlights the media appeal of the experimental and comical aspects of the 'virtual church'. Maria Ortigas, a reporter for CNN, also covered the story from the same angle. Her article, titled 'Cyber church: now God goes online', presents the Church of Fools as a sign of hope for a hopeless cause: 'Leaders of the Christian church in Britain fear an age old message is falling on deaf ears. But a "new means of communication" may just help them reach out and touch someone' (Ortigas 2004). Note the assumption in each article that the Church of Fools actually belongs to and works for British Christian leaders.

Both Wilson and Ortigas identify the safety of the Internet as an advantage over the potentially intimidating experience of walking into a physical building. According to Wilson, 'The thinking is that some people may be more prepared to wander into a website than a church on the corner of the street.' Ortigas quotes a conversation with a churchgoer who expresses a similar idea: 'It's non-threatening. [. . .] A lot of people don't like to go into a church, because they think it's threatening or they don't deserve to be there.'

According to the Church of Fools, the experiment did appeal to this intended audience of non-churchgoers. Figures published by the church record an average of 8,000 visitors to the site each day in the first two weeks, peaking at 41,000 shortly before May 25 (Church of Fools 2004a). A survey of 2,400 visitors was conducted by the church at the end of the project, and Jenkins reports that 39 percent 'were not regular churchgoers (if they went to church at all, they were only there for Christmas, Easter and family occasions)' (Jenkins 2008: 113). According to one visitor from the United States, 'I have a friend who had a crisis this week. No way would he ever go to a real church. But he went to yours and said his first prayer in many years' (Jenkins 2008: 113).

The Church of Fools website also used this survey to demonstrate the success of the project:

> We are keen to reach what we have dubbed "Generation X-Box"— the under 30s who are pursuing spirituality on the Internet, but may never darken the doors of their local church. At a time when traditional church is perceived as a place for old ladies, more than 50 per cent of our visitors have been under 30 years of age—and 60 per cent are male.
> (Church of Fools 2004b)

These statistics must be interpreted with some caution. I have not been able to find a copy of the full survey results, or any discussion of its methodological limitations. In a private communication in 2009, another church leader described the questionnaire as 'more of a poll than a survey', with nothing to prevent people from filling out the form more than once or doing so inaccurately. Indeed, the leader pointed out, 'among the responses I ignored in the analysis was a 300 line long piece of ASCII porn clip art.' Nonetheless, the Church of Fools was able to use their visitor statistics to claim at least some degree of success in attracting a new kind of audience into a Christian space.

Architecture and Space in the Church of Fools

The world of Church of Fools included two rooms, a church area and a crypt, connected through a doorway visible on the left in Figure 4.1. The main church was cross-shaped, with a wide nave and short transepts. The nave contained two rows of five pews either side of a central aisle flanked by translucent columns with rounded, Romanesque arches, leading to a chancel with apse, altar, elevated pulpit and lectern. Doorways were marked with pointed arches. The stone altar was topped by a golden cross and flanked by two golden candlesticks, and the church organ sat to one side. Behind the altar, a stained glass window displayed two of the logos of the Ship of Fools website, a cartoon boat being rowed in both directions at once and a bemused-looking image of the magazine's patron, St Simeon the Holy

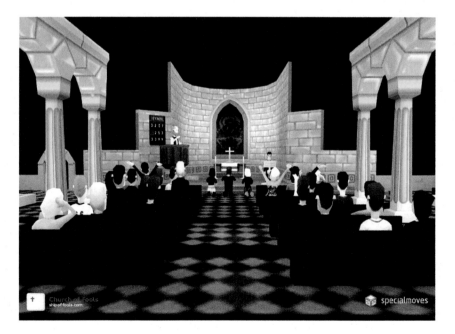

Figure 4.1 Worship in the Church of Fools, 2004. Image by Ship of Fools.

Fool. A hymn board hung behind the pulpit, displaying three absurdly high numbers in a gentle subversion of a common item of ecclesial furniture. The side walls included a set of contemporary images of the Stations of the Cross, each accompanied by a brief, contemplative essay. The Crypt area, accessed through a doorway but marked as underground by a flight of steps in one corner, contained a set of red armchairs and sofas, positioned facing each other, and three more armchairs in another corner. Several vending machines lined the walls. Worship was heralded by bells and accompanied by hymn tunes, but at all times the visitor heard what Jenkins describes as 'the ambient sound of an echoing church' (Jenkins 2008: 103)—a kind of gentle whispering hush.

The designers considered different modern and ancient architectural styles, according to Jenkins, but decided they needed to create something instantly recognisable:

> Since we wanted to appeal to people who never went to church, we decided that we wanted a church which said "church" as soon as you saw it. Which meant pointed arches, stained glass, pews and other familiar items from historic church architecture.
>
> (Jenkins 2008: 101)

This quote suggests that the designers of Church of Fools were trying to draw on a universal, nondenominational understanding of what a church might look like. At least some visitors disagreed, perceiving the Church of Fools as part of a Christian culture specific to the Church of England. Mark Howe's thesis, for example, refers several times to its 'Anglican visual metaphor' (Howe 2005: 34). There were no uniquely Anglican symbols in the church, but the combination of ancient architectural styles and bare stonework is indeed often found in England, characteristic of churches converted from Roman Catholicism and remodelled during the 16th-century Reformation and subsequent Puritan reform periods. The architecture of the church appears to have conveyed unintended cultural meanings to at least some of those visiting the space.

Creating traditional forms in a visual style better known for computer games was also intended to ensure that the space retained its novelty: 'we thought this ecclesiastical style would create atmosphere and give the whole thing a playful, experimental edge' (Howe 2005: 101). This is an interesting counter-example to Jim Barrett's concept of 'rhetorical holiness' (2010). In this case, symbols drawn from Christian tradition were being used to create a degree of distance from that tradition, generating humour by simultaneously signalling and playing with recognisable identity.

While the altar was never used, its image, particularly the cross it bore, added a symbol of spiritual sincerity. According to Jenkins, 'it was valuable to have the symbol of the cross as a visible sign of what we were doing'

(Jenkins 2008: 101). The Stations of the Cross contributed further to this signalling of intent. 'As one of our aims was to help create genuine moments of spirituality in Church of Fools, we decided to enrich the environment' by adding Stations to 'offer an opportunity for individual prayer and reflection' (Jenkins 2008). The Stations brought images and text into the environment, and 'they also signalled that we were attempting to create a form of sacred space' within a church that 'had the feel of a computer game.' The combination of humour and sincerity was important for the initial vision of Church of Fools, as Jenkins explained in his interview with the *Church Times*: 'At the heart it's very serious, even though it's cartoony . . . I'm sure there'll be some very funny moments, but we're playing a fairly straight bat on this' (Doney 2004).

These explanations indicate a desire to symbolically frame the church space in four different ways: as Christian, church, playful and spiritually sincere. The decision to choose a visual style that emphasises and undermines church-like seriousness at the same time is entirely characteristic of Ship of Fools, marking one point at which the new church is clearly drawing from the culture of the community that founded it.

The desire to frame space as sincere and holy through the use of recognisable church architecture and symbolism met with a positive response from at least some users. Anna, for example, is an American woman who identifies as a High Church, 'fairly up-the-candle' Anglican. Anna came to Church of Fools after noticing adverts and discussions of the church launch on the *Ship* website, where she had been a regular participant for some years. She participated in the 3D church as an ordinary congregant, later taking a leadership role after the closure of the 3D space. I was able to interview Anna in person when she flew from the US to attend a St Pixels gathering in 2008, and again in 2009 after she had married an English member of the community—one particularly intense example of the close friendships remarked on throughout my interviews in this community. Anna emphasised the importance of the reality of the space, the feeling that worship and conversation were genuinely taking place in a real church, and suggested that the appearance of the church—its rhetorical holiness, to use Barrett's (2010) terminology again—was one contributing factor to the development of this perception:

> I am an observant fairly High Church Anglican, so the fact that it looked like a church and felt like a church mattered to me [. . .] the church looked churchy, and I don't know about over here so much but we've got some churches over in the States, there's a brand new big one that's pretty rich, and it looks like a posh new fitness centre from the outside, and you think why? But that's not what I think of as church, it's not an auditorium, it's a church. And the 3D environment looked like a church.

The Avatar

Visitors to the Church of Fools could be represented as avatars (Fig. 4.1, Fig. 4.2), chosen from a range of pre-designed characters. Special avatars were created for important guests, like the Bishop of London, to reflect their physical appearance. Twelve male and 11 female figures were available for ordinary visitors, all using the same basic body shape but with a variety of skin tones and clothing. Notably, only three non-white skin tones are available for each gender, suggesting a strong assumption on the part of the designers about the audience they expected to attract. Clothing styles were mostly conservative, with two suits and a range of shirts available for men and trousers, floor-length skirts and full-sleeved shirts for women. The default male avatar bore a striking resemblance to Ned Flanders, the much-maligned Christian character from 'The Simpsons'.

An avatar could be made to walk around the space by clicking on the area of floor to which the user wished to direct it, while clicking on seats caused the avatar to sit. Clicking on the avatar itself brought up a range of gesture options, including four for worship—'kneel down', 'bless', 'Hallelujah!', and 'cross self'—and nine for social interaction—'clap', 'hands on hips', 'laugh', 'point', 'pull hair out', 'shrug', 'scratch head', 'shake hands', and 'wave'. Two avatars can be seen performing the 'Hallelujah!' gesture in Figure 4.2, raising their arms above their heads. It was also possible to turn

Figure 4.2 Avatars in the Church of Fools, 2004. Image by Ship of Fools.

the avatar 45 degrees in either direction, helping users orient themselves 'correctly' for face-to-face conversation.

Communication between avatars was limited to text and operated in two different ways. Ordinary visitors' speech appeared overlaid across the bottom of the screen and scrolled upward, while those leading services were able to speak in ascending 'thought bubbles' like those of the Ark. This latter option was been retained later for the single-user environment, where any typing appears in bubbles. Avatars could shout, speak or whisper, with shouting audible throughout the church, speaking only to avatars nearby, and whispering directed to a single selected other. The limited range of the speech command permitted many different conversations to take place in different areas of the church at once.

The site's designers chose to limit the number of avatars to 35 at a time, but permitted another 1,500 visitors to enter the church as 'ghosts' instead. A 'ghost' was represented by a translucent avatar able to move around and perform gestures, but visible only to that user. The congregation of visible avatars could be surrounded by a cloud of invisible presences, a second congregation of ghosts who could see but could not be seen. The presence of this cloud of witnesses was symbolically powerful for some, as described later in this chapter.

Avatars were simple, offered limited gesture options, and—due to the small number of choices available—were frequently identical to other avatars present in the church at the same time. Despite these limitations, at least some of the users of the environment identified strongly with their avatars, perceiving these visual representations as extensions of themselves. One might imagine that a High Church Anglican whose worship emphasises the physical environment and ritual of worship and focuses on the physical sacraments would find the Internet unappealing as a venue for church-building, and Anna admits that her initial reaction was unpromising:

> when they first started talking about online church, when it was a gleam in its papa's eye, I remember thinking that if I did not already know and like and respect some of the people involved my reaction would have been, "Oh, please!"—and that would have been that. I probably would not have checked it out at all, at least not at that time.

In fact, Anna found that the visual environment, including the avatars and their gestures, created a sense of reality that permitted the small virtual world to become, for her, a true expression of church. We will consider her comments on worship below, but her observations about the avatar itself are striking:

> what stunned me was how much I identified with that little cartoon dude [. . .] at any given moment, it was worse than wearing the same thing to the prom, at any given moment there might be three people in

there who looked a lot like you, but I really identified with her. And when you picked an avatar that's who you kept, because that's who you were in that community. And I think it fostered that sense that those people were really people and I was a real person.

The limited range of avatars and the constant experience of meeting others identical to yourself led to the emergence of brief rituals of community interaction. One regular visitor 'looked exactly like me, and it was a joke between us, we'd show up and say how lovely you look today, you know and stuff like that.' Rather than damaging the experience of immersion, this restriction was named and brought into conversation in a controlled and positive way by the use of in-jokes and so framed as a dimension of church culture.

Mark Howe's dissertation describes some of the different views among church leadership about the importance of the avatar:

> In a discussion among wardens about moving towards first-person rendering [. . .] an anglican minister said "I was surprised [. . .] how much I felt to 'be' my avatar". [. . .] One warden said that we had become "way too avatar-obsessed", while another responded that "Typing the command to cross myself and then seeing myself do it was as *real* and *meaningful* as doing so with my physical hand. I would find losing that immediate feedback of my gestures a real loss."
>
> (Howe 2005: 55. Original emphasis)

For some of these church leaders, an avatar was only a tool, and it could be improved or replaced as technology permitted. For others, the avatar was experienced as an extension of the actual physical body of the user. To cross yourself physically meant the same—and felt the same—as crossing yourself on-screen.

I heard a similar account in an interview with Barbara, a warden who had also led services of worship. On one occasion, she recalled, she moved her avatar into a standing position to preach in the church and found that her legs actually started to ache in real life—a problem eased only by sending the avatar to find a seat. Barbara discussed 'correct' and 'uncomfortable' ways to position the avatar body at length, using a code of proxemics that paralleled physical bodily activity. She felt a need to face the avatar she was speaking to, for example, and to find a seat when joining conversations in the Crypt.

Proxemics created other communication options that might not be so readily available or socially acceptable in face-to-face situations. It was possible, for example, to position an avatar to show that the user was listening but did not wish to take part in conversation. Cara, a warden in the church, commented in an interview conducted at a meet in 2007 that she preferred 3D spaces like the Church of Fools or Habbo Hotel because she could stand back from conversation and get a feel for what was being said without becoming involved directly, an option she felt was not available to visitors to text chatrooms. Because avatars could only hear speech uttered within a certain radius, it was also possible to hide behind objects in the church, preventing other avatars from approaching and so creating space for private discussion. Cara mentioned hiding behind pillars or joining a friend behind the church organ. Another interviewee, David, preferred hiding behind the vending machines in the Crypt.

Some visitors to the church established their own areas for specific kinds of conversation. According to Simon Jenkins, 'One group of three chairs came to be called "Atheist's Corner", because three atheists from the Netherlands regularly visited and sat there. They told us they enjoyed the church as a place where they could have intelligent debate about the issues which mattered to them' (2008: 102). According to my conversations with community members, these atheist visitors were aware that only a limited number of avatars were able to connect at once and carefully logged out before services to make space for others interested in attending worship.

Worship in the Church of Fools

Jenkins reports that worship patterns at the Church of Fools evolved during the project:

> Our original plan for Church of Fools was to run one service a week, on Sunday evenings, with a full liturgy, prayers, readings, a hymn and sermon. But due to the demand of our visitors, we soon started running daily services of morning and night prayer in UK time, and eventually also ran an evening service for US visitors, and other ad hoc services during the day and night.
>
> (2008: 108)

In September 2004, the Church of Fools website listed daily times for 'simple and short services' at 8:00 a.m. BST (GMT +1), between 10:00 and 11:15 p.m. BST, and at 9:30 p.m. CST (GMT—6). These services were led by members of the congregation. Guest preachers from a range of denominations were invited to offer brief sermons at the main Sunday services, and 17 texts are still available to read on the Church of Fools website (via the Internet Archive).[2]

The wardens appointed to run services created their own liturgies or used more informal patterns. Jenkins has a clear idea of the kind of worship that worked best in the Church of Fools, and claims that a particular style was soon adopted: 'short services, very short sermons, prayers and creeds broken down for audience participation, and plenty of opportunities for visitors to contribute with their own spoken words and gestures' (Jenkins 2008: 109).

According to Mark Howe, this semi-liturgical style emerged in response to features and limitations of the space. 'The architecture of the building itself certainly suggested an Anglican context', he claims (Howe 2005: 54), implying an expectation of liturgy, while the 'clunkiness' of the text interface limited the contribution that could be made by preaching. Anna suggests another explanation, linking the style with the church backgrounds of worship leaders as well as the requirements of the space:

> most of the people who were originally involved were English, and if they weren't Anglican, and most of them were, had a strong experience with that style. Versicle and response is what Anglicans have been doing for two thousand years, as long as there've been us, so that was what felt normal, reasonable and appropriate for most of us to start with. And then I was talking to Cara, and it's been years ago now, and she was saying her church does not do that but she has found that as a leader she needs to. So [. . .] there needs to be some component of that in virtually everything we do.

One particularly important ritual that emerged during the course of the experiment was the sharing of the Lord's Prayer. The congregation would be invited to type the words of the prayer in whatever form they preferred, leading to a jumble of different phrases and languages rolling up the screen. Jenkins includes a sample section of this ritual exchange, and explains why he found it so powerful:

> *Choris:* Our Father, who art in heaven hallowed be thy name
> *Babybear:* Ein tad, yr hwn wyt yn y nefoed
> *Jeff:* Our Father in heaven
> *Peter22:* Pater Noster qui es in caelis
> *Lillys:* hallowed be thy name
> *Karen:* thy kingdom come
> *Ilkku:* your kingdom come your will be done

> The experience of praying the Lord's Prayer together focused attention on our togetherness in prayer and worship, despite our distance in terms of geography, culture, language and faith expression. [. . .] Theologically speaking, it was like the coming together of the church on the Day of Pentecost, showing the unity of the church regardless of time and space. And it had big emotional impact.

> (Jenkins 2008: 109)

Worship in Church of Fools also made use of the range of gestures, integrated into new liturgies or deployed spontaneously by churchgoers. Jenkins mentions two examples, the 'tear hair out' and 'shake hands' gestures, used respectively to symbolise lament and the traditional liturgical ritual of

Sharing the Peace. He includes a sample prayer in which the tearing of hair features prominently:

Leader: Let's pray for the people of the third world
for people with no food, no clean water
for people who have seen their homes demolished
for people devastated by war
Please use the 'tear hair out' gesture as we think of them. (Jenkins 2008: 110)

The shaking of hands was also used creatively, as a way of interacting with the 'ghosts' who watched the service without being represented visibly. 'At a particular moment in the services, we asked the congregation to shake hands in mid-air as a way of greeting the ghosts'. According to one visitor, 'The whole ghost thing is rather beautifully symbolical [. . .] we're worshipping with unseen multitudes' (Jenkins 2008: 110).

According to Janet Wootton, one of the guest preachers for the Church of Fools, attempts to use the handshake gesture did always not go as planned (Wootton 2005: 107). It proved difficult to coordinate a handshake with another avatar, and it was easy to select the wrong gesture by mistake. When the worship leader called for everyone to share the peace, 'the whole congregation broke out in wandering around to face other people, and miscellaneously scratching their heads and shaking their hands at each other' (Wootton 2005: 107). Wootton describes services as 'oddly formal' (Wootton 2005: 108), 'fairly traditional' and yet rather 'chaotic' (Wootton 2005: 107), familiar and traditional and yet open to ritual experimentation, failure and disruption.

Different members of the congregation used gestures in different ways. Anna commented that 'the ability to kneel, the ability for my avatar to kneel, to cross myself, were huge for me', important 'in terms of making it feel real and normal and, in quotation marks, "churchy".' For Anna, 'it made it easier for me to get my head in it if that cartoon that was me in that context could kneel to pray. I was cross because she couldn't genuflect.'

David, a church elder offline, explained in our interview that he found the use of gestures helped make worship more 'corporate', increasing his awareness that he was sharing that time with others. David noted that 'I speak a lot with my body', and he used avatar gestures in the same way, as a form of expression. He also described the importance of gestures in more intimate terms. Where Anna referred to her avatar in the third person, as 'she', David emphasised that his avatar was actually him. 'It was good to kneel', he explained, 'because I *was* kneeling'. When raising his hands, 'you can feel like you're doing it, no, you *are* doing it'—'the virtual becomes the real'.

David also visited the church to pray when it was empty. The 'element of going somewhere and making an effort' was a commitment that helped focus his mind in prayer, but he also felt the church to be 'consecrated space':

'the fabric of the virtual building is already steeped in prayer and worship', he explained, becoming 'a place that is holy'.

Jenkins records one interesting example of personal creativity in the use of gestures, reported by a ghost. Accounts from lurkers who do not visibly participate in online activities are usually hard to obtain, but in this case the ghost later joined as a visible avatar and passed on their experiences. Using gestures and careful positioning of the ghost-avatar, the unseen observer had managed to create a way to join in with the prayers of the visible community:

> 'I could only get in as a ghost until recently. It gets frustrating not being able to interact, but I found a cool way to. When I ran across someone kneeling, I would kneel next to them and pray for whatever they were praying for. Sometimes they were praying "out loud" and sometimes not, but I would just pray for them.'
>
> (Jenkins 2008: 110)

Anna, the High Church Anglican, selected avatar gestures that were consistent with her behaviour in any other church. When I asked if she raised her hands in the 'Hallelujah' gesture she again linked her online practice with offline customs: 'No, because I don't do it in real life. I only did it if whoever the leader was said, now raise your hands for Alleluia. But it's not a gesture I do.' She reported that other users had behaved differently, however:

> There were people who never crossed themselves because they don't do it in real life, although I do know at least two people who crossed themselves routinely there and never did in their own church in their physical lives.

Mark Howe reports a different phenomenon, claiming that an 'unexpected emergent property of worship' was that 'it tended to "go high", almost irrespective of the churchmanship of the individuals involved' (2005: 54). According to Howe, everyone adopted gestures like kneeling to pray, even if they would never do so in a local church. He attributes this tendency, like the liturgical style of worship, to the limitations of space and software. Most nonverbal cues were impossible, so participants had to make extensive use of the options available to them as 'a useful way to maintain some semblance of cohesion'. Kneeling was not just a spiritual practice but an available gesture that could be used to signal comradeship with the rest of the congregation.

Causing Trouble: Trolling in the Church of Fools

Many of the quotations in this chapter derive from my own interviews with regulars who joined Church of Fools and were still active in the St Pixels community five years later. This level of intense commitment was not shared by all participants, and one great surprise for the managers of the project was the emergence of an enormous number of mischievous, hostile and aggressive visitors bent on causing more or less serious disruption and distress.

One word for such troublemaking is 'trolling', a term derived originally either from mythology or from a kind of fishing involving dragging bait behind a boat and waiting for a bite (for a historical etymology, see Phillips 2015: 15ff.). The troll acts or speaks in deliberately provocative ways, seeking to elicit a reaction. The term is now applied much more broadly, referring not just to a subculture of self-described trolls but often to any form of online aggression, particularly if the troll finds entertainment in the emotional reaction of their victims. The word 'troll' was used in the Church of Fools community in this broad sense, to refer to any kind of deliberately offensive or provocative activity.

According to Phillips, trolling encompasses a wide spectrum of behaviours, but the self-identified troll is always 'motivated by what they call lulz, a particular kind of unsympathetic, ambiguous laughter' (Phillips 2015: 24). This commitment to entertainment does not mean, however, that trolling is apolitical or empty of serious critique. Phillips argues that 'trolls believe that nothing should be taken seriously, and therefore regard public displays of sentimentality, political conviction, and/or ideological rigidity as a call to trolling arms' (Phillips 2015: 26). Anonymity is celebrated, and any confession of attachment is derided. Trolls often frame their activity as pedagogy, exposing folly and hypocrisy and teaching their targets a useful lesson.

For the kind of troll Phillips described, Church of Fools must have posed a tempting, perhaps slightly confusing target. This was a public display of religious conviction, described as an experiment in cutting-edge technology and human community, at a time when the idea of online churches was still new and unfamiliar. The Church's software was hopelessly compromised in security, open to a dizzying array of possible disruptions. And yet, the motivations Phillips describes—humour, anonymity, the undermining of sentimental and ideological rigidity—are all ideas we have already encountered in our consideration of the Ship and Church of Fools. The Ark's biblical reality show and the Church of Fools' vending machines and Ned Flanders clones could all be considered mild forms of trolling.

Trolling behaviour may also have been motivated by the cartoonish computer-game style of the environment. A video on the Church of Fools website included one brief exchange illustrating the confusion of expectations that this visual style could cause: 'This game has glitches', one visitor remarks, only to be gently reminded by Simon Jenkins that 'it's not strictly a game' (Church of Fools 2004c). The game style was a valuable asset for the Church of Fools, generating considerable publicity and creating an unintimidating, relaxed atmosphere that many visitors found very attractive, but common attitudes to computer games include the desire to push boundaries and find hidden software flaws to exploit and to humiliate other players with demonstrations of mastery and power. According to Jenkins, this could cause not insignificant misunderstandings:

> One visitor looked around with her five-year-old son on her lap. "Wow!" he said. "Who's on your team and which ones do you kill?"—a sentiment many traditional churchgoers will recognise.
>
> (Jenkins 2004b)

Trolling began as soon as the church was launched, and attacks are reported in a range of media sources. While the Bishop of London is preaching, according to Giles Wilson of the BBC, 'a new character enters the church and starts swearing, accusing the worshippers of the kind of activities forbidden by Leviticus' (Wilson 2004). The *New York Times* also noticed this unexpected event, opening its own article on the launch of the Church with an observation that 'Richard Chartres, Anglican bishop of London, is not used to having congregants wandering around in front of him swearing as he preaches' (Feder 2004).

The designers of the church had clearly not counted on the attraction for so many people of a once-in-a-lifetime opportunity to hurl abuse at a bishop. The software was set up to allow anyone to 'shout' statements to be heard by every avatar in the church, and avatars could move anywhere they pleased—including straight into the pulpit. In a brief article for the Guardian newspaper entitled 'The URL of the Beast', Jenkins reported 'sorties by small groups who want to post racist slogans, religious abuse and experience the joy of shouting "fuck!" in a church', focusing on one incident he considered particularly newsworthy:

> My face-off with the Prince of Darkness took place in the world's first web-based 3D church. [. . .] Disguised as a normal worshipper, I came across him ranting in our pixellated pulpit. I was logged in as a church warden, who has a smite button capable of visiting an Old Testament-style logout on the unrighteous. "What are you doing?" I asked him. "Who is this who dares approach the Evil One?" he demanded. "Well . . . I'm the church warden," I replied. "Ah . . . " he said, before becoming disappointingly contrite.
>
> (Jenkins 2004a)

News coverage of these encounters generated a new surge of visitors, peaking at 41,000 in a single day shortly before May 25 (Church of Fools 2004a).

Jenkins and Howe both describe a range of other misbehaviours, ranging from entering the pulpit—like the rather mild Satan in the quote above—to standing in doorways to prevent anyone passing through. Because avatars couldn't pass through one another, a team of like-minded troublemakers could effectively seal off areas of the church and trap other avatars in place.

A combination of kneeling and standing avatars could 'suggest oral sex' (Jenkins 2008: 111).

A number of avatars learned to combine the kneeling and 'Hallelujah!' gestures and deploy these in unexpected locations, creating a kind of cult devoted to the worship of the vending machines in the crypt. In a rather charming moment in the video 'Chat in the Crypt' (Church of Fools 2004c), six male avatars are kneeling in prayer before a line of machines. Simon Jenkins' avatar stands centre-screen and turns to camera, reporting on the scene behind him: 'And this, folks, is vending machines being worshipped . . . ' One avatar solemnly counts, and at a pre-arranged number the line leap to their feet, throw their arms in the air, and drop once more to their knees. The ringleader offers instructions: 'OK everyone on 3 hallelujah, and then Jebus will come!'—eventually admitting, after several hopeful repetitions, ' . . . jesus is really lazy today'.

The worship of vending machines is remembered with some fond affection by community members. Verbal forms of antagonism proved much more disruptive and were extremely difficult to stop. The 'shout' function and the ability to enter the sanctuary area were both quickly removed, but problems remained with less public forms of disruption—including 'men whispering obscenities at female avatars', using a communication option that no one else would be able to see (Howe 2005: 34).

A considerable proportion of the trolling experienced by Church of Fools was orchestrated by myg0t.com, 'The Harrassment Authority', a website community dedicated to causing disruption in online multi-player games— and attracted to the Church, perhaps, by its visual similarity to game environments. Using the Internet Archive, we can find a post on myg0t's homepage in June 2004 explaining 'how to ban evade Church of Fools' using a simple process discovered by one of myg0t's forum users (myg0t 2004). 'When you're banned', the post explains, you can now 'go back to raging' almost immediately. The myg0t website collected an archive of media articles mentioning the group, and as late as 2009 this page included newspaper articles about Church of Fools. 'We are not mentioned by name', the site boasts, 'but these articles where [sic] thanks to us' (myg0t n.d.).

The relationship between Church of Fools and myg0t appears to have been mutually constructive, with both sites defining their identities to some degree through their perceptions and understanding of the other. For myg0t, media publicity surrounding their attacks on Church of Fools was a triumph demonstrating the effectiveness of their tactics, while Church of Fools developed its own folk legends incorporating the persistent assaults from myg0t and similar sites into narratives of success. Several interviewees reported that one heroic church-goer had joined a troll forum, explained the importance of the church to its members and persuaded the hordes to turn their hostility elsewhere.

I have not encountered any discourse in Church of Fools describing trolling in terms of demonic attack, something I have witnessed in more charismatic or evangelical online churches. On the contrary, the presence of individuals seeking to disrupt church activity has frequently been described by regulars as evidence of the good work the church was doing. Some even found such hostility to be enjoyable in its own right. According to David, 'it's nice to get a troll now and then'. 'I loved talking to people who were not church people', he explained, and some of those who 'came in really to tease' stayed for longer conversations. Church members were 'gracious' to trolls, giving them a chance to understand the boundaries of the space, and 'sometimes that's what they want to find'; trolls 'didn't destroy anything', and their activity did not detract from his appreciation of the Christian fellowship he encountered.

One of the most interesting interviews I conducted regarding the Church of Fools was an encounter with Evan, a young American man who had himself been a troll (independently from myg0t). The viewpoints of disruptive or hostile users are often hard to access, unsurprisingly, as such visitors are much less likely to remain in the community or to participate in research conversations. Trolling can encompass a wide spectrum of behaviours and goals (Phillips 2015: 24), and Evan's account offers a rare glimpse of some of the more complex and nuanced motives that can drive what could be dismissed as mere thoughtless trouble-making.

Evan treated Church of Fools as 'a place where I could cause trouble without too many repercussions', and soon set about exploring how exactly he could cause maximum irritation. 'My first goal was to see how far I could push the boundaries', and he gleefully joined in with those praying to the peanut machine and kneeling in carefully selected spots to trap people in pews or doorways. According to his own evaluation, he didn't do anything 'major', like shouting 'Satan rules'. In fact, he caused the most trouble simply by asking logical questions of the more conservative and less technologically adept church leaders. Given enough provocation, some leaders could be relied upon to lash out and accidentally ban the wrong person altogether.

Evan's actions were only partly driven by a sense of irreverence and fun. Evan was a regular but discontented churchgoer in his offline life, and came to the Church of Fools looking for a space to ask questions and meet Christians he could respect. By the time of our interview he had stopped attending any physical church altogether, disillusioned by a combination of leadership change and congregational coldness. Church of Fools offered a new, different and far superior space to explore his ideas and questions. 'I went mainly for worship, when I wasn't going to cause trouble', and at times of worship 'if I was kneeling down, I meant it'—the avatar was 'not a toy, [but] a tool I was using to express what I was feeling at that moment'.

Evan encountered a number of Christians in the Church of Fools who recognised the sincere questions underlying his trouble-making and became close personal friends, giving him space to ask the questions 'I didn't feel comfortable asking my pastor'. The 3D environment kept his interest, but it was the people he met who 'taught me this is the way to find your answer', helping him to move away from the black-and-white answers offered by his home church and to develop what he now felt to be a more rounded and satisfying spiritual life. These friends encouraged him, developing his confidence and talents with great effect. Over time 'I grew out of causing trouble'; when he began to feel a real part of the community, that aspect of his activity 'just dwindled away'. By the time of our interview, he had started putting his computing talents to use helping with the programming side of the St Pixels website, had been permitted to begin leading his own Bible study, and had been appointed as a member of the leadership team.

Control in the Church of Fools

Not all Church of Fools visitors were so tolerant of the hostility they encountered. According to Frank, regulars 'didn't want to boot people out' but had no choice—'these people didn't want to be reached'.

Responding to this kind of behaviour, the leaders of the church established a team of 'wardens' with the power to remove avatars from the site. This practice was known as 'smiting', adopting an Old Testament term for the punishment of evil-doers. As Frank commented in our interview, it was 'kind of a tongue-in-cheek way to refer to it'. The appropriation of terminology familiar to those embedded in certain forms of Christian culture was a common strategy of both the Ship and Church of Fools and resonated with some visitors. David, for example, commented in our interview that he loved the term 'warden' because it was familiar to him from his church upbringing. Not all were so impressed: according to Mark Howe, the choice led to 'much confusion with non-episcopalian Americans who assumed that the term had something to do with prison warders' (Howe 2005: 34).

Howe's account of this period strongly emphasises the sacrifices of time and emotional energy made by the warden team in their attempts to protect the church space from their assailants. Most wardens were based in Europe, while most 'trolls' seemed to work on American time zones, so late-night shifts were frequently demanded. These periods could be lonely, tedious and draining:

> I remember one American mother describing how she had stood by the door of the church, alone, for three hours, removing trolls one by one, until they eventually gave up for the night, because she was not willing to let them spoil 'our church' or to simply close the doors.
>
> (Howe 2005: 58)

A difficult situation was complicated further by inclusive theology and inadequate software:

> Some wardens made a difficult situation harder for themselves in operational terms because of a deeply held conviction that banning anyone

from church was wrong in principle. This ruled out any of the more radical means of excluding users, and left them with a 'smite' button that was fiddly to use and, in the worst case, removed troublemakers for only a few seconds.

(Howe 2005: 58)

For Howe, this determination is theologically and sociologically symbolic. '[T]he sacrificial commitment shown by the leadership team', he claims, 'could be considered to be one of the signs of authentic church leadership'— and a clear rebuttal of any suggestion that online communities might lack a sense of mutual obligation (Howe 2005: 58). As in so many religious groups, the suffering of the founders of the community is used here as evidence of the rightness of their cause.

The work demanded of these wardens was too demanding to be continued indefinitely, requiring intense commitment of time and emotional energy. Some became erratic, ejecting innocent visitors for choosing the Ned Flanders avatar, standing too close to an actual trouble-maker or offending their personal sensibilities. As we have seen, Evan claimed he was sometimes banned for asking too many questions. Some wardens had to be replaced, others rested. Wardens I interviewed spoke with great fondness of one particular event, the 'Warden Olympics', when the whole church was closed for a period to let the support team relax and play games. Races around the church were slightly hampered by the enthusiasm with which participants started to 'smite' anyone who looked in danger of winning.

Such measures were only temporary, and neither church finances nor church staff could endure indefinitely. According to Mark Howe, 'One consideration when closing the experiment was that it seemed irresponsible to continue to ask individuals to give so much of themselves with inadequate technical backup' (2005: 58). The Church of Fools survived for one month beyond its original planned existence, and closed in September 2004. The last act was a service for the wardens; after the service, Simon Jenkins spent a few moments alone in the church, and then locked its doors.

The Afterlife of the Church of Fools

The core of the church community refused to disperse and moved briefly to a new setting hosted on the Ship of Fools website. Two Church of Fools members active at the time have suggested to me that the experience of existing as a church had developed a quite different culture from the Ship, dedicated to support and collaborative leadership rather than aggressive debate and strict moderation. Recombining the two communities in one site quickly became untenable, and the two leaderships came to acknowledge the need to separate again.

Reopening the 3D church as a multi-user worship space was temporarily impossible, requiring financial resources that were not available and extensive development work that could not yet be undertaken. A text-based website was created instead, churchoffools.com, offering forums, private messages between users and a text chatroom. This was ostensibly a temporary measure while work was under way on the creation of a new 3D space. Some of the characteristics of those forums will be discussed in the later chapter on St Pixels, but two dimensions of church culture are relevant here: the persistence of references to the 3D church, and hopes of returning there.

The dream of returning to 3D remained an undercurrent in site culture when I first joined and was raised repeatedly at meets and in publications over the following years. The website of the 3D Church of Fools included a question-and-answer section, created soon after the church closed, promising that the group was 'actively developing plans and models for the future—but it will take significant investment to make it happen' (Church of Fools 2004b). With development relying on the volunteer labour of a very small handful of computer experts within the community, the deadline retreated again and again.

This connection with a cherished past was reflected in the structure of the new forum site, where names and imagery recalled memories of the original 3D church. The site's discussion section, for example, was named 'The Crypt'. Forum members could select avatars, small square images to illustrate their posts, and these were collected from screenshots of the 3D church. When I first joined Church of Fools in 2005, I adopted an image of a red armchair, and it was some time before I realised that my armchair could once have been found sitting in the original Crypt. Another member added a capital letter 'Y' to her username as a reference to the hands-in-the-air 'Hallelujah' gesture.

Some of those who endured the move from 3D to text spoke of a great and enduring sense of loss. When I interviewed Evan in 2008 he admitted that his engagement with the text chatroom 'still hasn't got to that same level' that he had experienced in 3D. '[W]hen you have something in front of you [. . .] when you have something you can identify with it feels more personal.' Few interviewees told me they were still waiting for a new 3D space, but Evan was sure this aspiration was widely shared. He named close friends from the 3D church who would return as soon as the environment was ready: 'That's what everyone's waiting for . . . for the last four years that's what I've been waiting for, I know it's getting close.'

Barbara also reported a profound sense of loss from the absence of visual cues, but here the loss was spiritual rather than one of immersion. The text chatroom lacked visual cues for sacred space, she explained. She could experience times of prayerfulness there, but this prayerfulness arose from her own personal activity, not from the natural atmosphere of the space.

Cara spoke rather of the impairment of communication in text-based chat, where conversational boundaries were much harder to signal. In 3D she had liked to hide in secluded corners or take friends aside, creating bounded spaces that signalled her desire to converse with specific people or to remain silent, but a text chatroom forced her to join one single shared communication space in which no such subtlety was possible.

A small number of regulars transferred their 3D activity to new spaces away from the Church of Fools, trying to recreate and build on the experiences they had cherished there. Cara and some of her friends purchased and furnished rooms in the virtual world 'Habbo Hotel', building worship spaces and games to attract the interest of the predominantly teenage population as a kind of missionary outreach.

Eventually, in response to comments like those of Evan and Barbara, the leaders of the Church of Fools decided to reopen a limited form of the 3D space in 2004. It remained accessible until 2016. Users could choose an avatar, enter the space, move around, perform gestures and listen to snatches of music and bells, but the environment was a single-user space and no awareness of or interaction with other visitors was possible. For some users I interviewed—like David, quoted above—this solitary 3D experience remained an important part of their spiritual lives for years after the closure of the Church of Fools, offering a visual focus for prayer in a space richly connected with positive memories of spiritual and social experiences.

Conclusion

The Church of Fools was a short-lived experiment and seemed at times to survive only against the odds. It was, in some ways, poorly planned; its software offered too little protection against hostile interference and gave too much freedom to users, and its designers failed to foresee the numbers who would abuse those freedoms to disrupt the fledgling congregation. Control had to be exerted retrospectively, creating new make-shift systems to patch up some of the security flaws and social problems that had not been anticipated, and a sustainable system was never fully implemented.

It would be easy to blame designers and leaders for failing to see the problems that might arise, but their oversight is perhaps obvious only in hindsight. No other online church has experienced such intensity of attacks, before or since, and none of the churches studied in this book set out firm guidelines for dealing with troublemakers before the first trouble arrived. The successes of the Church of Fools were quite real, despite the challenges it faced, and can be seen in the church's most enduring legacy: a community which has remained vibrant for more than a decade. We will continue the narrative of that community in Chapter 6.

In Chapter 2, we surveyed five key topics: online and offline churchgoing; community; ritual; design; and authority. With three adjustments, this list can provide us with a useful framework to help compare the different case studies analysed in this book. First, Church of Fools attracted a much bigger audience than previous online churches had anticipated, and that size brought with it some serious challenges. We must therefore add an extra topic: scale. Second, our discussion of ritual in Chapter 2 focused on changes in liturgical form, because this has been a major interest for academic researchers. Church of Fools reminds us that this kind of collective ritual is only one part of the broader field of spiritual practices and experiences that can take place in a church. We also need to consider solitary prayers, sermons, the embodied experience of ritual participation and more. To signal this broadening of scope, we can widen this category to include all forms of spiritual experience. Third, authority in Church of Fools functioned on multiple levels, which deserve separate scrutiny. We will therefore divide the topic of authority into two, discussing internal control within the church and then its financial and administrative relationship to larger religious institutions.

These amendments produce a total of seven themes: the size of the church; the relationship between local and online participation; the kind of community generated by members; the forms of ritual and spiritual experience that they engaged in; the degree to which the design of the church replicated familiar forms; internal control; and external oversight, including funding. We can briefly summarise how each theme took shape in Church of Fools:

1. Scale. Church of Fools proved that an online church could attract extraordinary interest. Previous online ventures had gathered only handfuls of congregants, or had only encouraged direct email communication between visitor and pastor, but the Church of Fools attracted tens of thousands of visitors and scores of journalists. Online church could work on a much larger scale than anyone had previously realised.

2. Local Churchgoing. The majority of those attracted to the Church of Fools were already regular congregants at local churches—but some, perhaps many, were not. Church statistics and anecdotal reports showed that at least some visitors were not connected to religious groups offline, and that some of them found the online space to be a spiritually rich environment.

3. Community. Church of Fools also demonstrated that an online church could form something very much like a community, at least among its core of regular users. The friendships that emerged, the commitment shown by the wardens and the firm sense of belonging that kept the community alive after the 3D site closed all demonstrate the degree of emotional and social investment that online religion can support.

4. Ritual and Spiritual Experience. Congregants spoke enthusiastically in interviews of their experiences of shared worship and private prayer. The visual setting played some part in the success of these practices, as did the avatars and their gestures, the forms of ritual used, and the prayers typed between participants. A virtual environment could play a major role in generating the experience of being in a sacred space, at least for some visitors.

5. Familiarity. Tradition was a major theme of architecture and liturgical design. The problem of generating experiences of the sacred online and

framing appropriate activity could be answered by drawing on visual and ritual styles that visitors already understood. This could reinforce spiritual impact for churchgoers and indicate appropriate behaviour to non-churchgoers, and including a diverse range of familiar styles within a non-specific 'church-like' environment helped avoid alienating visitors with different experiences of church attendance. Reliance on familiar styles was not just evidence of poor imagination.

6. Internal Control. Discipline was a crucial and unanswered problem. Users took advantage of communication options in unexpected ways to cause disruption, and no real solution was found to the crisis this caused. A balance had to be negotiated between theological commitments and pragmatic concerns to create a system that congregants could reconcile with their idea of 'church'.

7. External Funding and Oversight. The Church of Fools received donations from Christian institutions to fund its start-up costs and benefited from association with a major denomination, but did so without surrendering its independence. The anarchic, ever-changing, theologically open culture of the church might not have been possible without this freedom, and its unique environment would certainly not have come to be without funding. On the other hand, this approach only supported a scant few months of operation. As we shall see in future chapters, other churches have negotiated this balance between freedom, support and obligation rather differently.

At the end of each of the five case study chapters, I will offer a similarly brief summary to illustrate how these themes were manifested. These are some of the core issues for online religion, and answers can be carefully planned or dramatically fought out in very different ways.

Notes

1 For an archived version, see http://web.archive.org/web/20040924025412/ http://churchoffools.com/. Accessed 26–08–16.
2 The full list can be found at http://web.archive.org/web/20040927223507/http://churchoffools.com/sermons/index.html. Accessed 01 September 2016.

References

Barrett, J., 2010. Religion in new places: Rhetoric of the holy in the online virtual environment of Second Life. *Working Papers in Teacher Education* 7, pp. 19–23.
Beckford, M., 2008. "Jesus Saves" piggy bank revealed. *Daily Telegraph*, 5 December. [online] Available at: <http://www.telegraph.co.uk/topics/christmas/3566932/Jesus-Saves-piggy-bank-revealed-in-12-Days-of-Kitschmas-collection.html> [Accessed 1 September 2016]
Church of Fools, 2004a. 41,000 go to church in one day. *Churchoffools.com*, 25 May. [online] Available at: <https://web.archive.org/web/20050205050222/http://churchoffools.com/news-stories/03_41000.html> [Accessed 1 September 2016]

———, 2004b. What kind of audience are you aiming for? *Churchoffools.com*. [online] Available at: <https://web.archive.org/web/20050311053636/http://churchoffools.com/got-questions/audience.html> [Accessed 1 September 2016]

———, 2004c. Chat in the Crypt. *Churchoffools.com* [online video]. No longer available. [Accessed 10 January 2010].

Doney, M., 2004. Computer church. *Church Times*, 14 May.

Estes, D., 2009. *SimChurch: Being the Church in the Virtual World*. Grand Rapids: Zondervan.

Feder, B., 2004. The first church of cyberspace: Services tomorrow. *The New York Times*, 15 May. [online] Available at: <http://www.nytimes.com/2004/05/15/nyregion/religion-journal-the-first-church-of-cyberspace-services-tomorrow.html> [Accessed 1 September 2016]

Howe, M., 2005. *Towards a Theology of Virtual Christian Community*. MTh. Spurgeon's College, London. [pdf] Available at: <http://www.cyberporte.com/virtual_christian_ community.pdf> [Accessed 1 September 2016]

Jenkins, S., 2004a. Satan loses his sulphur. *Churchoffools.com*, 15 May. [online] Available at: <https://web.archive.org/web/20050311025408/http://churchoffools.com/news-stories/02_sulphur.html> [Accessed 1 September 2016]

———, 2004b. The URL of the beast. *The Guardian*, 20 May. [online] Available at: <http://www.guardian.co.uk/theguardian/2004/may/20/features11.g2> [Accessed 1 September 2016]

———, 2008. Rituals and pixels: Experiments in an online church. *Online: Heidelberg Journal of Religions on the Internet* 3(1), pp. 95–115.

Myg0t, 2004. How to ban evade Church of Fools. *Myg0t.com*, 10 June. [online] Available at: <https://web.archive.org/web/20040615010348/http://www.myg0t.com/> [Accessed 1 September 2016]

———, n.d. Articles. *Myg0t.com*. [online] Available at: <https://web.archive.org/web/20090217142020/http://myg0t.com/?rage=articles/> [Accessed 1 September 2016]

Ortigas, M., 2004. Cyber church—now God goes online. *CNN: International*, 12 May. [online] Available at: <http://edition.cnn.com/2004/WORLD/europe/05/12/uk.online. church/> [Accessed 1 September 2016]

Phillips, W., 2015. *This Is Why We Can't Have Nice Things: Mapping the Relationship between Online Trolling and Mainstream Culture*. Cambridge: MIT Press.

Ship of Fools, 2003. Simon preaches, Job prays, Martha unimpressed. *The Ark*. [online] Available at: <http://ark.saintsimeon.co.uk/job/article.php?i=029> [Accessed 1 September 2016]

———, n.d. Ship stuff. *ShipofFools.com*. [online] Available at: <http://www.ship-of-fools.com/shipstuff/index.html> [Accessed 1 September 2016]

Wilson, G., 2004. In cyberspace, can anyone hear you pray? *BBC News Online Magazine*, 12 May. [online] Available at: <http://news.bbc.co.uk/1/hi/magazine/3706897.stm> [Accessed 1 September 2016]

Wootton, J., 2005. Reviews: Church of Fools—online church: www.churchoffools.com. *International Congregational Journal* 4(2), pp. 107–109.

5 I-Church

'*a genuine church, a real church, in a new medium . . . where people pray together and communicate at depths not often seen in parish churches.*'
—Colin Fletcher, Bishop of Dorchester and Chair of Trustees for i-church

In 2004, the year that Church of Fools first appeared, another project also made headline news around the world. 'I-church' was an online community founded by a diocese of the Church of England, run as part of that diocese and led by a web pastor. We see here a quite different kind of online church, operating in a different kind of relationship to institutional Christianity and reaching its own distinctive conclusions to the seven key themes I have just highlighted.

I joined i-church in 2005 and soon made a number of close friends. Indeed, for a time this was 'my' church, more so than any building I might attend in my own city. I have stayed with i-church friends in America and England and have met some many times, at conferences, meets and unofficial gatherings. For several years, the pocket of my winter coat contained a rosary of sandalwood beads designed and created by a member from South Korea. I once received a small teddy bear sporting a red jumper emblazoned with the word 'i-church', knitted as a gift by a member in England. I also made some arch-enemies in i-church, foes I sparred with daily for months or years, and never once managed to convince to change their minds. I can vouch from my own experience for the strong personal relationships, sense of belonging and intense emotion that can be generated in an online community.

Like any organization, i-church has changed over time, trying to adapt its vision, activities and community norms in response to new situations. We have already seen a short-term example of this adaptation process in our last chapter, when Church of Fools struggled to develop new policies and structures to deal with unexpected hostile attacks. To understand i-church, we need to follow its adaptation over a much longer period. I was an active member from 2005 to 2010 and a member of the internal church council from 2006 to 2009, and this chapter draws on my long-term participation to construct a narrative of the development of i-church. As we shall see, this history has included times of confusion, intense conflict and great optimism. By tracing the life of this one church, we can start to develop a more nuanced understanding of what institutional involvement in online religion really means.

The Vision: 2003–2005

The original vision for i-church came from Richard Thomas, who was at that point serving as director of communications for the Diocese of Oxford. Thomas had participated in online discussions between Christians and pagans, and—as he later reflected in his sermon for i-church's dedication service—he 'found these Internet-mediated communities to be every bit as significant as the local community of faith' (Thomas 2004a). If so, then online community could be a new way to fulfil the Church of England's mission to the nation:

> We have an historic responsibility, symbolised in our Monarch's dual role of spiritual and temporal care, of caring spiritually for the whole community, regardless of whether or not they come to Church . . . If Anglicans have a responsibility to the whole community, we would be failing if we ignored the new community of the Internet.
>
> (Thomas 2004a)

Thomas doesn't promise that the experiment will succeed—'sometimes it is difficult', he admits, 'to know whether history is being made, or whether one is simply engaged in a foolish, or even fool-hardy, endeavor.' Nonetheless, the Church of England has a duty to find out.

This enthusiasm for experimental community was widespread in the UK at that time. In the Diocese of Oxford, a £100,000 scheme called 'Cutting Edge Ministries' had been established to fund five new forms of church, and i-church was one of these projects. By 2004, similar initiatives were emerging around the country. The Church of England report *Mission-shaped Church* argues that parochial ministry is no longer adequate for contemporary British society, because 'communities are now multi-layered, comprising neighbourhoods, usually with permeable boundaries, and a wide variety of networks, ranging from the relatively local to the global' (Archbishop's Council on Mission and Public Affairs 2004: xi). In response to this sociological observation, the report calls for the development of new forms of religious community that can attract new audiences by engaging with their social networks. *Mission-shaped Church* describes examples of these 'fresh expressions of church', and encourages parish churches to continue experimenting. The report was widely discussed and highly influential and led to the creation of a national Fresh Expressions movement by the Church of England and the Methodist Church.

Mission-shaped Church presents its community experiments as a continuation of Anglican theology. The term 'fresh expressions' was chosen to suggest 'that something new or enlivened is happening', but also to suggest 'connection to history and the developing story of God's work in the Church' (2004: 34). Fresh expressions are needed to fulfil 'the Anglican incarnational principle' of mission to the whole of society (2004: xi), just as Richard Thomas argued above. There is at least one significant difference between the visions for i-church and *Mission-shaped Church*, however: while the report sees Fresh Expressions as a way to make the Church of England relevant to new audiences, the intended membership of i-church was not quite so clearly defined.

Early forms of the i-church website can be accessed through the Internet Archive, where the first record dates from January 2003.[1] In this initial version, i-church presents itself as 'a website and a community' seeking 'to give people an alternative way to engage with the life of the church, to learn more about the Christian faith and to express their Christian commitment.' By September 2003, this text had been updated: i-church was now intended specifically for those who 'are not able, or do not wish, to join a local parish church.'[2] By March 2004, the target audience had expanded to three categories: those who couldn't or wouldn't attend a local church; 'those who do not find all that they need within their own worshipping community'; and those 'who travel, either through their work or in their life-style'.[3]

Richard Thomas suggested yet another audience in an interview that month published by the *Guardian* newspaper, in which he argued that the Church of England must 'provide a spiritual community for people who relate with each other primarily through the Internet' (Press Association 2004). 'One of the defining features of our culture is the desire to self-resource', he argued in an article for the website *Thinking Anglicans*, and the Internet is 'the ultimate expression of that self-resourcing.' That independence is why so many people 'want to be part of a Christian community . . . without the hassle and clutter of participation in a local parish church' (Thomas 2004b), and creating a church on the Internet would be one way to meet their needs.

These different documents also explain something of what participation in i-church was actually going to involve. In September 2003, the website promised a two-tier membership structure, divided between Visitors and Community Members. Joining the second category would require making 'a commitment to prayer, study and action', the details of which would be decided 'in consultation with a member of the pastoral team'. In his article for *Thinking Anglicans*, Thomas reiterates this emphasis on commitment: visitors would come and go, but they would be served by a committed core community. There would eventually be meetings offline, including gatherings to share communion, and the church would be associated with a monastic community. The oversight of the diocese would ensure 'stability and guidance', and the monastic connection would provide 'a spirituality that will give it "bottom", a solidity that many Internet communities lack' (Thomas 2004b). This emphasis on tradition, structure and discipline suggests something rather different from the deliberately playful culture we encountered in Church of Fools.

On May 24, 2004, Alyson Leslie was announced as the new i-church web pastor.[4] Leslie was not ordained but had experience of online Christian ministry as the founder of 'WebChurch' in Scotland. Problems immediately began to emerge. In i-church's June newsletter, Leslie reported 'a response over 20 times larger than anticipated in terms of membership—and with 1000 more inquirers on top of that' (Leslie 2004a) and protested that she lacked 'the systems, processes or resources to immediately deal with the demand'. I-church was still determined to build a stable, committed community on monastic lines, and as yet there was no way for everyone to join in. Interested applicants were being turned away.

The first members of i-church were invited to travel to Oxford in July 2004 to attend a Dedication Service. Revd Richard Thomas delivered the homily, and his address gives some insight into his thinking in this turbulent period. The Internet, he argued, had created 'a whole new context for ministry' (Thomas 2004a), allowing Christians to develop 'new kinds of relationships with people we have never met.' I-church would not forget the limitations of this new community of the Internet, which must always be integrated into the everyday offline world:

> we create new communities and develop new understanding not 'in cyber-space'—that place does not exist, and the Church should not be promoting it as if it did—but through our Internet-mediated relationships with real people who live in real places and live real lives, with all the pain and opportunities that presents.
>
> (Thomas 2004a)

At i-church, visitors would encounter 'a quiet, unassuming Benedictine spirituality' (Thomas 2004a) focused on the principles of 'Stability' and 'Conversion of Life'. In the 5th century, St Benedict criticised monks who travelled from place to place. I-church would follow his example by demanding long-term commitment. Benedict called for prayer, study and social action, and i-church members would pursue all three as part of their daily discipline. Benedict emphasised regular worship, and i-church would worship throughout the day. Two Benedictine abbots had offered their support.

Thomas had already encountered opposition, he admitted. One critic had emailed him to declare that he was 'sick and tired' of the Anglican Church, which was now 'trying to set up a church where people don't even meet' (Thomas 2004a). On the contrary, Thomas insisted, the commitment of i-church members was already clear to see. Seven hundred people had applied for membership, and some of them had travelled all the way from the USA and from Australia to be present at the dedication service. Thomas assured his audience that these registered members were prepared for their lives to be transformed through long-term relationships of service and mutual accountability. If the sacraments are 'those things that make God, or his grace, visible', Thomas suggested, then the intense commitment of i-church members could actually become sacramental. The difficulty with this confident assessment is that online activity is typically fluid and low in commitment, as Thomas himself had previously acknowledged (2004b). I-church was proposing something intensely counter-cultural, and it was not yet clear if the level of commitment Thomas called for was actually feasible.

After this service, i-church decided that the solution to its unexpected popularity was to subdivide the community. By July 2004, the i-church website included to a 'Community' section,[5] only open to those who applied for full membership. This Community was 'organised in small "pastorates" of about fifteen to twenty people', each 'led by an authorised pastor.' Members also shared a common chatroom and forum, and—uniquely among the churches described in this book—all members were required to use a version of their real names, in line with the emphasis on mutual commitment.

The web pastor's next newsletter, in August 2004, announced that two 'pastorates' have been launched. The first group has connected on 'a trial discussion board and chatroom' (Leslie 2004b), but this proved difficult: 'few people have had experience of posting on message boards etc. I certainly underestimated the help people would need to use a fairly basic system.' The 'new community of the Internet' (Thomas 2004a) was apparently not the demographic i-church was attracting. Nonetheless, Leslie was positive: 'There is a real sense of concern, prayer, passion and care emerging in this group—which is thrilling.' A second pastoral group had just been created, and prayer was requested for the leader 'as he and his group get to know each other over the next couple of weeks.'

This optimistic letter was followed almost immediately by Leslie's resignation. Appointed in May for the launch in June, Leslie announced her departure in September, composing a detailed report for the i-church community. That report identifies three major areas of concern: high application numbers exposed a lack of resources; some of the expectations of members for one-to-one pastoral care could not be met by a single pastor; and the distribution of authority between diocese and i-church was unclear. The proposed system of small pastoral groups would be extremely difficult to scale. Each group required an authorised leader, and a community of 700 members would need no less than 40 volunteers. The web pastor had not expected to offer individual spiritual mentoring and support to congregants, but that seems to have been a primary expectation for many applicants. Meanwhile, her location far from Oxford made it difficult to negotiate changes in strategy with advisory teams based in the diocese. Faced with these apparently insurmountable challenges, Leslie chose to leave.

Richard Thomas was active throughout this period, seeking to encourage the fledgling community to develop in a more worship-focused and Benedictine direction. Thomas refers to monastic practices for examples and encouragements in his posts at this time, using the Rule of Benedict to support requests for disputes to be handled in a gracious manner, for postings to be humble and brief, and for worship to be at the core of community life, but his efforts do not appear to meet with answering enthusiasm for monasticism from the rest of the community.

By November 2004 worship was finally starting to take place in the chatroom. A forum thread started by one pastoral group leader states that members of her group 'have seen some very fruitful prayer walking online', proving that 'God really does move even through the PC!', and announces a weekly prayer meeting at 8:00 p.m. every Friday to which all are welcome. Those attending are asked to pray before they go online, and the group leader encourages them to 'Expect to meet with God' and to 'be open in your thinking.' Not all experiences were so positive, and engagement with these chatroom worship events was low. In February 2005, one member wrote on the forum that he had been leading Vespers each night for three weeks, expressed disappointment that he had encountered little interest, and protested that his prayer time was recently disturbed by another group seeking to hold an informal Bible study. In an interview, Olive recalled that when she joined the church in May 2005, two services were being organised every day by a member from Australia, who continued this practice for a year before asking others to assist. These events attracted a committed but very small group of worshippers; Olive recalled that regular attendance over the summer of 2005 was only three. These themes of excitement and frustration recur time and again in early forum threads; in some, almost every contribution expresses the poster's delight with i-church and its potential.

Stabilising the Community: 2005–2007

Ten months after Leslie's departure, a new web pastor was appointed. Russell Dewhurst had attended the dedication service and subsequently became a member, offering technical support. He was already ordained as a curate and now became 'priest-in-charge' of two Oxford parishes and web pastor of i-church. He took up the post formally in October 2005 and was licensed by the bishop of Dorchester on November 30 in a special ceremony in the chatroom. Based in Oxford, Dewhurst was able to meet representatives of the diocese far more easily than his predecessor. In a 2005 post to the i-church forums, he describes his role as three-fold, including pastoral work, technical support and liaisons with outside individuals and organisations; ominously, this combination of roles was even more onerous than the workload which the first web pastor had declared impossible to sustain.

This new appointment was followed by two other changes in governance. First, Richard Thomas left his post in the diocese and with it, his role in i-church. Second, the diocese agreed to increase the autonomy of i-church, appointing a group of trustees who would advise the pastor while retaining ultimate legal responsibility. I-church became a Charitable Company Limited by Guarantee, and its Articles of Association included a commitment to Anglican church rules and the ideas of Benedict. The pastor would receive extra help from an unpaid associate pastor and a new council made up of members. The council would be chosen through an online vote, and councillors would hold office for three years. This is the system used by local Anglican churches to appoint their Parochial Church Council (or PCC), a particularly striking example of i-church's desire to embed itself in the structures and styles of the Church of England.

The i-church website was redesigned again in November 2005, adopting a new logo (Fig. 5.1) created by Russell Dewhurst. This logo emphasised both the relational and computer culture aspects of i-church. The lettering, Dewhurst explained in a forum thread, 'is meant to suggest a person, as depicted in MSN and similar applications, because i-church is a group of people who meet on the Internet as a church . . . the current logo is supposed to be red, usually in chat programs, games etc. person 1 is red, person 2 is blue etc.' One member suggested a candle, but Dewhurst disagreed: 'it could suggest to some people that we are pretending to do things that other churches do, e.g. light candles. I've always felt we didn't want pictures of church buildings in the logo because that's not what we have.'

Some ordained members now started to post their sermons to the public side of the website, and Dewhurst contributed occasional articles. Visitors could post prayer requests, moderated and answered by the associate pastors. Dewhurst also restructured the forums to remind members of the original Benedictine theme, dividing them into 'Prayer', 'Study' and 'Social Action'. Social Action was the least popular section, largely because the community rarely shared a common mind and valued the inclusiveness of its membership and the honesty of its conversation too highly for any attempt to mobilize support for a cause to succeed. A fourth section, the Sofa, was eventually added to host social conversations and wordgames. Further forums were set aside for technical questions, or reserved for private access by pastoral groups, council, Moderators and others.

I-church stopped accepting new members shortly after the launch, waiting until the community seemed strong enough to weather periods of growth. Indeed, such was the determination to avoid the destabilising effects of newcomers that some would-be members were forced to go to great lengths

Figure 5.1 The i-church logo, 2005.

to gain admittance. Martha, one of the members I interviewed in October 2007, told me that she had first applied to join as soon as the i-church project was announced in March 2004 and emailed monthly thereafter to request admission, but was only allowed to join the community at the end of May 2005. I joined after ignoring a statement on the i-church website that no new members would be allowed—I emailed the pastor directly, and was signed up.

Forum posts from this time reflect tensions between those eager to open the community and encourage growth and those urging caution. In December 2005, for example, Dewhurst encourages members to discuss the possibility of finally contacting some of those who had applied to join:

> It's really important we grow, but at a rate that lets us remain a community where we know one another [. . .] I still think it's important we don't overextend ourselves. So I am very wary of doing interviews with the BBC, or posting articles to very popular websites—we're still not in a position to respond to the demand that might create.

One member, Peter, decided to keep a private diary of i-church through most of 2006. Peter used this diary to record his own personal history of the group, including daily activity and his own reflections on significant events, and he very generously sent the whole document to me by email. At the start of January 2006, Peter's diary records 128 registered members, falling to 105 by mid-month when the pastor decides to delete those considered 'inactive' and rising again to 230 by mid-September.

Dewhurst decided to conduct a membership survey at the end of 2006 and emailed all 250 registered members, receiving 114 responses and producing a report about his findings. According to this questionnaire, 60 percent of members at that time were male, almost exactly the same proportion as Church of Fools reported in its own visitor survey. The membership of i-church, however, was considerably older: only 13 percent were aged under 30, compared to 50 percent at Church of Fools. Fifty percent of i-church members were aged between 31 and 50, and 35 percent were over 50. Sixty percent lived in Britain and 20 percent in the United States, and 13 other countries were also represented.

More than 95 percent of respondents to the i-church survey described themselves as Christians, with one atheist, one agnostic and one 'other'. 65 percent were Anglican. 40 percent described their theology as 'liberal', while 12 percent said they were 'conservative'. This overwhelming Christian presence did not translate so evenly to church involvement, however. 93 percent of members had attended a local church at some point in the past, but only 50 percent still said they did so regularly at the time of the survey, and 35 percent did not attend a local church at all. These statistics are comparable to Church of Fools, where just under 40 percent of survey respondents did not attend a local church outside the major festivals of

Christmas and Easter. However, participation in i-church was not necessarily thought of as church attendance: 25 percent of respondents agreed that i-church was now their 'main church' and 50 percent said it was 'one of the churches that I belong to', but the other 25 percent considered it 'just an interesting website.'

Those who had ceased to attend local church were asked to explain why, by choosing one or more factors from a list of 13. Only 10 percent said that they could not find a church in their local area. Theological disagreements were more significant: half agreed that 'I do not need to belong to a building based church to live out my faith', half said that their local church had not provided spiritual 'nourishment', and a quarter disagreed with church teaching. Pastoral issues were also common: a quarter reported that their local church was unwelcoming, and the same proportion said their church did not meet their health needs. Health issues were widespread among respondents, and 20 percent reported some kind of 'mobility problem' or mental health condition.

13 percent of respondents said they worshipped 'frequently' in the chatroom and almost half (45 percent) worshipped there 'sometimes', suggesting at least 15 regular and 52 less frequent participants. Comments on this question suggest divergent perceptions of online worship: 'Rarely go to chapel for prayer but i-church still considered main church'; 'Chapel is dominated by a club like other churches, so not in accordance with Jesus' teaching'; 'Too structured'; 'Not formal enough'.

The survey also asked respondents for their opinions about the web pastor. Half agreed that the web pastor was 'very important' and only a handful thought that 'we should rely entirely on volunteers', but only 14 percent actually said they supported i-church financially. This was a very significant problem for the church, because the diocese had not committed to paying a salary indefinitely. The original expectation had been for i-church to become self-funding within three years, and that timeline was almost up.

My interviews with members illustrate these responses in greater detail. Martha lived in the southern United States and attended church nowhere else. She had been brought up Roman Catholic, but said she had been 'kicked out' at the age of 13 for asking too many questions. She hadn't attended church in 30 years, choosing instead to read the Bible on her own. She had used computers since the days of punch-cards and joined i-church as soon as she heard of its launch. When I asked why she stayed, she emphasised the strong relationships she had made, speaking of close i-church friends who 'would kill me if I left'. She now spent 2 to 4 hours in i-church every day, largely avoiding the theological discussion areas, which she said were colonised by 'experts' waiting to 'thrash' anyone who dared to disagree with them. Worship was a great pleasure, a kind of meditation that helped her 'tune out everything else'. She considered i-church 'my only church' and claimed the same would be true for around a quarter of the members she knew.

Lucy attended church well into adulthood, but disliked it so much—particularly her vicar—that she 'felt ill driving there'. A friend suggested i-church. She found the warmth of her welcome 'amazing', 'totally a contrast to what I was getting at b and m' (bricks and mortar, a common i-church term for local churches), but she had no intention of letting the Internet provide her with her main church experience. Unlike Martha, she felt the Eucharist was vital and cited this as a major reason for continuing to connect with a local church.

Esme described her i-church activity as an escape from the restrictions imposed by serious illness. She explained by email:

> Owing to the timing of medical treatment and other health issues I have over the years found it more and more difficult to attend a church building or even go to midweek house fellowships and bible studies. [. . .] It can be imagined what a help it is to me to be able to worship from my own home.
>
> The emergence of true churches on the Internet has been a boon for me. It has been something I have waited and prayed for. The feeling of worshipping with other Christians and talking about theological issues with like-minded people (and being instructed in other areas or argued with by those who know what they are talking about) has been restored to me.

For Esme, one of the most vehement defenders of the role of web pastor, 'the knowledge that those leading are from a true Church such as the Church of England or another denomination in communion with it [is] invaluable'. Scott agreed: three factors proved that i-church had a solid and trustworthy foundation, he said, and those were the link with the Church of England, the Rule of Benedict and the web pastor. He had chosen to join i-church, rather than another online church, specifically because it was Anglican. Martha also felt the web pastor was important, but only for practical reasons: 'you have to have a captain', she said, to steer the ship. Lucy, in contrast, considered i-church more inter-denominational than Anglican, had never interacted with the web pastor, and thought a good council of members could manage the church adequately without his leadership.

Peter was one of those who considered i-church 'just an interesting website'. Peter compiled the diary I have quoted, regularly attended worship, contributed daily to discussion threads, made firm friends in the community and eventually travelled to the UK to meet some of them, so his views did not reflect a lack of commitment. Nonetheless, he explained to me by email, 'online church was for me pretty much a fun thing to do . . . a social activity, rather than a genuine church membership.' This perception led him to resign in 2008: 'it began to feel to me like I wasn't being sufficiently respectful of what i-church was to some folks . . . people like me weren't really helping matters for those who depended upon the online church experience in a more important way.' Several other interviewees shared Peter's views, describing i-church as a community or website rather than a church, but explained their scepticism quite differently: no online group could celebrate communion, they said, and communion was a necessary requirement for any real church. Just like Peter, these members could be as committed and active as any other.

We can gain a rich picture of the worship life of i-church at this time from Peter's diary. Daily services took place at 10:00 a.m., 9:00 p.m. and 3:00 a.m. GMT, with a weekly Bible study. These services were shared between a small number of leaders, some responsible for multiple events every day. Peter comments on the particular commitment shown by one Australian member: 'There were many days when he prayed alone. And the poor man spent his wee hours every morning praying evening prayer!' This intense commitment was not unique; when the first 0300 service was held, Peter notes that the five in attendance included two logging on 'in the MIDDLE OF THE NIGHT from the UK!'

These services followed several patterns. One participant kept a complete transcript of the first 0300 service in February 2006, in which the worship leader typed out long passages from a book of Benedictine meditations. The participants' responses—Amen, peace be with you, Christ have mercy—were offered without any need for instructions, suggesting that those present understood traditional liturgy well enough to play their parts without prompting. A period of silent meditation was included, and the service ended by offering each participant the chance to contribute his or her own prayers. These were quite extensive, ranging from ten to twenty-nine lines in length.

In my own experience, it was much more common for an event to consist only of prayers typed by each participant, instead of using a formal liturgy. Services could also include a recitation of the Lord's Prayer, conducted silently with only the first and last line typed out. On one occasion, a very new member used his turn in the time of open prayer to begin typing in tongues, tapping out what looked to me like a long sequence of random letters. This went on for some time, until the other worshippers began sending each other private messages asking what was going on and how to stop it. The experiment was not repeated, and the member soon left the community.

Space was used to some effect in these events. The chatroom was divided into a 'chapel' and a 'cafe' in February 2006, and transcripts show participants moving into the chapel to start their worship and out again when worship ended. This transition was not firmly marked, and those present would often engage in some minutes of social conversation before someone suggested a move. Olive wrote an essay about i-church in 2009 as part of her training for ordination, and explained that moving between chatrooms 'was a way of defining what was for sacred purposes.' A new room, the Sanctuary, was added later for silent prayer: 'the convention was that mostly only one person would be there at once, and no chatting of any kind would go on if two or more were there.'

Those gathering for worship engaged in a game to mark the end of each service. Participants would typically roleplay some of the actions that might be shared by a local congregation, like finding seats, pouring pints and making coffee, and some made the role of virtual 'bartender' part of their daily contribution to church life. According to one regular I interviewed at the end of 2007, this daily activity was part of the routine, a sign of shifting gears between worship and conversation, and 'almost part of the liturgy'. As a reference 'back to the real world', such playful uses of words enabled those present to 'reach out and touch something we're familiar with', 'simulating proximity'.

Some experimented with voice-based worship and prayer, but reported mixed results. Over months of chat and email exchanges, Olive explained by email, one particular member 'became one of the people with whom I could share anything at all'. Eventually they tried to communicate by phone:

> It actually felt no different from when I talked to a couple of other people that I really don't know well. I was disappointed and surprised [. . .] In our next contact we used text and both noted that we could share things better that way [. . .] We seemed more open and honest [. . .] I could actually feel [him] with me much better than when I could hear him.

Another member reported a more positive experience:

> once or twice four of us experimented with sound. There was a man in the Windward Islands, one in Oxford and one in China, plus myself. I did the hymn-singing and being gentlemen the others did not complain.

Non-text media were used more successfully elsewhere. One i-church project involved asking members around the world to record chapters of the Bible to be posted online and linked into worship services, and some progress was made with the Gospel of Mark. At the end of 2006, a member began an ambitious project creating devotional videos and posting these to YouTube (http://www.youtube.com/user/ichurchvids). He reported with much delight as these began attracting hundreds and in some cases thousands of views.

In late 2006, one of my friends in the community suggested that I run for the council. There were reasons to think this might be a good idea: as a member of the team I would gain a better sense of how the church really worked, and as a participant observer I was already very active anyway in the church forums and chatroom. The i-church community had been generous in their support for my research, and working for the council could be a way to thank them. It would be rather unusual for an ethnographer to become so invested in the group being studied, but I felt confident that maintaining some critical distance would not be difficult; after all, the council was only really an advisory group. I was duly appointed in the next election.

The year 2006 was a high point for a particular vision of i-church community life. The church was led by an able and enthusiastic web pastor, supported by a council with every place filled, and looked forward to continued growth. The financial burden faced by the church was a serious concern, with the three-year diocese grant due to expire in 2007, but in most other respects i-church appeared to be a success. The survey had indicated that a major section of the church community attended church nowhere else, that a smaller portion considered i-church to be their main church, and that many members faced health and mobility problems that prevented them from encountering interactive, communal Christian ministry in local settings. I-church might not have fulfilled all of its initial vision for Benedictine monastic life, but it had managed to attract a committed core community.

Vision in Crisis: 2007–2008

A very rare face-to-face meeting was organised in Oxford in January 2007, gathering the pastor, trustees and council (which now included myself) to discuss church strategy and direction. Richard Thomas had expected local gatherings to be frequent, but the internationalism of the community made that considerably more difficult. Even this one meeting caused some dispute, because far-off members complained they were being left out of community activities.

At the vision meeting, participants agreed to drop the unpopular division between two tiers of membership. Previously, people joined the community as 'individual members', and then could ask to become 'community members' and enter a pastoral group. This was now rejected, as a theologically indefensible hierarchy of status. The lingering idea of a Benedictine monastery receded still further into the background of i-church culture. On the other hand, Richard Thomas' original vision for a community that served a wider audience was to be reenergised: a new site design was planned, with new open-access material and discussion forums, a move described as 'opening i-church to the world'. A key topic for the meeting was finance, and I had fully expected the participants to propose ending the salaried position of web pastor in order to scale back financial commitments to a level that could be met at current giving levels. Instead, the final decision was quite the opposite: to reemphasize i-church's commitment to the role of pastor, to start paying a web developer to help share the workload, and to meet costs by raising the profile of financial giving among members.

Before a new site could be implemented, events took an entirely different turn. The combined roles of pastor and web designer finally proved unsustainable, and Russell Dewhurst announced his resignation in May 2007, citing his desire to focus on parish work and return to the study of canon law. Without a pastor, the council began the task of turning itself from an advisory body into a decision-making one. From now on, decisions would now be made within the council by discussion and vote. A new lay chair was appointed to help lead council discussions, and she asked me to serve as her deputy. The council I had joined was rapidly becoming less and less like an advisory group, but the position did not sound too onerous and I gladly offered my services. As the interregnum period continued, and an attempt to appoint a new web pastor found no suitable candidates, it began to feel that this phase of church life would be a permanent one.

In some ways, church life flourished. The worship schedule continued to increase, as Ailsa Wright, one of the most regular i-church service attenders, has described (Wright 2008): there were now four or five daily services, led by a team of 17, with a weekly discussion group and special services for the major Anglican festivals. This proliferation of activity did not reflect any great increase in the proportion of church members who attended worship regularly, and congregations remained small, but more of those who did attend were now encouraged to lead.

These times of worship were powerful for some. In our interview, Lucy described the Compline service as peaceful, simple, and a good way to end her day. Heather, unable to attend church due to ME, wrote a moving account of her own experience for Ailsa Wright's chapter and shared it with me:

> I will never forget the day I first went into the I-Church [sic] chapel online. [. . .] Quietly but dramatically that evening during Compline, my messy lounge was transformed into a sanctuary. I experienced Emmanuel: God with us, sitting in front of my laptop! [. . .] I now lead Compline once a week. It isn't much but it means a lot to me to be able to do something—even if I'm wearing my pyjamas and laying on my sofa.

Another of the rare face-to-face gatherings was organised in Oxford, attended by members from the UK and the United States and by representatives of the trustees. New forums proliferated, activity seemed to increase, and new members joined the site. A new web developer was appointed, and work began on a new church website in consultation with the community. One i-church member was appointed to the board of trustees, ensuring that the trustees had direct participation day-to-day in actual i-church life (and vice versa).

Other indications were less positive. The church had no clear structure for decision-making, and the departure of the web pastor had left a maze of different individuals and groups in leadership roles with unclear responsibilities. The trustees had legal responsibility, but seldom used their powers to intervene directly. The council could make decisions, but a dozen people were involved in those discussions and consensus always took time. Such consensus was in theory guided by the lay chair and deputy—the deputy, remember, was me—but those two offices were not supposed to make independent decisions at all. Other departments, meanwhile, included the two associate pastors, who in the absence of a web pastor were no longer accountable to anyone; the moderators, who were deadlocked over the idea of introducing some rules to standardise their activity; and the leaders of the private pastoral groups, some of whom claimed that protecting the privacy of their members prevented them from letting anyone else know what their groups were doing. Each of these categories had some sort of authority, but now they had to rely only on common sense, friendship and trust to help work out how to exercise their responsibilities.

Meanwhile, church culture was shifting. The web pastor had played a very active role in church life and administration, but he had also occupied a role that was of considerable symbolic importance. As I saw it, the shared identity of the i-church community derived not from any shared values, shared history, or even a shared set of practices, for all these were regularly contested, but from common allegiance to a set of Anglican symbols. The web pastor, as a focus of universal respect, had acted to hold together the diversity of the group without providing the symbolic or material resources for any one view to become dominant. When he departed, this balance became unstable. I reflected on this possibility in my field notes at the time:

> I consider the absence of the web pastor to have removed one major source of unity and so encouraged the emergence of the tensions his presence had partially suppressed. It is not that new tensions have arisen, but that those present since the first launch of the church are now competing more warmly for dominance.

As my account of the division of responsibilities in i-church makes clear, the web pastor had also served as a location of final authority. With that position unoccupied, decisions could only be made by consensus. This lack of hierarchy may seem to some readers like a democratic ideal to be celebrated, but government by consensus also creates an expectation that the loudest or most popular voices will be able to state their cause and win decisions in their favour. In other words, those who wished for change now had a structural route to make that change happen, and when victory seems possible, battle is far more worthwhile. Should a suitably emotive cause arise, i-church could be poised for disaster.

That cause did indeed arise, at the very end of 2007. The sequence of events as I perceived them can be briefly related. One new member stated that she was autistic, and so had difficulty following rules and interpreting the behaviour of others. She then announced that the leader of a private group (a kind of pastoral group intended for 'spiritual direction') had punished her for a breach of etiquette by banning her from communicating with the other group members. When the i-church community reacted to this with shock and dismay, the group leader stated that his actions within the group were covered by the seal of the confessional and therefore refused to confirm or deny anything at all. The council embarked on its own internal discussion of what to do, in search of a consensus response, which proved elusive. Amid a maze of other subsidiary complaints and issues, now returning to the forefront of debate, focus turned on the council; were they not permitting the mistreatment of this vulnerable member, and in doing so, were they not showing they needed to be reformed? Complaints flew in all directions, followed eventually by legal threats and the public distribution by one council member (not me) of a series of private postings made by another (also, I am glad to say, not me) relating to the individuals concerned. Soon after, I received an email informing all i-church members that the website could no longer be accessed. The trustees had intervened, and the situation would now be resolved at a higher level.

These events can be interpreted along several different dimensions: according to the personalities involved; their differing perceptions of what kind of place i-church was; conflict between the values of safety, harmony, justice and self-expression; theological conflicts between models of episcopal and congregational leadership; the significance of deliberately creating exclusive and long-standing sub-groups within the church through the promotion of private forums; and so on. We could also apply the work of Penny Edgell Becker (1999), who suggests analysing conflict in congregations in terms of a finite set of underlying social models, each of which establishes how things are done, who is in charge of what, what matters most and how conflicts should be handled. The most severe crises, Becker argues, develop in congregations in which no one model is dominant, because here members cannot agree about how to fight, what is at stake or what counts as winning. That description certainly fits with my own experience of the i-church crisis.

We encounter here a serious methodological difficulty in our analysis of this conflict, because I cannot actually quote anything from the forums without the consent of the authors, and this was not a situation in which distributing consent forms would have been a good idea. I will therefore focus on the most straightforward issue, and point once again to the absence of a clear, quick, universally accepted source of decision-making. It was not possible for any one individual or group to announce a decision, expel a member or silence a conversation, because the authority to do so was too loosely distributed to be swiftly deployed and too hotly contested for any decision to be accepted.

Even in hindsight, I find my decision to join the council difficult to evaluate. By joining the leadership team, I had unwittingly chosen a side in a conflict that had not yet begun, and some participants always remained convinced that my research must therefore be suspect. I certainly encourage other ethnographers to think hard about what could go wrong with their fieldwork strategy, preferably before it happens. On the other hand, without such close access to the leadership process, I would have had an even more partial and distorted view of what was going on. All data is valuable, and no position can offer an entirely neutral or objective viewpoint; reflexivity is always an essential component in ethnography. It is no coincidence, of course, that I should consider an explanation rooted in structures of leadership and distribution of authority to be the most relevant explanation of a conflict that occurred when I was part of the structure of leadership.

Recovery: 2008–2009

Such a crisis demanded a reorganisation of the system of governance, a restating of the vision, purpose and unity of the church and new growth over time to replace the energy, optimism and good-will that had been sapped away by the dispute. The solution, in fact, was a return to the old system: the appointment of another web pastor. The trustees insisted that this had always been their intention, although—as we have seen—at least some in the i-church community had begun planning for a permanent existence without a leader and were taken entirely by surprise. This time the trustees declared their choice of pastor without public announcement or community consultation and announced a streamlined governance system in which they kept legal responsibility, the web pastor made decisions and the trustees, the council and certain co-opted officers would advise the web pastor as appropriate. The new pastor, Pam Smith, was ideally suited in experience and training: she had worked in team and parish ministry and had been a Church of Fools warden, a St Pixels leadership team member and part of the i-church community.

At another face-to-face meeting in Oxford in 2009, over a year after these events, the trustees described the absence of the web pastor as a crucial factor in the difficulties i-church had faced. According to the new pastor herself, 'there was just a huge insecurity' about who was able to make which decisions—a suggestion in line with the analysis I offered above. A pastor was able to make clear decisions swiftly and could take on a 'boundary-setting' role to enforce norms and create safe spaces. Both pastor and trustees suggested that the experience had shown the importance of appointing an experienced, ordained person to the role, both for practical reasons—such an individual would have been trained for community management during the process of ordination—and for theological reasons: according to one trustee, the church had suffered in the interregnum for the lack of a priest in leadership. The existing diocesan system had saved the church further damage, according to the chair of trustees, and without that structure i-church 'would have closed . . . it would not have survived in a recognisable form'.

All but a few council members and officers left over the next six months, finding the shift from decision-making to minor advisory group highly uncomfortable. They were replaced by co-opted officers more enthusiastic about their role in the new system and in due course, by a full election. I saw out my own 3-year term of office as a council member, which was almost up. A new web designer was appointed, working closely with the pastor. With one trusted person in charge, communication with the trustees became simpler, delegation to aides far more successful and decision-making swift and firm. Not only could the church start to recover from its troubles, but a new flexibility and speed could be brought to the long-running project of a new website.

One significant development instigated by the new pastor related to i-church worship. Services had proliferated to four or five each day but remained dependent on a small number of regular congregants. When some of these left the church or scaled back their commitments, service times began to run with no congregation at all, or no leader. In response, the entire worship team were put on indefinite leave and worship suspended. When services recommenced the packed schedule was replaced by just one weekly event, on a Sunday, led by the web pastor. The church had 'massively over-reached' itself, Pam Smith explained to me in one of our interviews, and needed to let projects and teams start to build up again organically as new and enthusiastic people joined the church or stepped forward from the membership. In fact, she suggested, a 'Fresh Expression' of church should not be built primarily around worship at all, but around community, mission and asking the membership what they actually wanted to support and offer (for a similar argument, see Male 2008).

A range of service times were tried, and a new 'worship co-ordinator' was appointed. In September and October 2008 I attended services at 9:00 p.m. on Sundays, but also at 10:00 p.m. and 9:30 a.m. midweek. Congregations ranged from 2 to 5 people. These half-hour events followed a liturgical pattern of set prayers, responses and readings, taken from Anglican or Celtic texts, followed by a time of open prayer. A homily of some 30 lines was added, a feature I had not encountered before.

A new website finally launched in October 2008, updating the range of available media for the first time since 2004. This new site followed some of the elements encouraged by Richard Thomas and by the Vision Meeting in 2007, creating a more vibrant and interactive public-access website with a range of multimedia resources.

Figure 5.2 shows the church website as it stood during Lent 2009. The new 'globe' logo was first introduced during the interregnum period and

Figure 5.2 i-church homepage, 2009.

shows Europe—and so Oxford—at the centre of the image. One interesting forum debate in 2007 had discussed the implications of an image of the Western or Eastern hemisphere, respectively taken to symbolise the origins of i-church and its current global reach. The logo is here circled by the words 'i-church' and 'ecclesia via media'. The 'via media' is an Anglican theological doctrine, outlined by Richard Hooker in the 16th century and popularised in the 19th by members of the Oxford Movement to present the Church of England as a 'middle way' between Catholicism and Protestantism, and here of course it offers a pun on the electronic media of i-church—a joke which would make sense only to visitors with a reasonable grasp of Anglican church history. The words were later replaced by the somewhat more prosaic 'Diocese of Oxford'.

The central horizontal bar shows the range of interactive options now available. In place of the sermons and articles once uploaded at sporadic intervals, the visitor can now access 'Public Forums', start his or her own blog, or join the 'Community', where the old private forums could still be found. Separate usernames could be registered for the public and community forums, and no requirement is made for real names to be used in the public site. At least a few of those regular members who had left the church during the events discussed above returned to post in the public site.

The lower half of the screen is dedicated to resources authorised by the i-church leadership and themed around the church year. The images of doors (Fig. 5.2) link to a project that ran during in the month leading up to Easter. Each day during Lent, a link was posted to a song, image or written reflection composed or created by an i-church member. From Palm Sunday to Easter Sunday, i-church published a Bible reading about the events of that day, a reflection on some aspect of that reading, and a series of illustrative photographs. A similar project was launched before Christmas 2009, creating an Advent calendar with a song, image or reflection behind each 'window'. Contributions came from i-church members, but also from Pam Smith's contacts in St Pixels and Second Life.

Figure 5.3 shows a screenshot of the full homepage as it could be seen in January 2010. The homepage has now been renamed 'The Gatehouse', and is coloured throughout in pastel shades, all resting on a white background. No images of churches are included—in keeping with Russell Dewhurst's design philosophy, quoted above—but there is a prominent stained glass window. Photographs of nature are included. A line of black-and-white images at the bottom of the screen illustrate a range of links to online resources and staff e-mail contacts, and these images combine suggestions of spirituality (candles), human companionship (a cup of tea, touching hands) and technology (a laptop). Text in the centre describes i-church as 'an online Christian community based on Benedictine principles', and invites the viewer to come to 'The Courtyard'—'the place where we interact with the world'. The public forums, now renamed 'The Courtyard', include prayer threads, discussion of theology and current affairs, wordgames and personal blogs.

Figure 5.3 i-church homepage, 2010.

Conclusion

At my face-to-face meeting with the trustees in 2009, we discussed the merits of i-church and the lessons the diocese had learned. The current chair, the bishop of Dorchester, declared his conviction that this was 'a genuine church, a real church, in a new medium'. The founders had hoped to use the Internet to create a way into church for those with no history of Christian involvement, but the presence of many who had been 'disappointed or damaged' by local churches was noted as another area of success with its own distinctive challenges. For one trustee, i-church had to be created on the Internet simply 'because that's where people are'—a line that could have been a direct quote from the writings of Richard Thomas, or indeed several of the other online church founders we will meet in this book.

I-church had taught the diocese a great deal, the bishop observed, helping Oxford to stay 'ahead of the curve' of Christian innovation. Reliance on existing structures had been a strength and a weakness: 'we just kind of took the models we were familiar with and tried to rethink them', but 'something we had totally failed to grasp was the nature of the Internet', particularly that 'online and diocese do not sit well together', divided by the increased speed of communication and relationship fostered by the Internet. At the same time, the Anglican emphasis on good structure and clear accountability ensured visitors to i-church knew that the details behind the vision had been worked out, that someone was responsible for what took place and that the site would be stable, safe and long-lasting. 'I don't think we know where this journey is taking us', he later observed, and flexibility was vital in engagement with an ever-changing medium—another theme that Richard Thomas had stressed in 2004.

If we return to the seven themes identified in Chapter 4, we can see that i-church and Church of Fools differ significantly on several counts.

1. Scale. I-church did not initially want to attract a congregation of thousands, and church leaders was disoriented by the high levels of interest in 2004. Small-scale intensity was crucial to the initial vision of the group, and i-church has continued to search for a workable model of online small group.
2. Local Churchgoing. Once again, the majority of members combined their online participation with local church attendance. However, a sizeable proportion of participants had left local churches for various theological, pastoral or health reasons before discovering i-church. Many members actually didn't think of i-church as a 'church' at all, despite the Church of England's approval.
3. Community. I-church did develop a core network of participants who shared strong interpersonal bonds, firm commitment and a sense of belonging, but the initial vision of a monastic life of discipline proved much harder to put into practice.

4. Ritual and Spiritual Experience. Relatively few church members worshipped regularly in the chatroom, but prayer forums played a significant part in community life. At our meeting, one of the trustees praised the 'absolute focus on prayer'—'the support is amazing', she claimed, creating a 'solid' foundation for the community. The bishop concurred, reflecting that i-church had become a space 'where people pray together and communicate at depths not often seen in parish churches'.

5. Familiarity. Tradition is again extremely important, just as in Church of Fools, but the focus here is quite different. Instead of producing a visual imitation of church architecture, i-church followed the organisational structure and liturgy of the Church of England. Church of Fools used familiarity in part as a form of satire, but humour was not one of the goals of the creators of i-church.

6. Internal Control. Compared to Church of Fools, i-church encountered very few 'trolls' and was able to develop a much more discursive, participatory leadership style, usually structured around a diocese-appointed, salaried pastor. As we have seen, this structure of governance had both strengths and weaknesses, particularly in crisis situations.

7. External Funding and Oversight. I-church is a formal part of a diocese of the Church of England, answering to a board of trustees who intervened directly on rare occasions. As the bishop commented, the challenges of meshing a web community into a diocese were significant, not least because building an online church as part of an established religious institution slowed the pace of decision-making and implementation. There were also clear advantages, however, including finance, a recognisable identity that appealed to many members, and—in a crisis—a solid and final location of authority. Most importantly, the narrative of i-church reminds us that institutional strategies change over time, developing and adapting in response to perceived opportunities and new challenges. I-church eventually established a manageable system of governance under the oversight of the diocese, but it took a long time to get there.

Notes

1 'i-church.org', January 22, 2003. http://web.archive.org/web/20030122165855/http://www.i-church.org/. Accessed 10–01–10.
2 'i-church', September 23, 2003. http://web.archive.org/web/20030927001016/http://i-church.org/. Accessed 10–01–10.
3 'i-church', March 26, 2004. http://web.archive.org/web/20040326145714/http://www.i-church.org/. Accessed 10–01–10.
4 'i-church', May 24, 2004. http://web.archive.org/web/20040524234845/http://www.i-church.org/. Accessed 10–01–10.
5 'i-church', July 30, 2004. http://web.archive.org/web/20040730192202/http://www.i-church.org/. Accessed 10–01–10.

References

Archbishop's Council on Mission and Public Affairs, 2004. *Mission-shaped Church: Church Planting and Fresh Expressions of Church in a Changing Context.* London: Church House Publishing.

Becker, P., 1999. *Congregations in Conflict: Cultural Models of Local Religious Life.* Cambridge: Cambridge University Press.

Leslie, A., 2004a. A letter from the web pastor. *i-church*, June. [online] Available at: <http://web.archive.org/web/20040807001909/www.i-church.org/news/200406_pastoral.php> [Accessed 1 September 2016]

———, 2004b. A letter from the web pastor. *i-church*, August. [online] Available at: <http://web.archive.org/web/20040814024824/http://www.i-church.org/news/200408_pastoral.php> [Accessed 1 September 2016]

Male, D., 2008. Who are fresh expressions really for? Do they really reach the unchurched? In: Nelstrop, L. and Percy, M., eds. *Evaluating Fresh Expressions: Explorations in Emerging Church.* Norwich: Canterbury Press. pp. 148–160.

Press Association, 2004. Church of England to set up "Internet parish". *The Guardian*, 5 March. [online] Available at: <https://www.theguardian.com/technology/2004/mar/05/religion.news> [Accessed 1 September 2016]

Thomas, R., 2004a. Dedication service for i-church: Homily by Revd Richard Thomas. *I-church.* [online] Available at: <http://web.archive.org/web/20040814025842/www.i-church.org/events/20040730_sd_sermontext.php> [Accessed 1 September 2016]

———, 2004b. Why Internet church? *Thinking Anglicans*, 5 March. [online] Available at: <http://www.thinkinganglicans.org.uk/archives/000499.html> [Accessed 1 September 2016]

Wright, A., 2008. i-church: The unfolding story of a fresh expression of church <www.i-church.org>;. In: Nelstrop, L. and Percy, M., eds. *Evaluating Fresh Expressions: Explorations in Emerging Church.* Norwich: Canterbury Press. pp. 123–134.

6 St Pixels

Figure 6.1 The author, as seen by a member of St Pixels. Cartoon by Xander, 2008.

Church of Fools has moved four times since 2004, shifting from a 3D virtual space to one text-based forum, then another, and eventually onto Facebook. The church renamed itself 'St Pixels: Church of the Internet' in 2006, and still uses that name today. Some of the most active participants during my research had first met years before in the 3D church, and many of those are still active in the group in 2016.

This chapter will focus primarily on the state of the St Pixels community in 2009, the period of my most intensive ethnographic research. By 2009, St Pixels was quite a different kind of space from the 3D church, offering a wider range of communication channels—including forums, chatrooms and blogs—and organizing regular offline gatherings. The community was also considerably less anarchic. The membership was still diverse, at least theologically and geographically, but that diversity was now almost entirely Christian; there was no equivalent of the Church of Fools' Atheist's Corner, no vending machine cult and no swarm of hostile clones of Ned Flanders.

I will begin by outlining the development of Church of Fools after 2004. I will then introduce St Pixels by considering its site design, avatars and usernames, leadership system, discussion forums, blogs, worship activities and the importance of play. To end the chapter, I will bring these themes together to describe a worship event that took place during a particular face-to-face gathering, using that case study to explore some of the rituals, practices and norms of the community. St Pixels has continued to change since 2009, and I will explore its more recent activity in the Conclusion to this book.

From Virtual World to St Pixels

The 3D environment of Church of Fools attracted media attention, many visitors and a loyal core community. When the project came to an end, participants realised that creating a new, improved virtual space would require financial resources that were not available. A website was created instead, churchoffools.com, offering forums, private messages and a text chatroom as a temporary measure while plans were put in place for a return to 3D. Some of those who endured these moves experienced great disappointment and loss (see Chapter 4), but this was also a time of creative adaptation.

The new Church of Fools text site—nicknamed 'flat church' by one of my interviewees—developed the interaction range of the group in several significant ways. New discussion forums were created, named 'the Crypt' in reference to the social area of the old 3D environment. Other new forums were dedicated to prayers and praise reports, celebrating community birthdays and playing games. Text-based worship appeared in the chatroom, and—just as in i-church—this began as an informal experiment by community members. Worship continued to use some of the elements developed in the 3D Church of Fools, including liturgical responses, times of open prayer and the simultaneous recitation of the Lord's Prayer in different forms. Additional channels of interaction also emerged, taking community interaction beyond the website and in some cases offline. Some contacts were arranged through the church website, like the annual 'Secret Santa' exchange of small presents by post (discussed below). Other channels emerged unofficially, including email, MSN conversations and telephone calls. Face-to-face gatherings proliferated and became a key part of church culture.

A basic set of rules been applied during the 3D period, based on the Ten Commandments used in Ship of Fools. As the church began to encounter difficulties, these rules needed to be adapted and expanded. Leadership team member Mark Howe recalls that 'each new problem seemed to demand an extension to the list of proscribed behaviour', until 'the whole system started to feel pharisaical' (Howe 2005: 52).

Now that the heady, exhausting waves of visitors and mass attacks had ended, the style of leadership could shift to gentle encouragement of good behaviour. The Wardens were replaced by newly-appointed 'Hosts', and the Commandments were replaced with a new, more positive list of six 'Core Values': respect; tolerance and diversity; constructive dialogue; personal reflection and corporate worship; responsibility; and accountability (Howe 2005: 69–70).

At this stage, the Core Values made only the briefest reference to theology:

> Church of Fools is a Christian church. You are welcome to join us, whatever your beliefs, though you should expect the organised activities to have a Christian emphasis.

As Howe points out, '[t]he advantage and drawback of this approach was that it enabled each reader to use their own working definition of Christian and church' (2005: 53). This discursive approach to doctrine was typical for Church of Fools, but offered only the most cursory theological foundation or boundaries to guide church activity and participant behaviour. A more elaborate statement was soon developed through church discussion, designed to provide a theological justification for the six Core Values:

> God is revealed to seekers by many different means, including creation, the Bible, the life of Jesus and the Spirit-filled witness of the Church. Church of Fools is one expression of that historical, international and universal Church. We aim to create sacred space on the Internet where we can seek God together, enjoy each other's company and reflect God's love for the world. Those of any belief or none are welcome to take part in our activities, providing they accept the Christian focus of our community and respect other participants.
>
> (Howe 2005: 53)

This paragraph attempts to summarise Christian teaching without excluding any shade of Christian belief and practice. It does not specify valid forms or interpretations of revelation, and foregrounds social activity. Sacred space encompasses all church activities, including fellowship.

Church of Fools relaunched as St Pixels, 'Church of the Internet', in May 2006. The new St Pixels website was designed by community members. Members could now write their own blogs, and could design new avatars— now all human, with adjustable faces and outfits. A new chatroom called LIVE (Fig. 6.2) offered visual and audio capabilities designed for worship. LIVE was designed to resemble the ground plan of a medieval church, with a few concessions to humour and functionality. Visitors logged in to the

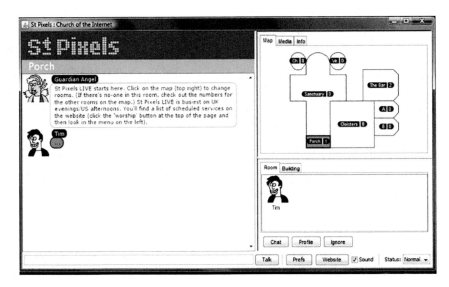

Figure 6.2 LIVE, the St Pixels chatroom, 2009.

'Porch' and could then move to other rooms, including 'the Sanctuary'—a cross-shaped space with an apse, like the design of the 3D Church of Fools. There were also chapels, meeting rooms and social areas called 'Cloisters' and 'The Bar'.

Just like Church of Fools and i-church, St Pixels courted attention from established media industries to publicise its online experiments. The launch of the new site earned the church an invitation to host BBC Radio 4's Sunday Worship programme in 2007. Speaking to the *Guardian* newspaper about this high-profile event, Mark Howe described St Pixels as 'quite a breakthrough' and promised 'to show how technology and spirituality can interact at every stage online' (Wainwright 2007). Broadcasting text-based Internet worship over the radio posed a challenge, however, particularly when the radio audience was accustomed to the highest and most traditional standards of church music. St Pixels members had to meet in person at a church building in Manchester, accompanied by a choir, and organized a service that—in order to satisfy the expectations of their radio listeners— was much more conventional than their usual online events.

As church spokesperson Steve Goddard pointed out to the Guardian, in-person meetings like the Manchester broadcast did not appeal to all members: 'everyone adopts a character online to participate in the services, and there are definitely some who do not want to "uncloak". The anonymity of our worship is important to them' (Wainwright 2007). Many St Pixels members relished the chance to breach their online anonymity and meet up in person, and we will consider an example of such a gathering at the end of this chapter, but not everyone felt the same way.

StPixels.com: The Website

St Pixels was a public-access website, open for all visitors to read. The site was divided into seven sections: Discover, Interact, Blog, Discuss, Reflect, Worship and Support Us. Highlighted content—news, discussion threads, interesting blog posts—was selected from the site by the leadership teams and posted to the homepage.

'Discover' offered information about the site, including the latest version of the Core Values. 'Interact', described as 'the heart of the St Pixels community', hosted word games, information about meets and a section for 'support with various challenging situations' entitled 'Stand by me'. 'Discuss' was the main debate forum, while 'Reflect' was used to discuss occasional themes selected by the management. 'Worship' included information about LIVE events, prayer and praise report threads and discussions of spirituality and social justice. 'Support Us', finally, included information about site finances and donations. The most significant innovation from the old Church of Fools forums was the 'Blog' section, where all members could start their own personal blogs.

The boundaries between these site areas were closely guarded by the Hosts. One of the site's Core Values was 'Constructive Dialogue', and this included the reminder that 'different parts of the site are intended for different types of interaction'. The boundary between 'Discuss' and 'Blog' was considered particularly important, and blog posts that Hosts saw as particularly controversial were regularly moved and turned into discussion threads. Constructive dialogue was taken to mean that all participants in a discussion must be equal, so any attempt to use a blog to give extra weight to the author's voice was not permitted.

St Pixels conducted a survey of its users in March 2008, receiving 113 responses. Only one quarter of these had belonged to Church of Fools. Most were newcomers who had encountered St Pixels through media coverage, but 14 percent had heard of the church through a word-of-mouth recommendation. 79 percent of members came from the UK and 19 percent from the US. Almost 80 percent were aged 30 to 59, with the highest proportion, 34 percent, aged 50 to 59. Under-18s were not permitted to join. St Pixels members in this sample were apparently older than the visitors to the 3D Church of Fools, and closely comparable in age to the membership of i-church. The gender balance had also shifted: now only 40 percent were male and 60 percent female, reversing the proportions reported in Church of Fools and i-church.

78 percent of respondents attended church once per month or more, and 15 percent did so 'occasionally'; this contrasts strikingly with Church of Fools (where 39 percent were said to be non-churchgoers), and with i-church

(where 50 percent said they were not regular churchgoers). 69 percent said St Pixels would be an adequate replacement for local churchgoing, but 93 percent still attended a local church at least on occasion. Almost all St Pixels respondents described themselves as Christian, but the survey was more diverse in theology than the statistics reported at i-church. 40 percent described themselves as 'evangelical' and the same proportion as 'liberal', while 30 percent selected 'charismatic' and 'traditional'; 10 percent identified as Catholic.

Avatars and Usernames

Avatars and usernames are of particular interest to online community researchers. In designing a profile, users seek to create something they can recognise as their own, that maintains a preferred degree of distance or transparency between their online and offline activity and that others will respond to in a desired manner. The designers of a community site are therefore likely to put great thought into the kinds of avatars and usernames they make available for users to choose from, in order to promote the kinds of self-expression, identification and anonymity that the designers consider most likely to support the culture they are trying to promote.

In Church of Fools and St Pixels, the Core Value of 'Respect' addressed the question of privacy, reassuring users that 'you do not have to reveal more of yourself than you wish . . . People are comfortable here saying what they actually think, as opposed to what they know their bosses, etc. want to hear. We want to keep it that way.' Personal control over the degree to which one's identity is shared with others was considered a necessary condition for honest, safe and personal conversation. On the other hand, there were limits: the Core Values also included 'Accountability', which ruled that no one could have more than one username.

Distinctions between acceptable and unacceptable forms of pseudonymity occupy a particularly important place in the norms of all the churches studied in this book. Each church permitted some degree of acceptable dissimulation in avatars and usernames, varying from group to group, but forbade any form of communication deliberately intended to deceive. Users (and researchers) must establish the range of pseudonymity accepted within a specific community in order to appreciate the kind of relationships members form with their avatars and with each other. St Pixels tolerated some degree of distance between online representation and embodied self but drew the line at the multiplication of selves and usernames known as 'sockpuppeting'. As we shall see in Chapter 7, the congregation of the Anglican Cathedral of Second Life took a different approach to this issue. Several Cathedral visitors operated two or more avatars, and these 'alts' were generally accepted as opportunities to explore a new identity or make new friends.

Registered users of St Pixels could create a cartoonish avatar (Fig. 6.2) by selecting options for a series of layers, including head shape, skin tone, hairstyle, eyes and nose, mouth and clothing. Different ranges were available for male or female avatars, often including strong gender markers. Males could select a skin tone indicating an unshaven face, for example, while the mouths of female avatars were originally limited to a range of full red or pink lips. Male choices included a jacket, a shirt and tie, a T-shirt and a football shirt in three different strips; female choices were all conservative, with covered shoulders, and included the jacket and T-shirt but also outfits with bead necklaces or lacy collars.

My own avatar resembled my physical appearance in shape, skin tone, hairstyle and clothing as closely as the software permits. This attitude was common but not universal. Frank's avatar was 'pretty close' to real life, with a pony tail hairstyle, and smoked a cigarette—although Frank would have preferred a cigar, his normal favourite. The avatar was 'about as close as I could get', a 'caricature based on reality'—'I don't really try to hide who I am'. William reported that he habitually changed the colour of his avatar's clothing to match the shirt he was wearing that day, freely admitting that this was 'a bit silly'.

At the opposite end of the scale, privacy-conscious Harriet was highly aware of her anonymity and committed to safeguarding it, and continued this preference into her avatar design. Harriet expressed the least confidence in agreeing to an interview, querying my research at length beforehand and insisting we speak through an instant messenger text program to avoid sharing phone numbers. In fact, the interview was a great success; Harriet expressed herself fluently and quickly through typed text and answered my questions informatively and at length. When I asked if her avatar resembled her physical appearance, she responded 'no!!! [. . .] i do not have grey hair' and explained that this was part of her protection of privacy: 'avatar is not like me—anon!'.

Even the simplest avatars can become objects of emotional investment and identification, hotly defended by their owners against management interference. On one occasion in 2005, the Church of Fools leadership decided to 'upgrade' the avatar images used on the forums without consulting members. They were startled to find themselves embroiled in a rebellion that later became known as the 'avatar wars'. Mark Howe reports 'complaints of "who stole my avatar?"', and explains that 'few of us expected the sustained anger on the part of some users who had been deprived of *their* avatar. One user complained that without her avatar she could no longer be herself and no longer be a full part of the community' (Howe 2005: 37). William, one of those most angered by the decision, recalled in our interview that he had lost something he had personally identified with. For the leaders, these images were insignificant—Howe describes them as 'poorly-drawn' and 'the size of a postage stamp'—but for at least some users they represented something highly significant, symbols of community membership and personal identity. According to Howe, it was here that the church leadership 'came to realise just how intense virtual community can become.' A different kind of avatar war erupted again when the new St Pixels cartoons were introduced in 2006: in this case, women in the community objected so strongly to the gender stereotype of full, red lips that community management eventually agreed to introduce a wider range of mouth options.

Several members of St Pixels developed a reputation as cartoonists, producing scenes in which St Pixels avatars cavorted in entertaining and usually somewhat disreputable ways. This chapter opens with one particularly elaborate example (Fig. 6.1), a cartoon created for me by a member called Xander. He has signed his work, so in this case I have not disguised his username. Xander regularly created cartoons of the avatars of community members, and sold these in various formats to raise money for St Pixels. We will find another cartoon below (Fig. 6.3), produced by another artists for a face-to-face gathering in 2009.

I was twice startled by unexpected divergences between avatars and realities. First, I noticed that a sizeable minority of users selected avatars with dark skin tones and interpreted this as evidence that St Pixels included a degree of ethnic diversity. I subsequently learned that the community was almost exclusively white, but that some members varied their skin tone according to the season—using dark skin and sunglasses to indicate a suntan, the arrival of summer or return from a tropical holiday. Second, I was surprised at a meet to encounter a number of women my own age, despite my belief for several years that I was almost the only member under 30. The avatar designs available to women had all signalled, to me, middle-aged or older identities, particularly through the choice of hair and clothing; this was a limitation unintentionally created by the (middle-aged male) designer, not an intentional choice by community members. Both cultural and software influences are relevant to online appearance and through appearance, to perceptions of identity.

St Pixels members were also required to choose a username. In Church of Fools—both 3D and 'flat church'—registered members usually selected usernames quite different from their real names. This tendency is common across the Internet, but not always accepted in online churches; i-church, for example, has always insisted that a username must be some variant of the member's real name. As we have seen, Church of Fools did not usually allow members to change their usernames, but in late 2005 some long-term participants began asking to switch their pseudonyms to reflect their real names. The leadership team agreed on a temporary username amnesty, and I was one of those who began using my real name in the online community. The use of real names remained popular (but not universal) when the church relaunched as St Pixels. From my own point of view, using my real name online represented a greater transparency and a firmer connection between my online and offline selves, reflecting the confidence I had by then developed in the safety of the online environment and my own competence at navigating it without mishap.

I interviewed several St Pixels users who did still use pseudonyms, and they explained that they had selected these usernames primarily for simplicity or personal significance. The effect of the name on others was mentioned only as a secondary concern, and it was extremely rare for members to choose usernames with any obvious religious connotations. When I asked Chris why he had selected his username, he responded, 'Oh, I've had that for ages'; preserving one name allowed people he interacted with to recognise him across sites. Harriet invented a new word by combining parts of the names of her two cats and liked the outcome—'my name is spiky like me'. Beth adopted the name of a character from a favourite book because she was 'very computer illiterate' when she registered and 'very afraid' to reveal her real identity. Carol selected a flower for her username, a choice that influenced her real-life perceptions: 'I look at [that flower] differently now [. . .] its just part of this huge joke that makes St Pixels work'.

The Leadership

The 3D Church of Fools developed a three-tier structure of leadership: a management team appointed by Ship of Fools, wardens appointed to undertake moderation duties and worship leaders. This structure continued in an expanded form in the text-based Church of Fools and in St Pixels. By 2009, the management team included 7 people, all long-term members. There were 17 wardens, now called Hosts, separated into separate groups for each of the seven site areas. Hosts' avatars were marked with a halo. The worship stream included no fewer than 32 volunteers. St Pixels also became a limited company in 2009, with a community-elected Board of Directors. The site announced that this change would 'protect the people running St Pixels against being personally liable if anything goes wrong' while giving any future external partners 'confidence that we're a regular organisation with a common legal structure'.

The hosts for each stream had three major tasks: content management, encouragement and moderation. Content management occurred particularly in the Discuss area, where any discussion threads had to be submitted for approval before they were posted to the website. Hosts discuss the submission, edit it if necessary to clarify the question asked and attach an image to illustrate the theme. Discussions could take a day to be approved and were less frequently started than in Church of Fools but aimed to be more tightly focused, more interesting and more visually appealing and tended to attract a far higher number of responses.

The task of 'encouragement' was emphasised by several Hosts I interviewed. For Bella, for example, hosting means 'you're inviting people into your space' and making sure they're treated well, but 'very seldom' stepping in to moderate. When moderation was deemed necessary in a forum thread, hosts posted a statement explicitly labelled as 'Hosting', citing the Core Values and calling on participants to return to acceptable behaviour. 'Encouragement' and 'moderation' are endpoints on a continuum, and Host response to any specific incident was likely to involve a combination of informal guidance and formal reprimands. One host reported that the balance between these different positions had to be argued out among the leadership from time to time, between those who favoured leading by example and those who preferred to enforce clearly stated rules.

By 2009, the site's Core Values statement had been updated from the early version discussed above. Each of the values was now accompanied by a somewhat longer and more detailed explanation, with a clearer theological basis. The value of 'Constructive Dialogue', for example, now included the following statement:

> We believe that exchanging opinions and experiences can help each of us to learn about God, others and ourselves. We therefore do everything possible to cultivate a climate on the site that is conducive to such exchanges.

Readers were warned to 'Expect your beliefs and assumptions to be challenged, and consider unpacking them in order to help others understand you better'. In other words, any opinion could be expressed, regardless of theology, so long as the poster was willing to engage with disagreement; any disagreement could be expressed, so long as the poster refrained from personal attack. This was the balance that the Hosts were required to encourage and enforce.

A new official category, the Mediators, was created in late 2007. Mediators were completely independent of the leadership system, offering a chance for members to take any complaints to a neutral body, and they were appointed by democratic vote among members. Two served at any one time. Members with any kind of grievance were instructed to seek a private conversation with the other party, then to take their objections to the management team, and to contact mediators only as a last resort.

Discuss and Reflect

Forum debates took place in two sections of St Pixels, 'Discuss' and 'Reflect'. 'Reflect' was used only rarely, for themed discussions organised by the site leadership. In 2006, for example, a discussion of the report *Mission-shaped Church* dedicated separate threads to each of its chapters. In 2007 and 2008, Reflect threads were used to discuss aspects of membership surveys organised by the leadership, and a solitary thread running from 2008 to 2009 discussed the place of the Bible in the St Pixels community, amassing 252 replies. These are the only four themed conversations Reflect had featured between 2006 and 2009, but each became a major focus of attention.

'Discuss' was much more active, dedicated to community conversations around seven themes: 'Church Life', 'Everyday Life', 'Current Events', 'Culture', 'Opinion', 'Talk Theology' and 'That Book'—the Bible. This list separates sections for philosophical discussion from sections intended for discussion of real-world experience, a distinction echoed by many of my interviewees. The inclusion of a 'Church Life' section suggests that participants were expected to have considerable experience of church attendance—as we have already seen in our discussion of the St Pixels membership survey.

The somewhat ambivalent reference to the Bible is also noteworthy. The introductory paragraph to 'That Book' emphasises the community values of respect, diversity and constructive dialogue, and carefully avoids any suggestion of doctrinal boundaries:

> Here is where we can study the Bible together and discuss what it means to us. [. . .] Through these discussions you can share your interpretation of a passage or read about someone else's take.

The focus here is on sharing interpretations and personal meanings, rather than teaching or learning, and no privileged authority is given to any particular version of Christian teaching. The implied assumption that readers will have a personal interpretation of the Bible to share further underlines the churchgoing experience expected of community members. There may be new Christians or non-Christians reading these pages, but none of the Discuss areas make an explicit attempt to educate, attract or engage such viewers.

My interviews with members suggested that many viewed the Discuss areas with mixed feelings. Evan, for example, explained that he visited Discuss 'a lot' to read postings by others he considered intelligent and well-educated, but he also noted that his own comments were ignored and 'pretty much snuffed out'. Indeed, his ideas were usually voiced by others and 'dissected and destroyed' before he got around to posting at all, and he would typically hold back from a thread if one particular member had already contributed—'he's a really smart man'. Discuss was 'more in your face' than other areas of the site, Evan explained, but this was one of its good qualities—'I like that'. We see here a member negotiating a particularly dangerous part of the site, where a misstep could lead to public belittling or worse. He does so by paying attention to which ideas have been covered and who has commented on them, judging the weight of contributions according to his perception of the intellectual reputations of different posters.

This deference to perceived intellectual prowess was not universally shared. Beth explained that she used to read every discussion, but now 'it all seems so technical', 'beyond me' in complexity and focused on 'education and not people's experiences'. She now scanned discussions instead, looking for particular posters that 'I always read'. These favoured posters were 'not theologians, not educated in a formal way in the Bible'. One, for example, was 'calm and fair' in everything she wrote, and another was praised for being 'so irreverent and off the wall', 'very different from how I think I am'. Like Evan, Beth now preferred to read rather than write, but she followed a carefully worked out practice of skim-reading based on her understanding of the reputations of different posters and was much less admiring of combative display.

Attitudes could change over time, as posters gained confidence and experience or lost interest and patience. Angela usually logged in to St Pixels over her breakfast porridge to survey the night's postings, considering her responses through the day before deciding what to add. 'I found the discussion area very interesting' at first, she explained, 'because I'd pretty much never thought theology, I thought faith'. She wasn't shy, she explained, but she considered herself 'academically fragile' and particularly sensitive to being 'shot down', and she struggled at first to join in with such a 'challenging and difficult' environment. Over time, however, she 'gradually became tougher', and now 'I join in with the big boys and girls'. Discuss had been 'a learning experience', and part of that learning involved her own intellectual confidence. Angela was interested in 'other points of view', but she also 'wouldn't say that any of them have changed my mind about anything.' Where her views had shifted, she attributed this to the gradual process of following her own trains of thought over time.

One common motivation for participation in discussion was the perceived lack of any such opportunity at home or in a local church. For Sandy, Discuss was a chance to express herself in new and exciting ways. She 'was basically in Discuss most of the time' when she first joined the site, 'several times a day'. 'It was like a big valve opened up', a chance to release 'thoughts that hadn't been expressed for years.' Discuss offered space for 'intellectual activity that I craved' after years of caring for small children. Over time, her attitude changed: Sandy eventually moved on to other kinds of community activity, because 'I don't have that need so much any more.'

For Daniel, the need for escape came from a church that refused to countenance the range of ideas he was beginning to find interesting. Part of a conservative evangelical church, he began asking complex and provocative questions about the Bible and Christian doctrine. 'There was a need for me to probe these things', he recalled, but to do so openly could cause trouble at church. Instead, he started to join online forums, concealing his name to protect his privacy. Over time he moved away from his theological conservatism, using the Internet as a resource to help think through his new ideas. 'I don't think it [the Internet] triggered it', he reflected, 'but it puts alternatives and options at your fingertips'.

I also encountered a much rarer but still highly influential point of view: the desire to save St Pixels from its theological and spiritual inadequacies. Vaughan was perhaps the most notorious example of this group, attracting a high profile within the community through his frequent, uncompromising attacks on other posters. Vaughan had engaged in theological debate online for more than ten years by 2009, moving between text and voice chatrooms and forums in search of interesting conversations and spaces to make a difference. He claimed to enjoy 'the cut and thrust' of argument, and particularly wanted 'to reach out to those people who are in cults', making something of a personal project of talking to Jehovah's Witnesses. Vaughan saw joining St Pixels as part of that larger online mission, another way of 'getting alongside people' to see how they think and engage them in debate. According to Vaughan, his presence in St Pixels was much-needed:

> I personally think there are many on there, I wouldn't like to put a percentage on it, who are religious but don't know Him [. . .] Don't get me wrong, I pray for them, I do care about them [. . .] I'm trying to reach out to these people.

According to Vaughan, St Pixels members reacted with particularly telling disdain to the Bible. When he presented what he considered to be clear reminders of biblical truth, other posters tended to become uncomfortable, dismissing his messages as his own personal opinions. On the other hand, he claimed, he was supported by a silent audience who appreciated his courage and candour. Vaughan assured me that other members frequently sent him private messages to say they agreed with his views, but didn't feel 'strong enough' to join in with the public debate. In sharp contrast to some of the community members introduced above, Vaughan's extensive experience of online debate made the attempts of St Pixels members to shoot down his arguments seem 'pretty tame in comparison', 'water off a duck's back'. Indeed, he admitted, his willingness for confrontation could be a weakness— he might feel more empathy for someone he could visibly see was nervous, but he could be much less sensitive online.

Blogs

Every member of St Pixels could write their own blog, claiming a section of the site to host an archive of their entries. Each blog displayed the avatar of its author above the list of entries, and bloggers could also choose to upload an image or photograph. Blog entries were open to comments for 30 days, and the website listed the most recent updates. As in the Discuss section, the stream hosts could select particularly interesting entries to highlight on their section homepage.

As we have seen, St Pixels discouraged bloggers from posting controversial positions. In an announcement, the Hosts explained that policy as follows:

> Blogspace is still personal space; a place to share with a space for other members to comment, share their own experience, offer support or whatever. What it should not become is a place to post opinions on controversial subjects, because you won't be challenged and we are officially discouraging that sort of blog.

In the 2008 membership survey, around 30 percent of respondents said they had written a blog post in the last month and just over half had commented. I analysed 30 days of posting from February to March 2009, and again around 30 percent of people who logged in during that time—76 people in total—wrote at least one blog post.

These 76 bloggers posted 262 entries between them. The most active blogged daily and four others posted more than 10 times, but most were far less frequent contributors. 34 people posted only once. These occasional bloggers were often still regular writers, posting one or two entries each month over long periods of time. Because so many people contributed a small number of entries apiece, the section thrived; because the section was thriving, anyone who posted an entry could be almost assured of gaining an audience and a few comments.

I conducted a thematic analysis of these entries, coding each into one or more categories as appropriate. A small but varied range of themes emerged from the coding: 'diary' entries, mentions of church attendance, formal presentations of theology, accounts of lived spirituality, and creative postings. I will discuss each in turn, ending with mention of two rather different contributions.

164 entries (63 percent) were 'diary' posts, describing events from the author's daily life. 62 bloggers wrote at least one entry of this form. Less than one-third of these diary posts, composed by one-third of the bloggers, could be described as negative or downbeat in tone; the remainder were neutral descriptions of events or cheerful celebrations. St Pixels can function as a support group and a safe space to describe unhappy experiences, but this is by no means a dominant activity.

Another major theme, addressed in 51 posts (19 percent), concerned involvement in a local church. Again, negative entries critical of churchgoing experiences accounted for less than one-third of the total (16 posts). 25 bloggers mentioned churchgoing, and only 6 of them said something negative. St Pixels blogs could be used to criticise the limitations and frustrations of local churches, but a much larger number of bloggers chose instead to talk openly and positively about their experiences.

Expressions of faith in this sample were encountered in two forms. 17 entries outlined a doctrinal position, often an interpretation of the Bible. More commonly, entries included prayer requests, described devotional practices or referred to the author's perceptions of God at work in their lives. 57 posts by 32 authors shared this kind of everyday lived spirituality.

Ten bloggers posted 'creative' material, including their paintings, needlework, poems, music and stories. These blogs were relatively few in number, amounting to only 7 percent of the total, but they were well-known around the St Pixels community, referred to by members in online and offline conversation. Interviewees spoke about these creative posts with great warmth. Several mentioned a blogger who posted a series of lengthy fantasy stories about the social and religious lives of a family of toy 'trolls' she owned, and other posters were also praised for imaginative, funny and entertaining contributions. For Beth, images from other countries around the world gave her a new opportunity to see landscapes she had never visited and people she had never met.

The most prolific poster did not fit into any of these categories. Liam blogged a daily hymn verse, without comment. The practice of blogging hymns was first adopted by Ben, the elderly man we encountered earlier in this chapter. Liam took up the practice after Ben's death, as a tribute to his memory and an ongoing service to the community. One interviewee described Ben's postings as 'a little encouraging nugget to begin the day', 'a mini-devotional' and many commented warmly on their enthusiasm for this St Pixels tradition.

One final category received only one entry in this 30-day period: the 'good-bye' post. Members of online communities sometimes choose to mark their departure with one last post, outlining everything that's wrong with the community or its leadership, bidding farewell to favoured friends and vowing never to return. This combination of elements can be adjusted to display the resigning author in a favourable, even heroic, light, as one able to operate as a sociable, well-liked and well-adjusted community member but driven out by forces beyond his or her control. February's departee was a good example, using his blog to blast the site for its inadequacies. An impressive 63 comments included pleas to remain, good wishes for the future, cynical analyses of the motivations of such a post and arguments about the merits of the original complaint. The blogger in question swiftly retracted his resignation, citing the numerous favourable comments as the factor that changed his mind.

Interviews with St Pixels members included discussion of favourite blogs, motives for blogging and benefits for readers and authors. Warm appreciation of 'diary' postings was particularly common. Carol liked 'the ones that are about people's lives.' Patricia, the blogs coordinator, explained that she would 'rather read about someone's personal life than a theological discussion'. Her favourite blog on the site was 'creative' and truthful, 'telling a good story', and 'really makes you feel you're part of [the blogger's] life'. Beth admitted that 'I have a little difficulty with the blogs that seem to be begging people to comment on them', saying 'tell me I'm OK, tell me I'm doing the right thing', but also recalled some such blogs as among her favourites—'I felt like [one blogger] needed support and I felt like just by reading them I was supporting [her]'. In a forum thread about the merits of blogging, Aaron shared a similar perspective:

> Blogs give members the opportunity to share parts of their lives, their joys, sorrows, worries, mountain top experiences or depth of the valley times. [. . .] other members in their turn are given the opportunity to respond, offer support, a word of congratulation or share a laugh. In simple terms, to share in the lives of others as people do off line.

For some bloggers and blog readers, posts offered a chance to share faith and prayer. In my interviews, April mentioned praying over what she read, and Beth spoke of her particular love of certain bloggers who she felt were 'strong Christians'. Angela posted to the same forum thread as Aaron, offering a view that emphasized the spiritual benefits of blogging:

> I did keep a journal once—but the difference is in the interaction—I LOVE the comments and prayers—the comments help me to think more clearly and the prayers are just wonderful.

Carol was one of many to suggest that blogging helped strengthen bonds between writers and readers. Blogging gave 'insights into people', she explained, 'it helps you build up relationships'. On the forums, Brendan argued 'Blogs are one of the biggest builder of community we have, along with the chats we have in St Pixels LIVE.' The chatroom was immediate, but 'Blogs give the opportunity to give more depth to the thoughts. Emotion can be expressed better here, more joy, more love, but also more frustration at a personal situation, and more anger in a rant.' Of course, insight into others is not always welcome: according to Vaughan, St Pixels blogs often 'disappoint me' by posing questions 'you wouldn't expect a Christian to ask', such as whether people needed to be saved.

The act of writing down one's experiences and thoughts can also be therapeutic and formative, helping authors come to terms with events and clarify their thoughts. One member's post to the forum thread about blogging expresses these different motivations particularly well:

> It's a great opportunity to be able to explore different ideas and stages in my life/spirtual journey. It also encourages me to write about what is on my heart. [. . .] Whether anyone listens or not—it doesn't really matter. [. . .]
>
> Why do I blog??? Something gets in my mind and starts to niggle. [. . .] Writing a blog helps me to clarify my thoughts and emotions. I was feeling quite down, when I wrote one, but by committing it to type and being more focussed I was able to see things were by no means as bad as I felt they were. [. . .] On the other hand writing about my Mum enabled me to face things that I had really buried, and to acknowledge the huge gulf between where she was and where she is now, and to allow some of the grief to reach the surface.

Worship

The 2008 membership surveys also indicated a high level of involvement in the Worship areas, including prayer, praise and support threads and services in LIVE. Three-quarters of respondents (73 percent) visited a chatroom worship event once per month, and 61 percent posted to the prayer, praise and support threads.

Themed forums were one of the oldest forms of spiritual practice in St Pixels, dating back to the text-based Church of Fools website. The core threads, 'Members Prayer' and 'Members Praise', offered space to post prayer requests and positive experiences. The Praise thread had received almost 600 posts between 2007 and 2009. These posts were clustered, with each praise report receiving a rush of quick responses. The Prayer thread was far more active, receiving 430 posts in just two months in 2009. Postings dealt particularly with the health or employment needs of friends and family, both in the St Pixels community and outside it, and could include names or initials to identify those to be prayed for.

Prayer and praise threads were liberally embellished with a range of small images offered in the site software. These usually showed faces in various colours, displaying a range of static or animated expressions—☺, 🎱, etc. In prayer, one particularly important image appears: not a face, but a small flickering candle. This simple visual, 🕯, featured in almost every post and often appeared with only a name or no text at all—a silent votive candle, signalling a prayerful response to whatever had gone before.

Other 'Worship' forums focused on education or sharing experiences. 'Meditation and Sharing', for example, included posts requesting help from God, experiences of healing and desires for the future, largely posted without comment. At least some members—the exact number was not published—joined a private network of St Pixels 'prayer partners'. 'Spiritual Journey' blogs were created by five members, including a US Army chaplain in Iraq, to describe their life experiences and perceptions of God, and could be raw, emotional and intensely personal.

St Pixels also created a monthly Social Justice Prayer Focus to draw attention to issues outside the community. Each theme was introduced by a brief article, discussed and taken by the community as a focus for prayer. Topics ranged from worker safety and religious freedom to the plight of refugees and access to clean water. At least one Focus developed these prayers into more concrete assistance, raising £1000 for a water charity by auctioning off gifts and artistic creations donated by community members. Members contributed books they had written and blankets they had knitted, as well as ornaments, souvenirs and other prizes.

The LIVE chatroom (Fig. 6.2) was designed to facilitate the role of the worship leader, who could use special tools to upload prepared images and texts, post them to the Sanctuary and cue audio recordings of speech and music. The worship leader's avatar appeared behind a wooden pulpit in a separate section at the top of the chat space. This function helped to keep the service intelligible, separating the leader's words from congregation prayers or responses.

Worship in LIVE could follow a very wide range of patterns. Thirty worship leaders were active in 2009, each developing their own independent styles. The full calendar included 26 events each week: a daily service at 2100 GMT, silent prayer weekdays at 0845 and 2045, a mid-afternoon service four days each week, the Jesus Prayer at 0730 Mondays, the Rosary 0800 Wednesdays, a 2100 CDT (Central Daylight Time) service for American members on Tuesdays and Thursdays and the occasional Bible study.

Silent prayer is perhaps the most surprising addition to the schedule, an event for which people logged on to their computers twice daily to do nothing at all for 15 minutes. The appeal of such an action clearly reflected the sense of space, shared presence and shared focus that was experienced in the LIVE worship space: being logged in to the same chatroom at the same time as others could create an atmosphere that helped participants to focus on prayer even without any posting activity designed to foster such an atmosphere.

The basic structure of the main daily service, at 9:00 p.m. GMT, included a homily, hymns, responses and scripted or spontaneous prayers. We will encounter an example at the end of this chapter. These are all elements that would be familiar to regular churchgoers, particularly from the Anglican or Methodist traditions, and—as we shall see—participants often liked to sing along to songs they recognised. Members of the St Pixels community were almost all familiar with traditional styles of church worship and able to understand, appreciate and benefit from a traditional format.

Colin commented on this familiar structure in our interview, and offered three explanations: church software offered a limited range of creative options; congregations were predominantly composed of people who either attended a local church or had done so in the past; and the use of a standard pattern for worship helped leaders to put services together quickly and efficiently. Bella, one of the worship leaders, suggested two other relevant factors: the traditional church backgrounds of the worship leaders themselves, who naturally created worship patterns that suited their own 'comfort zones', and copyright restrictions affecting the range of music that could be played. Another advantage to familiarity is its predictability: in a setting where participants could log in and out at any time without warning, an immediately comprehensible worship style is a distinct advantage.

Almost all interviewees who attended worship services reported their experiences with warm enthusiasm. 'Online worship absolutely works for me', Angela said. Bella spoke of LIVE worship as a 'forced time window of half an hour' to focus on God, a 'God-shaped space' she rarely found in her busy schedule. Rose described worship as 'an extension of her personal prayer life', and Tina too was enthusiastic about the power of online prayer: 'I find the prayer times to be pretty powerful', 'I've felt the Holy Spirit there'. 'I'm not a great pray-er', she added, 'but I've been really touched by all those different kinds of prayer in St Pixels'.

Some were less impressed. For Liam, 'some of [the services] are excellent and some of them are appalling'. He objected most to those that used 'churchy language and pious phrases' instead of the Scriptures, and commented that 'St Pixels is far too introspective in the services, far too spiritual . . . devotional rather than anything else', focusing on personal prayer to the exclusion of any reference to current affairs and the problems of the world. Colin described St Pixels worship as 'remarkably . . . deplorably traditional', attractive to experienced churchgoers but meaningless to anyone else.

Three interviewees described themselves as non-Christians who had stopped attending local churches, and they all disliked LIVE worship. One described the style as 'arid', and another explained that 'I just can't connect with it, it's not my thing, it just doesn't do anything for me'. The third objected that St Pixels services were 'just the same as going to church', with 'hymns and prayers and someone saying something', and 'not something I enjoy at all'—just as Colin had predicted.

Play, Conversation and Friendship

We have already discussed three major motivations for St Pixels membership: discussion, sharing lives and prayer. A fourth motive, sometimes overlooked in studies of religion, was fun. We have seen the importance of play and humour throughout this chapter, and this section will focus on some of the specific forms of play shared at St Pixels. Friendship was perhaps the most important motivation of all, and this section will also outline some of the major channels for communication between friends within and outside the website.

The main focus for playful interaction in St Pixels was the 'Bouncy Castle', a forum dedicated to wordgames and light-hearted conversation. Participants composed limericks, poems and jokes, asked questions of Frank, a self-designated expert who promised 'a completely inappropriate solution' to any dilemma, or participated in organised sweepstakes to guess the results of upcoming sports games and award ceremonies. These competitions often included small prizes, sent out by mail to the winners. The exchange of post between members was a long-running tradition, first introduced for 'Secret Santa' events in which participants were asked to send a small Christmas present to a randomly selected recipient. My first gift arrived from California in 2007: a stuffed reindeer, a bag of chocolate and a miniature red armchair just like the image I had chosen for my avatar when I first joined the forum. Around 50 participants took part in the 2008 gift exchange, contributing to a 417-post thread volunteering to join in, expressing excitement and anticipation, and eventually describing, praising and posting photographs of the gifts received. Participation in the Bouncy Castle was not universal—only one quarter of respondents to the 2008 survey posted monthly, and 90 percent of postings during the 2008 calendar year were created by just ten individuals—but the most popular games attracted a quick stream of responses.

Playfulness extended far beyond this dedicated forum, appearing in the selection of usernames, the cartoon style of avatars, and even the name of the site itself. For Frank, play was 'definitely a prominent part of St Pixels' and had great theological significance, as a way for Christians to show that 'God gave us a sense of humour'. His 'expertise' thread gave him great pleasure—'I laugh my tail off whenever I go on'—and added 'a little bit of levity' to the site. Interestingly, Frank suggested that the site was 'if anything too serious' now, a view expressed by several of the longest-standing members of the community in conversations and interviews. The emphasis on play, foolishness and the expression of genuine Christian spirituality through irreverence can be traced back through Church of Fools to the Ship, but some sensed a gradual shift over time away from this atmosphere towards an increasingly 'church-like' solemnity.

Much light-hearted conversation occurred in the chatroom. LIVE frequently took up hours of participants' time, and was the primary form of St Pixels interaction for some interviewees. Services were usually followed by long hours of conversation. Harriet took this observation further than most, claiming in a chatroom interview that 'i almost live at st p it seems—there till 4:30 am this morning :-)'.

Many of those I interviewed spoke very warmly of the importance of LIVE. April suggested that chatroom conversation helped participants get to know one another better than any other online medium: it 'makes the friendships more real', she explained, 'it's like I'm almost shaking their hand'. For Carol, LIVE conversation helped her 'get to know people in a completely different way', because 'you get into deeper relationships much more quickly' without distractions of physical appearance. St Pixels was so important to her, she explained, 'because I can open the window, and there is communication. It's opening a door on a different world'. Ursula described one occasion when her children were upset and she logged in to LIVE to find friends to pray with her. 'The response I have to say was fantastic . . . Let's face it, would you call your vicar at 11 o'clock? Probably not.'

During my research, the friendships I encountered extended beyond St Pixels through a wide range of other channels. In the 2008 survey, 44 percent of respondents had used instant messaging at least once in the past year to communicate with another member, 58 percent had sent an email and 29 percent had made a telephone call.

Social network sites are not covered in the survey, but Facebook in particular became very important for community life. Wordgame applications on Facebook became extremely popular among St Pixels members, who challenged one another to endless competitions. Several members registered for Facebook specifically to join these contests, designing profiles under their St Pixels usernames and avatars and avoiding any information that could identify them offline. This negotiation with the technical requirements of the Facebook platform enabled them to communicate with friends without mixing their online and offline social worlds or giving up their control over the presentation of their identity. These examples were rare: over 120 members were members of the St Pixels group on Facebook in 2009, and only the smallest minority created special profiles to do so. For most, connecting St Pixels friends into their wider social networks, managed under their real name and photograph, was apparently quite unproblematic.

St Pixels surveyed its membership in 2007 as well as 2008, and one of the most striking shifts between those two surveys was in the percentage of respondents who had attended a face-to-face gathering. The proportion who organised their own informal meetings remained fairly stable at around one-third, but attendance at organised meets rose from 36 percent to 78 percent. Twenty-one organised meets were advertised on the St Pixels website in 2008, and a similar number in 2009. All but one of these meets occurred in England or Scotland. American members face a greater organizational challenge, but some have flown great distances to visit one another, travelled across the Atlantic, or organised meetings to coincide with other travel plans. Another popular option for American members was the 'phone meet', gathering participants for a conference call.

The main annual meet since 2005 took place at Morley in Derbyshire, England. Each year, the manager of this Christian retreat centre—a member since the first days of Church of Fools—invited the community to spend a weekend socialising, playing games and worshipping together. The 2009 gathering was attended by 43 members and planned and celebrated in a 400-post thread, including photographs, updates during the meet, fond memories after the meet ended and assurances that each member had arrived home safely. Members unable to attend contacted the gathering by telephone or computer, and these devices were passed around from hand to hand to let the caller speak with as many people as possible. A laptop was carried all over the house to let a member in California see each participant through a webcam. On previous meets, packages of sweets, pictures and handmade gifts were posted from America to be left on the pillow of every guest. Those unable to attend demanded a toast be announced for absent friends, and those who took part faithfully took photographs of this event to post to the website.

At the meet itself, visitors addressed one another by their usernames, each wearing a laminated badge showing their avatar and username. Some members brought partners and children, and if these had not already signed up to St Pixels—which several had—they were awarded honorary names, avatars and badges. Two members brought cakes. Continuing the connections between online and offline interaction, each room in the retreat centre was named to represent one of the areas of the LIVE chatroom, and a cartoon was created to ornament each door—invariably a scandalous depiction of St Pixels members misbehaving (Fig. 6.3).

Most of the weekend was left empty for informal conversations, cups of tea, countryside walks and playing games, but worship services, prayers and Eucharists punctuated each day. A sing-through of Handel's Messiah was arranged, drawing on the experiences of many with church choirs, and a Taize service was held one evening. One of the most important of these worship events took place at 9:00 p.m. each day, when guests assembled from their conversations, country walks and games of croquet to participate in a service in the St Pixels chatroom—an event we will consider in the next section of this chapter.

Figure 6.3 'The Bar', image designed for the Morley Meet. Cartoon by Julienne Jones, 2009.

Almost all who attended meets said they were not surprised by the people they encountered. Irene found it 'remarkable' how well she had known people before meeting them. Some had surprised her with respect to age or looks, but most had been 'just like their avatars'. For Patricia, online conversation allowed her to get to know people as they really are, without the distraction of appearance; people are 'pretty open to bare their souls' online, building extremely strong friendships on the basis of this honesty and openness, and when she came to meet those people she found they were 'very much like their online personalities'. That said, respondents also frequently suggested that meeting face-to-face gave more complete understanding. Ursula suggested that meeting 'helps fill in the picture'. She considered St Pixels a space where she could be 'thoughtful, flippant, stupid, all the things I am in real life', but 'I filter it a bit' to appear nicer—'I don't think the true bitch fiend from hell comes out there'. Others suggested that meeting face-to-face gave reassurance that people truly were as they appeared to be, strengthened existing relationships and changed subsequent online conversations by adding extra nuance, an accurate mental picture of a person's appearance and voice and a range of shared experiences.

Worship at the Morley Meet, 2009

To end this chapter, I will discuss one of the online worship events organised at the Morley meet in 2009. At 9:00 p.m. on the evening of February 20, the group of 43 logged on to their laptops, used PCs in the retreat centre's office or followed the service on a large projector screen. They were joined in the chatroom by another 21 people from around the world. Participants were divided roughly 2:1 between women and men, a ratio I found on almost every visit to LIVE. The chance to communicate between the gathering and the larger online community was a common topic of conversation—'It's great to have Morley + non-Morley peeps together :-)'—and distant participants asked frequent questions about who had arrived, who was misbehaving, and what the gathered members had been doing. 'Morley accentuates my 'maverick' streak!! :-)', one woman declared.

I had started recording field notes, and this was reported with good humour: 'O Lord tim has got his pen and paper out'—'nooo!' I consistently found community members willing to tolerate and support my research with patience and amusement, and this evening was no exception.

A few minutes before 9:00 p.m., a peal of church bells rang out. The sound could be heard in any area of the chatroom, letting everyone know that worship was about to start. The oldest member of St Pixels, Ben, was extremely popular and well-respected, and he was well-known for the pleasure he took in this bell. According to members who spent time with him in LIVE, he would log in most evenings to say goodnight and type 'it tolls for me' when the bell rang. Following his death in 2008, the community began to refer to the bell as his specific sound, turning an existing daily practice into an informal memorial. As the bell rang on this occasion, several of those present in the chatroom typed his name: 'Ben's bell'.

The service on the 20th lasted just under three quarters of an hour, ending at 9:40. The first hymn was heard in silence among those gathered together in Morley—but not, apparently, by some of those joining the service from around the world. 'singing :)', one woman typed. Lyrics were posted by the worship leader, line by line, and some responded by typing out some of these phrases. As the hymn played, images appeared on the media screen: candles, an X-ray of a hand, figures praying. The first hymn was followed by responses, and sections for the congregation to repeat were indicated in capital letters:

LORD, SEARCH ME
GUIDE ME
LEAD ME

HOLD ME
EACH AND EVERY DAY
AMEN

Next came a Bible reading from the book of Ecclesiastes, spoken by another member of the community and illustrated with an image of a Bible text magnified through a pair of glasses—a photograph taken at Morley during a previous meet. The bells that summoned participants to the chapel were recorded at Morley's parish church. Hosting worship from Morley, using images photographed at Morley and heralding each service with the recording of the Morley bells were practices that functioned to connect every LIVE service, throughout the year, to this time of physical gathering.

This showcasing of community-made resources also demonstrates the importance of various forms of craft-making within the community. St Pixels blogs are regularly used to share photographs and discuss crafting hobbies, as we have seen, and some members are well-known in the community for their creation of cartoons (Fig. 6.1, 6.3). The selection of worship leaders also encourages creativity, and the role is often taken by lay Christians seeking to explore and develop gifts in homily-writing and prayer. The leader of this event, for example, had no experience as a worship leader before coming to St Pixels.

During the second hymn, more people posted responses: 'Fantastic tenor line to this', 'good job no one can hear my singing :)', 'singing the alto at home :-)', 'the Lord can hear each one of us singing as a choir :-)'. One woman sitting near me began to sing, and others joined in or hummed the tune. Keystrokes were used to signal movement, /o/ or \o/, indicating arms swaying or raised to heaven. The decision to sing involved the physical body of each participant in their online worship, while these keystrokes invoked imagined bodily movements. In both cases, these members showed considerable familiarity with Christian culture, remembering song lyrics, tunes and harmonies and referencing the kinds of embodied performance that might be expected in a local church service. The singer beside me was startled by the sudden appearance of a private message, sent by another participant in the room: 'love the singing!'

The worship leader led the group in another set of prayers and responses, and then embarked on a ten-minute spoken homily, reflecting on the passage from Ecclesiastes to demonstrate the importance for Christians of involvement in politics and social justice. A photograph of a cake decorated with Pixels avatars—baked for another Morley meet—emphasised the importance of commitment and generosity in Christian life. Congregants shared their appreciation—'Amen', 'good words'—and repeated their thanks as the homily concluded: 'thank you [. . .] you really spoke to me'. For one of my interviewees, this homily 'really knocked my socks off . . . it really really worked for me, that sermon, that service, that day'.

More music and singing followed, described enthusiastically in typed messages, and the service ended with prayer. The service to this point had been conducted amid a gentle to-and-fro of conversation, spoken, typed and sent through private conversation channels, but off-topic communication now completely ceased. Instead of walking from room to room, joking and commenting on the words on their screens, participants now performed an embodied display of full attention. Spontaneous contributions from the congregation focused on naming individuals in need of prayer and flowed for many minutes, amassing scores of contributions. Those without computers called out names for others to type on their behalf, and other conversation was silenced with murmurs of 'shh', 'no talking'. This phase of the service ended with the Lord's Prayer, typed by all participants simultaneously in multiple different versions and languages.

The unique sacredness of prayer emerged again on another occasion, when I asked church management for a complete transcript of chatroom activity during a service. I had hoped to analyse this for evidence of conversation patterns before and after services and to look more closely at these times of prayer, which move too swiftly for accurate observation—simply counting the number of prayers shared, for example, is a great challenge. My request was not approved: a transcript did exist and could be shared with me, but only if a team member first deleted all individual prayers from the record. Even though these prayers were almost exclusively names without further detail, I had already seen them while attending the service in person and I promised not to quote them directly, sharing a text record of this specific part of the service was seen as a violation of community trust.

The service ended after 40 minutes with another round of appreciative thanks. Those logged in embarked on conversations and welcomed newcomers who had arrived after the service had finished. Participants remained in LIVE all evening but slowly drifted from the Sanctuary to The Bar, creating separate conversation groups. Those at Morley proved reluctant to relinquish their laptops, leading one computer-less individual to ask 'Would it be more sociable if we went and got our machines?' Online, conversation attended to the life of the community, discussing controversial recent blogs. An American member bemoaned the difficulty of organising face-to-face gatherings in the United States, where users live further apart, and asked for a 'phone meet'. A Host walked over to poke gentle fun at my rather earnest fieldnotes: 'Are you taking notes on this inane conversation?'

This account shows some of the ways in which technology can be designed to facilitate worship and worship designed to suit technology. Different patterns of multi-channel, multi-media communication emerged, with members conversing simultaneously through the chatroom, private chat windows and speech, each channel used to pass comment on the others. The shift in mood and focus that occurred across channels during times of prayer indicates the importance of this spiritual practice within St Pixels, a community in which sincerity and frivolity can follow closely on one another. Finally, this account demonstrates the close relationship between moments of face-to-face gathering and the annual and global rhythms of the online community as a whole.

Conclusion

We see in St Pixels an ongoing negotiation between different social, technological, demographic and theological factors influencing community growth. Church of Fools, i-church and St Pixels are three quite different kinds of online church, each favouring different sorts of activity and leadership, receiving different levels of funding and creating a community of a different size. To some extent, they also differ in demographics and in commitment to local church attendance. Nonetheless, each of them succeeded in generating experiences that members consider spiritually valuable, relationships they consider significant and a deep sense of belonging.

If we return to the seven themes identified in my discussion of Church of Fools and i-church, we see that St Pixels has developed new answers to some and retained the same approach to others.

1. Scale. St Pixels continued to demonstrate that online religion could appeal on a scale large enough to sustain an online community, albeit one numbered in hundreds of participants rather than tens of thousands. Like Church of Fools and i-church, membership growth was closely tied to coverage in mainstream media.
2. Local Churchgoing. St Pixels seemed to have consolidated its appeal to those already committed to Christian communities, but lost some of the diversity once displayed by Church of Fools. The curious and sometimes-hostile visitors to that experimental space had largely evaporated, and only a few self-described non-Christians could still be found.
3. Community. St Pixels was much more stable than Church of Fools, richer in its range of synchronous and asynchronous media and more firmly interconnected through social network sites, email, instant messenger and face-to-face gatherings. Like Church of Fools, St Pixels valued playfulness and games and inspired long-term commitment from its core members. My interviewees often spoke of their friendships with one another as the most important benefit of their participation in the community, just as they did in i-church.
4. Ritual and Spiritual Experience. My interviews and observations showed that chatroom worship, especially typed prayer, was valued by a significant group of regular participants. At the same time, critics complained that the style of services was too traditional. Participation relied to some extent on familiarity with the liturgical forms and music being used, appealing most to those who already liked the style of traditional Protestant churches. Services in LIVE included spoken sermons, recorded music and pictures, but not—of course—the avatar gestures possible in Church of Fools.

5. Familiarity remained just as crucial as in Church of Fools, if not more so. Worship was based on traditional liturgy, in a chatroom designed to look like a liturgical space. Some of the logic had shifted, however. Instead of trying to reassure those who knew very little about church-going, a familiar style was now favoured because it seemed natural to those who knew a great deal, and because such a format could easily be put together by untrained worship leaders.

6. Internal Control. The issue of control became less significant with the cessation of large-scale trouble-making. The church consolidated administrative authority in a management team directly involved with daily church life, able to make swift decisions and prepared to delegate widely. This leadership claimed no authority over doctrine or matters of faith, and Hosts were expected to encourage respectful behaviour without trying to regulate the ideas being expressed.

7. External Funding and Oversight. St Pixels functioned independently from established denominations, without receiving further funding from the Church of England or Methodist Church. Running costs were far lower than for Church of Fools or i-church, and design work was carried out in-house. Members proved willing to donate finances or labour to keep the church running. A few community members continued to work on the idea of returning to some kind of graphical environment, as discussed in my earlier chapter on Church of Fools, but the lack of funding and full-time design staff proved a serious barrier to progress. As we shall see in the conclusion to this book, St Pixels eventually chose to develop in a quite different direction.

References

Howe, M., 2005. *Towards a Theology of Virtual Christian Community*. MTh. Spurgeon's College, London. [pdf] Available at: <http://www.cyberporte.com/virtual_christian_ community.pdf> [Accessed 1 September 2016]

Wainwright, M., 2007. Let us pray . . . at St Pixels, the virtual church with bar and bouncy castle. *The Guardian*, 12 April. [online] Available at: <https://www.theguardian.com/technology/2007/apr/12/news.radio> [Accessed 1 September 2016]

7 The Anglican Cathedral of Second Life

I remember the moment where I said, you know what, I think we need a Cathedral. And I remember someone saying no, I think the Cathedral's too big, we need to start with a small parish and build up. And I said no [laughs], this needs to be really big.

—Mark Brown, interview, 2009.

The Anglican Cathedral of Second Life sits in Gothic splendour atop a sunlit hill, dominating a small island in a virtual ocean. Visitors come in many forms, from tattooed centaurs to respectable middle-aged ladies. At the busiest times in the Cathedral's ten-year history, gatherings came together every day of the week for casual conversation, organised discussion, private prayer or corporate worship. This chapter will trace some of the outlines of the culture of this Anglican isle, introducing the 'virtual world' of Second Life, the vision behind the creation of the Cathedral and the main activities and practices that shaped life on Epiphany during my main period of ethnographic research in-world (2008–2009). Particular attention will be paid to four topics: worship, architecture, the avatar and the motivations guiding visitors to the island. An additional issue, the relationship of the Cathedral to offline Anglican structures of authority, took shape after my ethnographic research and will be discussed later in this book (see conclusion).

Second Life was first opened to the public in 2003, and encouraged users to build a world of their own with 3D graphics, animation, sound and text. Users could buy and sell these items using a special in-world currency that could be exchanged for real-world money. This creative freedom attracted great media publicity, covering the first real estate millionaire, the virtual activities of a string of real-world corporations and universities, reports of 'Second Life addiction' and a series of sex scandals. Registered members quickly ran into the millions.

This media interest did not last. Following a peak of coverage around 2007, it became clear that some of the initial hopes for Second Life would not be fulfilled. The BBC published an obituary in 2009, titled 'What Happened to Second Life?' (Hansen 2009)—and then another one four years later (Howell 2013). According to Jeremy Howell's sombre commentary, bands had expected Second Life to be their launchpad and corporations opened stores there, 'but most of these ventures have now been abandoned' (Howell 2013, video, 01:15). Howell suggests that Second Life was too difficult to use, didn't attract a large enough audience and didn't make money for companies that opened stores in-world.

What Second Life did offer, however, was a space where individuals could create new designs, explore striking landscapes and meet new friends. Users may have shown limited interest in clothing from real-world brands, but wild and creative styles flourished among independent producers, supported by an extensive network of blogs advertising and critiquing the latest trends. Religion proved particularly well-suited to Second Life, and small gatherings soon began to meet for religious purposes all across the world. As we shall see, the Cathedral of Second Life has been shaped by its own unique set of personalities, contexts, opportunities and challenges, but it still shares many of the features we have already observed in Church of Fools, i-church and St Pixels.

Introducing Second Life

Up to 2011, Linden Labs—the owner of Second Life—released quarterly reports regarding the total number of 'user hours' logged in-world, the peak number of concurrent users, land owned and transactions conducted. In the last quarter of 2008, during my ethnographic research, 112 million 'user hours' were logged with a peak of 76,000 users logged in at the same time. These users owned 1.76 billion square metres of land, and 'spent more than $100 million USD on virtual goods and services' (Linden 2009).

A range of standard shapes—'primitives', or 'prims'—form the basic building blocks of creativity and can be tweaked, combined and decorated with 'textures' created by the designer. With patience and skill, these tools can be used to construct complex and elegant objects, from trees and flowers, houses and cars to clothing, hair and jewellery. The designer of an item can sell it to others or give it away, and stores, markets and 'freebie' boxes abound throughout the world.

Visitors to Second Life must create an avatar, and while most start out human and bland, it is commonplace (indeed, expected) that serious users will soon acquire a more creative body, skin, hairstyle and wardrobe. These avatars tend to be human, but need not be so; animals are common, as are mythical creatures, robots and anything else that can be dreamed up by a skilled designer. The basic avatar can perform a range of movements, including flight, but more complex actions can be designed and sold for private use or fixed into the surrounding environment as 'pose balls'. Seats offer 'pose balls' with a selection of postures, while nightclubs offer ranges of dances. A more extravagant user can invest in land, for a private home, store, club, garden or whatever else appeals—a source of income, or a gathering space for friends and visitors. A search function can be used to hunt for people, groups, places, classified ads, land sales and events, and also displays a regularly updated showcase of impressive spaces chosen by the world's managers.

Aside from this creativity, consumption and display, the most important activity of Second Life is communication. Avatars can gather together and communicate through typed text or voice, and friends can add one another to a contact list. Private messages can be sent to anyone in-world, and this contact list helps make that personal communication easier. Groups can be created to help communicate with large numbers of people at once, often to publicise times and locations of upcoming events. The name of one group can hover above the avatar, another opportunity for identity display. User profiles can list information about Second Life identity, groups joined, favourite places, real life identity and so on, an easy-to-access directory of what that user wishes the world to know. In many cases the first information I gained about a new acquaintance included details of their religious activity, sex life and hobbies that take some time to learn face-to-face.

Religious practitioners can use the freedom of Second Life to experiment with new roles, setting up their own retreat centre or pulpit at minimal financial cost. Opportunities for creative visual design have encouraged the emergence of hosts of small churches, chapels, mosques, temples and prayer gardens, often beautifully crafted. Communication between users is easy, through text or voice, so the environment is well-suited to preaching. Animation is less straightforward, but complex gestures and movements can be encoded in objects and activated with a click—so users can instruct their avatars to undertake a yoga routine, meditate, dance or assume a posture of prayer. These experiments are unlikely to attract very large audiences, because of the limitations of the technology, but religion has remained one of the more vibrant sectors of Second Life activity since its early years.

Given that Linden Labs makes its money from land, it's unsurprising that the designated term for Second Life users is 'Resident'—a loaded term favouring heavy users and land-owners over casual visitors. Referring to users as 'Residents' helps to construct the ideal Second Life-r as a house-owner and conversely, to construct the non-houseowner as marginal or uncommitted. Unfortunately, no other name seems preferable. 'Player' and 'user' are inappropriate for a social world, while 'visitor' implies a lack of ownership over the space and 'member' suggests a problematic notion of corporate identity. The term 'Resident' has been widely adopted in Second Life and will be reluctantly used here, but the significance of this particular construction of the user should not be overlooked.

Residents frequently distinguish between 'sl' (Second Life) and 'rl' (Real Life) when referring to their offline activities. This 'rl' language will also be used in this chapter, again because it is meaningful to Residents and because no obviously preferable alternative is available. I do not suggest, of course, that life outside a virtual world is more 'real' than what goes on inside it.

My research in Second Life began at a face-to-face gathering in 2008 in Guildford, a city in the UK. This event offered a chance to meet some of the leadership team, and I was able to interview the pastor of the Anglican Cathedral of Second Life, Mark Brown, and several other leaders and participants. Following this real-world introduction to the Cathedral community, I spent time learning the basic skills and cultural knowledge required to function in-world, meeting people, becoming known and letting my new acquaintances know about my research project. Sandy, the leader in charge of Epiphany Island's design, agreed to erect a noticeboard next to the church door announcing my research as an additional way to advertise my presence. I quote exactly from my in-world interviews throughout this chapter, including original spelling and punctuation, and preserve line breaks to show how statements were written.

During my ethnographic research, I visited Second Life several times each week. I primarily spent time on Epiphany Island, but to gain more of a sense of Second Life's wider cultures I also visited different religious spaces, landscapes and music venues, looking for intriguing constructions and interesting people. I did not try to become a 'Resident', however, at least in the sense that word implies. I did not rent land, buy a house or learn the skills needed to design objects in-world. These investments of time and resources were not necessary to be accepted as a member of the particular community I was studying, where many of the regular participants and leaders were not landowners or designers. I did still need somewhere private to conduct interviews, and a fellow researcher, with much more advanced design skills, kindly allowed me to borrow her skybox—essentially a flying house, which because of its great elevation was unlikely to be discovered or disturbed by visitors.

Introducing the Anglican Cathedral of Second Life

When I first visited Epiphany Island in 2008, the surrounding seas were clear and blue and the sky above was only ever speckled with the thinnest white clouds. It never rained and snowed only when the church's owners wanted it to—which they did, every (northern hemisphere) winter season. Across a narrow causeway, the next island was dotted with small houses, churches and Christian spaces. No other land was in sight. The Cathedral (Fig 7.1.) was built in grey stone and planned in a traditional style, cruciform with a long nave crossed near the east end by short transepts. An apse closed the east end of the church in a half-dome. A mighty square tower rose from the crossing and flying buttresses supported the walls all around the perimeter. The nave was filled with rows of wooden pews, pillars supported the roof and glancing beams of light shone in through stained glass windows onto the floor. Furnishings were also traditional, including an elevated pulpit and a lectern resting on the wings of a brass eagle. The sanctuary area included a high altar with altar rail, where an incense burner hung from its stand. Outside the highly carved main doorway, a broad plaza offered space to gather. Across the square, giant banners displayed the 'Compass Rose' symbol of the Anglican Communion. To one side, benches surrounded a fireplace in winter, or a pool of water in the summer.

A deep chasm cut the island in two, spanned by a bridge leading to a much smaller chapel, also traditional in style but furnished with informal cushions rather than pews. Elsewhere on Epiphany the visitor could find gardens, a labyrinth of hedges, a small cove, and a jetty with rowing boats. Seasonal changes included the addition of a rabbit to roam the island at Easter time and wreaths and flowers to celebrate Christmas. At least two art exhibitions have taken place on the island, including one collecting sculptures created in-world on the theme of the Holy Spirit. Birds circled constantly overhead, and a few other creatures—a rabbit, some squirrels—roamed across the grounds. If the visitor's speakers were turned on, gentle sounds of birdsong echoed around the island. As we shall see later in this book, almost every detail of this description is still accurate today.

Epiphany Island was the creation of a group called 'Anglicans in Second Life', led at the time of my research by Mark Brown. Brown was then the CEO of The Bible Society in New Zealand, and considered personal research to be a vital part of his work. In 2006 that research took him into Second Life, where he discovered something he found startling: the world of Second Life was attracting some 600,000 visitors every two months at that stage, but was served by only one church.

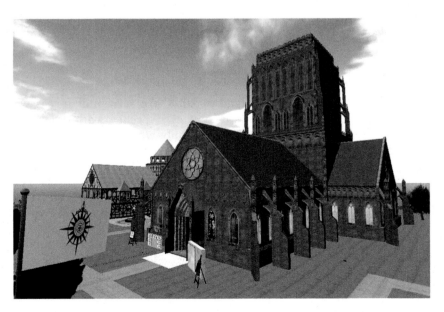

Figure 7.1 The Anglican Cathedral of Second Life. Image by Mark Brown, 2009.

I thought, well, a—where is everyone? Where's the missionary organisations, the Baptists, the Catholics, the Anglicans, why aren't they here? Well, the answer to that is fairly simple, they don't have a reputation for being early adopters and this is the cutting edge I would say.

There is an implicit theology of mission at work here: Christians must be present on the 'cutting edge' of culture, or their message will not be heard by the whole of society. We will encounter a similar understanding in each of the five case studies considered in this book. The idea that Second Life itself represented the cutting edge of digital communications was widespread at this time, encouraging investment from a wide range of commercial companies, education institutions and other industries.

Brown searched for Anglican groups and encountered 'Anglicans in Second Life', which at that stage had just 15 members. The group agreed to meet, and their discussion led Brown to suggest establishing a new church:

And at that meeting, it was really clear to me, I remember the moment where I said, you know what, I think we need a Cathedral. And I remember someone saying no, I think the Cathedral's too big, we need to start with a small parish and build up. And I said no [laughs], this needs to be really big.

Inspired by this vision, another member of the group contacted a young German student, who offered to build the Cathedral:

I remember the moment when I said, well, what are you going to charge? And he said Mark, in his broken, well, it was text at that stage, but I know his English is broken, but he said Mark, I can see this is historical, and I'll do this for free. He spent five months building it, and it is quite an awesome structure when you understand virtual architecture, it won an award in Second Life, he won quite a bit of money and donated much of it to the community.

Brown became the pastor of the new church, and was later ordained curate and priest by his Anglican bishop in New Zealand to support his virtual work. He stepped down as pastor of the Cathedral in 2009, looking for new avenues for his online ministry, and was recently appointed president of Scripture Union USA.

During my ethnographic research, most evenings found a group of people talking in the plaza outside the Cathedral, and services were almost always preceded and followed by long conversations. It was not uncommon for Brown to lead the congregation in a display of avatar dancing after services, but even without these energetic pursuits these conversations can last several hours. Mark Brown and his second-in-command, Sandy, celebrated one another's avatar birthdays (the day they first registered to use Second Life) by erecting signs and banners. As Sandy put it, 'what motivated me to stick around was really the opportunity to meet people', like-minded Residents from all over the world, 'people who are interested in the same things I am', 'people with a similar religious sensibility, I suppose.'

I found many hints and indications during my research that the growth of the Cathedral had not always been quite so easy or harmonious. Early participants referred to acrimonious disputes, departures, power struggles, scandals and the relocation of the Cathedral from one place to another. These stories were by no means consistent, and the same events could be retold as a scandal by one participant and an unremarkable mishap by another, or with quite different sets of heroes and villains. It is important to remember that the kinds of disagreements experienced by i-church (Chapter 5) are by no means unusual among online churches.

We can construct some kind of picture of the community from a survey conducted by church leadership in 2008. This survey received 79 responses[1] and findings were reported in 'Christian Mission to a Virtual World', an essay by Mark Brown published online in April of that year. Some 60 percent of respondents were aged between 31 and 50, 15 percent younger, and 56 percent were male (Brown 2008: 4). These are very similar statistics to those reported in i-church, but the congregation seems to have been older than Church of Fools and attracted a higher proportion of men than St Pixels. Just under 20 percent attended a service at the Cathedral once a fortnight, 35 percent once a week, and 10 percent more than once; if we take these statistics as a proportion of the 79 respondents we can ascertain that at least 50 individuals were attending Cathedral services twice a month or more. 67 percent of respondents attended a local Anglican church and 16 percent a church of some other denomination (Brown 2008: 6).

17 percent of respondents said 'the SL service was the only church service they attended' (Brown 2008: 6), a figure representing some 13 or 14 people. Brown quotes one example: 'I have been housebound for the last 2 years due to disability, so, at present, this is the only church service I attend.' However, I did not meet a single individual in this category during my participant observation in Second Life, nor could any of the church leaders I approached suggest such a person for me to interview. I met several non-Christians on the island, but these did not come to services. I did meet one woman who had once attended only the Cathedral, but she had subsequently left, and at the time of our conversation she had begun attending a local church again. These figures Brown gives are not sub-divided according to frequency of attendance, so many of those who do not attend a local church may have been infrequent attenders at the Cathedral as well.

Worship in Second Life

The first service of worship at the Cathedral was organised in July 2007, and the number of events gradually began to increase. By mid-2008, three were being held each week. In 2009 the schedule expanded to six services, plus a discussion group outside the Cathedral, a Bible study in the conference centre and a smaller voice-chat Bible study gathered on a ring of black leather sofas placed precariously on the very top of the Cathedral tower. At the beginning of 2010, the schedule expanded again to 27 weekly meetings, now including daily Morning Prayer, six meetings for Evening Prayer, four services of Compline and two mid-week evening services. We saw this urge to multiply at work in Church of Fools, i-church and St Pixels: once again, enthusiastic members of the congregation were volunteering to find new times and new styles of worship to add to the calendar, trying to ensure that every time zone was accounted for.

In keeping with the visual style of the building, Brown adopted a traditional Anglican style of liturgy for his own worship events, based on the service of Evening Prayer. He added modifications as he felt necessary:

> if you were a strict liturgist, you'd frown at what we do. [. . .] I kind of look at the liturgy and say, well, you know, I don't think, obviously we don't need that, I don't need that, and I try to shorten it a bit, Evening Prayer, it's usually, if you're traditional it doesn't have a sermon, I have a sermon.

These sermons were brief, but not otherwise distinctive from talks one might expect to hear in a local church. Nadja Mizcek reports the same observation in her own studies of Church of Fools and two Second Life churches (Miczek 2008). The success of the Cathedral might be mentioned and future vision discussed, but I heard no teachings about how to act in Second Life or how to live Christian lives online. These were issues that community members discussed regularly, expressing strongly held but divergent opinions, but preachers did not touch on them.

Cathedral services included a time of open prayer, another innovation Brown considers very successful:

> those sessions can sometimes go on for a good ten plus minutes, to fifteen minutes, and they are very moving, I mean people pray for their close relatives with cancer, it's really out there. Now they are connecting with people from around the world.

In our interview, Brown expressed some reservations about this format and hoped that more innovative liturgies might be devised in future:

> what we probably need to get to is actually finding people who will write liturgy for Second Life. Now, that's not just words, that could be places, it could be music. I mean, there is actually a lot of scope for creativity, but at the moment, baby steps.

Despite this expressed intent, services continued to follow established patterns. Andrew, for example, explained that his services 'use a variety of liturgies, usually Celtic, liturgies from the Iona community, Northumbria Community', an approach that he described as 'deliberately experimental' while remaining 'almost like Anglican Evening Prayer' in structure, with the addition of a meditation and 'a time of open prayer'. This may be experimental, but it is a kind of experiment clearly rooted in established offline worship practices. Epiphany Island's hedge labyrinth also demonstrates this continuity: like Celtic liturgies, the labyrinth is a popular element of contemporary Christian spirituality that purports to connect the participant with ancient history.

My interviews suggested that the reassuringly recognisable worship style was welcomed by those attending, and that the criteria used to assess the success of worship were little different from those operating offline. Diane, for example, described Sunday Compline as 'a restful service, and a wonderful way to transition from one week to the next', and justified online worship biblically: 'I am a great believer in "When two or more are gathered in My name, I am with you."' Ed explained that he valued the look of the Cathedral and the Anglican style of worship because it made the event seem more 'real': 'for a service I like the feeling that I am "in" a church'. The visual representation of a church was also important because it enabled Ed to see that other people were present.

I encountered a minority of visitors who hoped to find some kind of ideal, purified church online, separate from politics, intrigue and conflict, but no one I spoke to had come online seeking the kind of totally new, artistically creative 'liturgy for Second Life' that could theoretically be achieved through the use of available building and animation tools. The continuity of online and offline worship here is a deliberate and welcome choice, not a failure of creativity or imagination. I observed similar deliberate continuities in my studies of Church of Fools, i-church and St Pixels.

The traditionalism of services also extended to the provision of animations. Each pew included animation options. A visitor sat in these pews during services, could choose to kneel and was invited to stand for the reading of the Gospel. Mark Brown made the additional investment of buying a personal animation that he could operate to cause his avatar to cross itself. I encountered no examples of liturgical innovation involving avatars at the Cathedral—aside, perhaps, from the occasional outbreaks of dancing Mark Brown and others sometimes encouraged to entertain the congregation after services. This was a different approach from that taken by Church of Fools, which also created a virtual world with pews and liturgical services, but used gestures like the tearing of hair and shaking of hands as part of worship, prayer and social interaction (see Chapter 4).

In interviews, some Cathedral congregants explained that their use of gesture animations was stifled by the lag problems associated with animating an avatar in Second Life, and this was certainly my own experience—standing up in a crowded room could stall the program completely. Others explained that they disconnected their camera view from their avatar and zoomed in on the service leader, cutting out the rest of the environment and so speeding their connection.

Those who did use gestures in worship followed their 'real life' practice with minimal innovation. Ashley, a High Anglican, explained 'I've never been one for the handswaying in rl so I don't do that here'—'I guess its all what is most like rl.' For this user, animations make the experience of worship seem more 'real' by copying the actions that accompany the 'real'—an attitude I encountered among some Church of Fools members.

In a small number of cases, interviewees told me that their avatar performance was accompanied by physical actions performed in front of the computer. Fred, a High Anglican church organist, said Compline at home every night and crosses himself at the appropriate points throughout. When he attended worship online, he did the same. Interestingly, though, he added that this practice of physical action could be superseded by the avatar: 'maybe if I could animate my avatar I wouldn't do it in rl'.

Outside these times of set worship, visitors to the Cathedral also engaged in informal times of prayer. These prayers might be shared with specific individuals or groups or pursued privately. Henry, a regular visitor, suggested in our interview that 'there is a core group of people who hang around and welcome people', a practice that 'has resulted in spontaneous prayer at times', while Mark Brown claimed that private prayer was common: 'I know people who go there and pray before they start work every day.'

Every Saturday visitors to the Cathedral were welcomed to an open discussion, focused on what it means to be Christian in Second Life. This pursuit of contextual theology through open discussion instead of authoritative teaching was reminiscent of Church of Fools, i-church and St Pixels, although leadership members were present to supervise the interaction. On February 7, 2009, the Saturday discussion centred on the question of online prayer, and the nine participants kindly agreed to let me quote them here.

Most of the conversation addressed practices of group prayer. June, one of the regular visitors to the Cathedral who took part in my interviews, explained that 'Kevin [another regular] and I sometimes meet to pray' and added by private message that 'I don't, in fact, pray with others in rl but do in sl'. Several others also claimed that Second Life had helped develop some aspect of their prayer. Diane felt 'more comfortable' and less self-conscious praying in groups in Second Life. This comfort came partly from anonymity—'you don't feel so much the people looking at you', Kevin explained—and partly from control. 'maybe in SL', Diane suggested, 'we have more control over our friends, because we can just leave when we are uncomfortable'. For some this new spiritual confidence carried over into 'real life'. According to Diane, 'SL has made me a little less shy in RL, about Prayer as well as walking up to strangers and introducing myself!'. For Kevin, 'SL helps me discover the power of praying together with other people'.

Thoughts were also offered on the practice of private prayer. Mandy introduced herself as the pastor of another Second Life church, operated on behalf of an Anglican church located in the United States. Mandy found praying online to be 'comforting' and 'satisfying'. 'I often come to SL to do my RL prayers'—'I've found SL to be a great addition to my spiritual practice', 'just helps me be reminded that I need to stop and pray'. Presence in Second Life, particularly at places like gardens that could be perceived as 'beautiful' or at sites designated at 'spiritual', helped participants to focus. Sandy agreed: 'I think it helps take me out of the day to day world and concerns'.

Another explanation was offered in an interview with Sam. Sam prayed both on the web and in Second Life, and his goal was not focus but connection:

Sam: when i read morning prayer online over breakfast before the kids get up, i feel like i am connected to everyone else who is reading it as well as opposed to just reading out of a book

Sam: one thing i have done quite a bit in the mornings is to log in to SL, visit the cathedral, and read morning prayer while my avatar is sitting there

Sam recounted an experience in a 'real-life' church, when a time of private prayer was interrupted by the presence of another visitor, creating a powerful sense of connection. Being visibly present in a church-like space recalled that special moment and added to his perception of connectedness.

Many of those I met spoke of the importance of the avatar in Second Life prayer, and their conversations shared three main themes. First, participants argued that the avatar offered a powerful sense of co-presence, of actually being with other people—as Sandy explained, 'when I am talking to someone in SL, and our avatars are together, I feel like I am "with" them'. Second, they explained that the movements of the avatar actually help to set aside a period for prayer: as June put it, 'When I'm praying with someone, the kneeling stops the coversation and starts the praying'. The avatar here acted as a communication tool, a nonverbal way to frame a particular period of time within a specific activity context; kneeling signals that prayer is expected, not talk. Third and finally, the movement of the avatar contributed to users' sense of focus. Olive, who participated in i-church as well as the Cathedral, commented in our interview that she had enjoyed navigating the island's labyrinth: 'the concentration was good I think [. . .] it helped me to think, to be still, even though my avatar wasn't!' These comments qualify my earlier observations regarding lack of innovative use of gestures in worship: at least in private prayer, familiar gestures like kneeling or walking may be used in familiar ways but with new and distinctive meanings and purposes.

One dissenting voice was heard in the discussion quoted above. One participant insisted that it was not place that made prayer possible but people.

Indeed, according to this participant, it would be difficult to pray at all with people he did not intellectually agree with. 'I find that the people are what make it', he argued, 'I like the places, but without the people, Its just a place.' Those who had been discussing their search for 'spiritual places' in Second Life did not disagree completely, but incorporated his view into a more nuanced explanation of their own. As Sandy explained, 'the people imbue the place with that atmosphere.' To make sense of worship, we need to consider the space in which it happens.

Architecture, Space and Design

Mark Brown's explanation for his determination to build a Cathedral is worth quoting at length. He broke down his reasoning into three sections: branding, publicity and spiritual appeal. First, the church design should be 'very clearly Christian, an icon, a symbol of Christianity'. Second, he hoped that his design would create publicity:

> I wanted to create buzz, and guess what, it has [laughs]. You know, when the media got hold of it I've been on TV, radio, gosh, I don't know how many, seriously, I don't know how many times, radio in the US, Australia, New Zealand, you know, newspapers, weblogs, a huge number of blogs, and a big part of it is (a) Anglican, (b) Cathedral?, and (c) high technology, that creates a buzz. If I just build another, I don't know, just an open space with some pillows on the ground and a cross in the corner, I don't think it would have got the same.

It's interesting to note here that Brown saw a more informal style of church design, something breaking with traditional patterns of architecture, as less innovative and exciting than the continuity represented by his cathedral. It was the juxtaposition of the stereotypically ancient and established style of Anglican cathedral-building with the 'cutting edge' of fashionable technology that created media appeal; note the parallels here with Church of Fools.

Third, according to Brown, a traditional design was actually best suited to contemporary spirituality:

> the third reason is my very simplistic assessment of post-modernity with its fascination with tradition and what I call deep Christianity, the lectio divina, the meditation, the kind of saints, the mystery of the Middle Ages, that's all in, I mean that's kind of in at the moment. The second interest of post-moderns is technology, you know, synchronous communication, blah blah blah. So I thought, here's a way to combine the two. It's pretty crude, but let's give it a go.

The Second Life Cathedral did not actually pursue any of the traditions Brown lists—there were no meetings for the Lectio Divina style of Bible reading, for example, and no public devotion to saints, although the inclusion of a labyrinth on the island does summon something of 'the mystery of the Middle Ages'. What the Cathedral actually offered was a collection of spaces in which architecture and design had been used to imply tradition, structuring space according to well-known, instantly recognisable symbols, categories, themes and patterns, and these spaces communicate a connection with tradition, with something larger and more ancient than the gathered congregation. For Brown, this connection helped to provide 'grounding':

> [The Cathedral] grounds what is actually a fairly amorphous experience, it is literally out of body. And I think if you're too esoteric in your architecture, in your presentation of the church facility, you'll just trip people out. It'll appeal to people who feel comfortable in that kind of very esoteric world, but my experience is they're a fairly minor part of the population. So it's a trick, a perception trick, of course it is, it doesn't exist, but it tricks people into believing that actually it's a real cathedral. And the evidence of that is that I know people who go there and pray before they start work every day.

Worshipping online, communicating with God, in the company of people scattered across the world, while remaining alone, is a strange and novel experience. The recognisable reality of the Cathedral offered some foundation to that experience, a connection with more familiar and embodied experiences, and that foundation reassured the visitor that the Cathedral could be a genuine place of holiness and prayer. This architectural referencing of reality is closely related to the discussion of worship above, particularly the idea that animations of the avatar can help to enhance the sense of being in a 'real' church. For some, at least, this 'perception trick' was central to the creation of sacred space for authentic worship.

Interviews with other leaders echoed Brown's comments. Andrew, a Methodist minister in the UK, entered Second Life hoping to investigate the possibility of establishing a 'Fresh Expression', a new kind of church, in the virtual world. He did find churches active in the world, unlike Brown, but he found their style off-putting: 'A number of them felt very American to me, they had that style, and I was a little uncomfortable with that'. Andrew shared Brown's interest in post-modern traditionalism as a cutting edge, culturally relevant alternative:

> If I was going to create a Christian community it would involve having a recreation of a church, something recognisable, because of the post-modern fascination with the old, and the sense of this, of the old coming into the new, I thought was, had resonance . . . I think in this particular instance [traditional style] is a strength, because of the pre-occupation with many people in Second Life to create something that reflects the real.

Another leader, Sandy, argued in our in-world interview that

Sandy: there seems to be an attraction to that kind of tradition.
Sandy: really, you can see evidence of that all over SL

But she added that 'people in Sl really appreciate a nice build, one that obviously has a lot of care and thought put into it.' For Sandy, the Cathedral's design succeeded not just because it looked old but because it is showed a real investment of talent and dedication.

While the Cathedral was built according to a preconceived understanding of social trends and the role of architecture in religious experience, the grounds of Epiphany Island have been allowed to evolve more gradually. Sandy was in charge of site design at the time of our interview in mid-2008, and reported that 'I (that is we) figured out what would be included on the island by listening to what people like to do there.' Parts of the island, notably the labyrinth, were built to house objects created by or given to the church by community members. Other sections were redesigned to respond to preferences expressed by visitors:

Sandy: well, i the original design of the island, there was a meditation garden, that people really liked.
Sandy: so, we wanted to bring that back [. . .]
Sandy: we knew that people come to Epiphany for it's meditative atmosphere,so that's
           where we got the idea for the meditation chapel. [. . .]
Sandy: but overall, people like to come there for fellowship, so, I wanted to design areas where people could gather together as well.

Andrew emphasised the freedom the Cathedral offered to its visitors:

Some of it is what people can make of it, and so people can explore their spirituality by exploring the labyrinth, some can go to the little chapel if they feel that the cathedral is too big, if they're wanting a much more intimate sense of being with God they can be there, they can explore the grounds, walk amongst the trees, take the boats around the island, so in some ways the ground is there to make of what you will.

These accounts present design as a response to visitor preferences, but the decisions described also aim to shape activity in a more active sense. If people came to Epiphany for its meditative atmosphere, it was at least partly because the environment already created there encouraged that form of activity. Visitors were encouraged to explore their spirituality, but certain specific forms of spirituality and of social activity had been identified from a much wider range of possible options, and these forms were prioritised and resourced to direct community life toward an ideal form that leaders wish to cultivate. This ideal form developed in conversation with community norms and practices but not purely in response to it.

Virtual architecture is not empty and passive but actively structures the kinds of activity that take place in the spaces it creates, contributing to particular moods and practices. As sociologist Mark Nunes argues, space must be understood as a social product, a dynamic process involving material forms, conceptual structures and lived practices (Nunes 2006: xx). The 'meditative atmosphere' of Epiphany Island arises from a combination of the materiality of the user at the computer screen, the 'virtual architecture' that structures the island, the concepts symbolised by the image of a traditional church in a natural environment, the understanding of Christian life that values meditative peace and the user's actual practices within that virtual space.

One interviewee, Paula, voiced some particularly interesting criticisms of the design of the island, seeing this design as a reflection of a controlling and aggressive leadership style. The key issue here is not the accuracy of her perception but her understanding of the connection between architecture, self and control; in Nunes' terms, the relationship between material form, conceptual structures and lived practice. According to Paula, the island once held a garden she particularly liked:

Paula: It was a rose garden
Paula: with statues
Paula: pretty and feminine

This area was designed by a particular member of the leadership team who left the group before I first registered in Second Life, in a series of events described by several interviewees as a 'power struggle' (Sandy). Her departure was marked by the destruction of the areas she had built. According to one current leader, the departing individual had removed everything she had built herself, selfishly deleting her work from the island. For Paula, however, this removal was a leadership decision, a traumatic event that marked the entire island with an unmistakable sign of masculine violence and control:

Paula: they ruined the island
Paula: they derezzed [her] garden
Paula: and placed a huge gorge there
Paula: it almost felt like a rape to 'excorcise' her
Paula: It did the trick
Paula: she no lionger comes
          [. . .]
Paula: but I got told it was derezzed as [she] had left and they wanted 'control'
Paula: the objects could have been given group ID

Creative work reflects more than simply a material form and the effects of form on practice. Creativity is an extension of the self, and the mistreatment of creative work can be perceived as mistreatment of the creator. The positioning of creative work within the community is interpreted here as a communicative act, a statement regarding the acceptance or expulsion of the actual creator, drawing the boundaries of community membership through manipulation of the environment. From this perspective, it is not surprising that the process of design decision-making was controversial for several interviewees, and that three expressed not just regret but anger that their own creations had not been accepted into the Cathedral's grounds.

Another objection was raised by Mark Brown himself, in our interview. Adopting a familiar style of architecture makes one key assumption: that the visitor is in fact familiar and comfortable with that style. According to Brown, 'what I've found is that, um, actually, um, I think people who are not used to cathedrals come in and feel a bit intimidated and a bit confused, why did you build a cathedral?' I encountered similar concerns in my interviews. Quentin, based in Australia, questioned the geographical breadth of appeal of such a design: 'one of the problems even about the look of the place is that it is very English or European. It does not cater for Asians Africans or South Americans for instance.'

For Quentin, to design a church in a recognised style is to limit the church's audience to those for whom that style is familiar and significant, an important decision for a supposedly global religion like Christianity. Familiarity can also be a limitation for a church seeking broad theological appeal: Paula claimed that the design of the cathedral indicated a High Church affiliation that excluded her from participation.

We have already encountered a number of non-Christian members of St Pixels who disliked the worship there because it reminded them too much of being in church, so these drawbacks of reliance on the familiar are not unique to the Cathedral. Ultimately, Brown dismisses such objections: 'I think the proof's in the pudding, is that actually we are, we're growing. So you have to kind of say well, I would, I would, suggest, it's anecdotal but I would suggest that part of the success is that we have a cathedral.'

Despite these reservations, the actual aesthetic appeal of the Cathedral was unchallenged. Even Paula was unstinting in her praise, describing the build as 'beautiful' and the builder as 'inspired'. 'Aesthetically', she claimed, 'it is fantastic'. The attempt to create mood through the design of space also received general appreciation. According to Kevin, 'Architecture helps set the atmosphere—peaceful, not too jokey or trivial'. For Olive, the difference in style between the cathedral and the smaller chapel that stands alongside it created a difference in atmosphere relevant to the activity of prayer: 'I like the whole feel of this [chapel] area', she explained, particularly the light colours and big windows—'there's a sense of uncluttered space', compared to the relatively 'fussy' Cathedral, and as a result 'I think it would be easier to pray here'. Again, atmosphere was created through the use of recognised architectural styles—minimalist rooms illuminated by natural light, in a manner Olive considered attractive and calming.

A rather different perspective was provided by one of the two non-Christians I interviewed. Rachel was an 'eclectic witch' from Scotland who agreed to a series of three interviews in-world; we will encounter the other non-Christian, an American Buddhist called Stephen, later in this chapter. Rachel's Second Life activity involved much attention to the dynamics of space, and our interviews were conducted in a pagan 'Henge' high in her private skybox, during a pagan gathering around a fire, and amid the meditation spaces of a Buddhist zone. Rachel was a frequent visitor to the Anglican Cathedral, as she explained:

Rachel: i visit more often than you think probably. . . .
          i'm on sl every day..so i could almost guarantee i make an appearance once a day . . .
          that doesn't mean to say i stay long each time,but its a place i go to. esp..at the end of the day..when i need some 'lag-free' space to IM my goodnights etc..
          otherwise i take a walk around the gardens probably about twice a week.. and the same for inside..
          tho not necessarily on the same visit :-)

The activity described here is primarily solitary—the cathedral was a suitable space for sending private messages because Rachel knew she would be alone and undisturbed there at the times she chose to visit.

Off-world, Rachel also enjoyed visiting churches:

Rachel: most of them are built on ground which has ben sacred for possibly thousands of years..
Rachel: the 'energyu' i talk about when i discuss them has been part of the earth since time began . . . just because an 'all good god' has claimed it for his own..it ain't gonna keep me out:-)

Despite this apparently physical and historical explanation for the 'energy' of church spaces, Rachel believed that this spiritual power could be found in the virtual world as well:

Interviewer: so do you find that "energy" in sl religious spaces too?
Rachel: surprisingly yes..
Rachel: . . . i have a theory that it is something carried in the 'love' that the people who actually built them have somehow transferred
                 [. . .]
Rachel: but its a spiritual energy..which can possibly be transferred thru the web..electricitty
                 [. . .]

Interviewer:	is it possible that the "energy spots" you've said exist on earth might exist in sl too?
Rachel:	yes, thats entirely possible..i'm not sure if they exist at the 'actual place' of 'worship' or possibly the place just 'focuses' your mind into a collective consciousness type of thing?

These energy spots could be found in the Second Life Cathedral, 'and not just the building,but the whole island'. Rachel discovered this energy by 'instinct', when searching for a space to sit quietly, 'just "chill" and feel.. by myself without being alone'.

When I asked about Second Life church services, Rachel commented that 'they annoy me on a personal level', because her non-Christian contributions were unwelcome. She preferred to sit at the back of a physical church, leaving partway through and looking around the graveyard. Nonetheless, the architecture of the Cathedral and the spaces that surround it created an atmosphere that she could perceive as 'energy', comparable in effect to the experience of visiting an ancient holy space in 'rl'.

The convergence of material form, conceptual structures and lived practice in the creation of architectural space is found also in the creation of the visible self, the avatar. Here too we see central values of the community deployed to structure practices of creation and display, good and bad use of resources and to mark boundaries for the group.

Presenting the Self: Avatars and Usernames at the Cathedral

Second Life requires the new Resident to construct a representation, an 'avatar', to act as a visible presence in-world. The basic tools of the registration process enable the user to create a simple human form and select a range of clothing, but more sophisticated looks—including detailed skin, complex hairstyles, fashionable clothing and if required, designer body parts—can be sought out among Second Life's many stores and markets. The creation and display of identity illuminates group themes and values and offers insights into the sometimes-complex relationships between Second Life and the 'real world' outside.

As I observed in my study of St Pixels (Chapter 6), online communities permit some forms of pseudonymity and forbid others according to shared norms that can differ from group to group. The Cathedral community tolerated a greater diversity of avatar design philosophies than St Pixels, but not everyone agreed on the exact limits of acceptable behaviour and self-presentation.

In my interviews with Cathedral-goers, explanations of avatar design fell into four major categories. For some, the avatar should be as realistic as possible, as a matter of honesty; these respondents sounded much like those I met at St Pixels and i-church. For others, some degree of improvement was acceptable to create an 'ideal me'. A third group used their avatars to explore an aspect of their identity that they could not embody in 'real life', or to experience a new and different kind of identity. Finally, a small group used their avatars as a kind of play, without attempting to reflect their physical selves or self-perceptions at all. This spectrum of representation runs from realism to pure fantasy, and the range of ways to relate 'Second Life' and 'real life' was almost as broad.

Henrik Bennetsen suggests that Second Life philosophies can be characterized as either 'augmentationist' or 'immersionist', respectively perceiving Second Life as an extension of existing Internet technologies or as an independent reality (Bennetsen 2006). Andrew expressed a very similar view in our interview in Guildford:

> I think there are two distinct types of people in Second Life. There are those who want to be themselves, it's almost as if it's a Facebook presence, they are here to socially interact as themselves, it's just they are different media. Another group of people want to come to Second Life because it is a Second Life for them, it's a way of exploring a different life, or perhaps aspects of their own lives that it is, that they can't fulfil in real life.

Andrew claimed that both types of people are found at Epiphany, and that both approaches are welcomed. However, he was confident that those who displayed elements of fantasy eventually set those aside in conversation at the Cathedral, letting something of their true self show through. Some might appear in 'full role-play mode', complete with clerical collars and robes, or take on more outlandish forms, but they still engaged in sincere conversation:

> There are also those who appear outrageously, as fantasy characters, but I find they don't tend to come to the church as that fantasy character, you can still talk to them and find out where they're from, something of themselves, so it's simply the avatar that they usually use, but they're coming to the cathedral for something that is, that is real.

As Bennetson and other commentators recognised, immersionist and augmentationist viewpoints are endpoints on a continuous spectrum. My interviewee Ashley expressed this well:

Ashley: sl is in this weird middle ground between fantasy and reality
Ashley: that is hard to explaing
Ashley: Its not purely fantasy
Ashley: but its also not purely reality
Ashley: its somewhere right in between
Ashley: thinking about it too hard makes your head explode

Olive was a good example of the 'realism' school of avatar design. Her avatar at the time of our interview was relatively short, middle-aged and heavy-set, and she explained that 'I made mine fatter to be a little bit more realistic'—'I'm inherently honest'. Tanya, on the other hand, commented that 'My avatar is an ideal me'—in fact, 'I think she is hot:)'. Tom shared a similar view: 'SL is great as you have an awful lot of freedom to express fantasy—e.g. in RL I've always wanted hair and beard like this'.

Of course, Second Life also permits avatar creation well outside the parameters of 'human' identity. Rachel's character, while human, displayed a cat's tail and vampire teeth. Vivian appeared as an angel, or a mermaid swimming in the church fountain. Others at the Cathedral chose avatars based on gnomes, centaurs, human-like 'furries' and natural-looking animals, and the group discussion of prayer that I quoted above was quietly observed by a hippopotamus. These kinds of dress and behaviour were generally accepted as part of the culture of the Cathedral.

A more significant issue for the Cathedral community was nudity. Genitalia and naked bodies of all shapes and sizes are readily available in Second Life, and occasionally make their way into church settings. My conversations with Cathedral members suggested that such events were much disliked, but that naked avatars were ejected from the island because they also tended to seek to disrupt and offend with the words and behaviour, not specifically because of their nakedness. A very wide range of interpretations of avatar design was permitted, in the hope—based on experience—that even those trying to role-play and seeking provocation would engage in sincere conversation from time to time.

The most interesting avatars for the researcher are those which play closely with the fine and blurring line between reality and fantasy, passing as realistic while incorporating hidden or publicly displayed elements of role-play and the fantastical. It is here that misunderstanding and deception are most likely, and community trust most vulnerable. Observations of these blurrings and passings help to identify some of the boundaries of an online community, regarding what is acceptable, what is unacceptable, and what is valued as authentic or genuine.

For Fred, a teacher from Texas, Second Life offered the chance to explore a new ethnic identity:

Fred:	I knew what I wanted from teh start.
Fred:	I knew I wanted to an Asian, tall, slim
Fred:	I'm white not so tall in rl
Fred:	with an average build.
Interviewer:	so not asian irl?
Fred:	no
Interviewer:	what made you want this particular look?
Fred:	I love Asian cultures
Fred:	My friends even hae described me as an Asian trapped in a white body

I did not see Fred's Asian-ness questioned or challenged by other visitors to the Cathedral, and his racial experimentation appeared to be accepted as a valid form of self-representation. Stephen's avatar experiments, on the other hand, became a topic of much greater controversy. Stephen is a white American who describes himself as a solitary Buddhist, but according to his own account, he first appeared at the Cathedral as 'a black catholic priest asking for church wine money'. On another occasion, I encountered his priest avatar at the Cathedral trying to raise funds to build a church with its own strip club. Stephen later returned to the Cathedral to roleplay as a Korean Zen master in flowing robes. On each occasion he adopted a stereotyped, racialized form of speech and tried to act in character. 'I couldn't make a friend in the world as the black priest', he noted ruefully. He explained his actions in terms of a misguided voyage of self-discovery:

Stephen:	anyway . . . i was kinda exploring myself
Stephen:	through my avatar
Stephen:	seeing, or testing, how others would react to me
Interviewer:	did you expect anyone to believe you?
Stephen:	believe what?
Interviewer:	believe you were a real priest, black guy, korean, zen master etc
Stephen:	oh no, in fact it sometimes became embarrassing
Stephen:	when i would be asked
Stephen:	i'd have to answer that i'm just being an irreverent jackass

For Sam and Ashley, Second Life offered the chance to explore not ethnicity but gender. Both are male, but both have created female avatars. Sam hoped 'to experience life as a woman', exploring an important side of his real-life self: 'i have always identified with what would be feminine roles and traits. . . .. communal actions, nurturing and such'. Ashley explained that 'I thought it'd be interesting to be the opposite gender', but claimed that his actual behaviour is unchanged—'It is hard for me not to be me'. While Sam claimed that avatar appearance was unimportant, Ashley created his ideal woman, designing the avatar according to 'basically what I find attractive'.

Ashley reported that his adventures had introduced him to a number of social differences in the treatment of men and women, from a new ease in making female friends and 'a lot of men flirting with me in really degrading ways' to new rules of conversation: 'I find that strong opinions are not as welcome from me', because 'a lot of people do not like a woman having strong opinions.' Ashley believed that his new female self had introduced him to some of the realities of living in a gendered culture, but his account strongly suggests that gender norms were not actually being undermined in Second Life. Stereotypes and cultural expectations remain, just as the past decade of Internet scholarship would lead us to expect, even though the boundaries of who may act male or female may have been shifted or weakened.

Alicia Spencer-Hall describes a slightly different case of avatar role-play in her own study of Second Life religion. One of her interviewees, a middle-aged male member of the Church of the Latter-Day Saints, had chosen to appear in Second Life as a small boy. He looked 'childlike', he explained to Spencer-Hall, because 'I like to think it fulfils the Savior's admonition we become as little children. A form of "sack cloth and ashes" I suppose. In RL, when I pray, I imagine myself as a little child before God' (Spencer-Hall forthcoming). Like Fred and Sam, this user described his self-representation as a means to express an inner truth concealed by his outer appearance, but in this case that truth is spiritual. By designing and operating an avatar, the user hoped to achieve the identity represented by that avatar.

One of my interviewees, Paula, spoke about her creation of an 'alt'. The alt is an entirely separate Second Life character, with a new name, profile and look. Paula's main avatar took considerable time to create, closely resembled her and operated mainly in Christian regions, but seemed permanently entangled in complex and acrimonious struggles and disputes over her attempts to gain recognition as a leader and creative designer. Eventually 'I wanted to start afresh', and the new alt, Wendy, was created to spend time in areas related to Paula's secular career. As Kevin pointed out to me, 'you can easily create a new avatar if your old one gets into trouble'. Paula designed Wendy to be taller, younger and more confident than Paula herself—and was startled to realise that the avatar she had created actually closely resembled her own 'real life' daughter.

My only other encounters with alts, apart from Paula/Wendy, were through gossip, rumour and intrigue. Several Residents I spoke to voiced suspicions that old opponents in the Cathedral, or visitors who had just left our company, had behaved so strangely that their characters must surely have been alts—seeing an alt as less authentic than a primary avatar, an instrument rather than a full persona, and therefore highly suspect. For some, double identities were a threat to the community and a danger to the trust between members.

The community expressed the most intense hostility to two groups of individuals: griefers (those deliberately seeking to cause offense, like the 'troll' visitors to the Church of Fools) and false clergy. False clergy were a perennial issue for people I interviewed from the Cathedral community, and the ease with which anyone can create a new character, buy some vestments, buy a church and set themselves up as a pastor is perceived by some as cause for grave concern. The issue of most interest for our discussion here is not the actual ordained status of these leaders, which would be difficult to determine, but the shared perceptions of authority and deceit among the Cathedral-going congregation that these themes reveal. For Ashley, for example, confidence in the licensed authority of pastors was key. One Second Life church leader, according to Ashley, 'has not been to a day of seminary' and copied his sermons from the Internet, but falsely claimed to be a 'real life' pastor. The Anglican foundation of the Cathedral offered Ashley a guarantee against such abuses:

Interviewer:	so why does it matter for you that [Mark Brown] is recognised as a real priest, and has his church recognised by a real diocese?
Interviewer:	is that important?
Ashley:	yes
Ashley:	because I think that by putting yourself out there as a spiritual leader in sl
Ashley:	you give yourself an air of authority
Ashley:	and people will listen to what you say
Ashley:	and if you dont' really have the bible knowledge and the temperament for the job
Ashley:	that can be dangerous
Ashley:	which is why [the untrained pastor] worries me

Along with this hostility to unlicensed clergy, certain kinds of church-like activity also met with disapproval. The Cathedral's architectural space was designed to closely resemble a real-world church, and so included an altar, but performances of weddings, Eucharist or Baptism—all practices offered at other Second Life churches—were ruled out by the leadership (see Chapter 2). This issue was divisive for the community, particularly the celebration of weddings between Residents who meet, declare themselves in love and set up house together in-world. While the Cathedral leadership refused to approve such events, several interviewees excitedly told me about their adventures in romance, and others directed me to spirited and acrimonious debates over this question on the Cathedral's blog (for an example, see Chapter 10). Second Life romance can also include Second Life sex, a possibility that raised urgent questions about the nature of sin in virtual worlds.

These three concerns—clerical authority, virtual sacraments and sexual sin—all feature in Jana Margueritte Bennett's recent theological analysis of digital media, *Aquinas on the Web*. Bennett visits *Second Life* to find out if sacraments are being offered there, and encounters a presumably-fake priest offering to hear her confession and a man who asks her for sex; 'thus ended', she says, 'what I had hoped would be an interesting theological conversation' (Bennett 2012: 124). For Bennett, this experience demonstrates that Christians should evaluate online churches through their familiarity with older theologian traditions. The Internet can be deceptive, risky, isolating and trivial, and—in the oldest traditions of Christian digital theology—Bennett uses the example of an online church to demonstrate these dangers.

The question of griefing was also important for the Cathedral when I first arrived. Services were mainly undisturbed, but visitors to the discussion group and Bible study frequently provoked intense arguments, mocked Christian earnestness or displayed avatars the group considered inappropriate. Tanya ran the Saturday Bible studies, and distinguished between the merely argumentative and actual griefers. Those who dominated, 'pushing their beliefs', were perceived as a problem, but not as griefers; that title was reserved for those with 'a 20 foot penis hanging out', 'also stupid remarks about how Jesus should have smoked more pot', or 'how all Christians are idiots or that we are all going to hell'. Tanya's distinction separated those with serious but misguided intent, those who wanted to discuss their views, from those who only wanted to cause confusion and distress. Rare though these clashes were, Tanya still found them upsetting: 'it puts a sour taste in your mouth when you get a griefer'. Tanya admitted that Mark Brown's view was more lenient than hers, 'because you never know when a person will stop being a griefer and come to be a friend'. Stephen's progress from racial stereotyping to his current activity, running a serious Buddhist retreat centre in Second Life, would be a case in point.

In conclusion, then, attention to the construction, display and deployment of avatars at Epiphany Island shows an interesting convergence of fantasy and reality. Visitors to the island may represent themselves in a variety of ways without group censure, but the recurrent theme was authenticity, a perception of the avatar as an extension of the self, a channel through which the self can be expressed and known. As Tom and most other interviewees put it, 'I don't see SL as an alternative or substitute for RL, I see SL as an extension of my RL'. Even those like Ashley who role-played extensively in their Second Life activity seem to revert to a strict realism when they come to church, frequenting only religious communities they would join in 'real life' and favouring the activities they would pursue there. The cardinal sin within the Cathedral community, the issue about which complaint was most often voiced, was to reject the authentic communication of selves by entering into genuine communication with another Resident and then rebuffing that openness by insulting, snubbing or disrespecting them, claiming unwarranted spiritual authority over them or showing them insufficient support and appreciation. Community life was predicated on the assumption that the avatar is an extension of the true self of the user, and that rejecting the avatar is a direct and particularly callous mistreatment of the user.

Joining the Cathedral: The Value of Anglican Space

Almost all of those I met were attracted to the island not because it answered some general post-modern desire for tradition, as Mark Brown had suggested, but because it offered a space to meet Anglicans with whom they expected to share considerable common ground. Even Rachel, the Scottish witch, was attracted to this Anglican identity: 'the fact it was "anglican"...

.. ... sounds stupid . . . but i didn't want born again yanks annoying me:-)'.
Here is another quote, from my interview with Diane:

Interviewer:	how did you come across the cathedral?
Diane:	Search for Anglican, if I remember
Interviewer:	why did you run that search?
Diane:	The Episcopal Church is very important in my life
Diane:	and when I was thinking of things of interest to search on, it just naturally
	came up within the first 5 or so

In the other online churches discussed in this book, members explained they had sought out that space to satisfy their curiosity or to meet particular religious needs. In contrast, the interviews I conducted with Cathedral-goers indicated that any spiritual benefits were often unexpected. Their primary purpose in searching for church spaces online was simply to find Anglicans in Second Life, like-minded people they could associate with. June, one of the most active congregants at the Cathedral during my research there, was a good example:

Interviewer:	so what made you look for anglican sims?
June:	because I'm an Episcopalian
June:	and I did wonder if there would be a chance to chat with people from elsewhere
June:	whether I would get a different take on what's happpening
June:	I didn't come here looking for a church. I have one of those in rl
June:	I came for a place to meet people

Three other motives for coming to the Cathedral were also important. The first has been discussed above—the occasional appearance of griefers, visiting the community to protest perceived grievances with Christianity or simply to enjoy causing offence. Role-players were similar in this respect, visiting the Cathedral in search of a space to play out a particular identity in a context where local regulars will respond predictably to the play.

The second category concerns prayer. It was not uncommon for people to visit the Cathedral seeking a space to pray, often in a time of personal trouble. This might not require regular return visits, attendance at services or time for conversation, so such visitors could easily have escaped notice during my times of participant observation. Rachel was one example, visiting the island to experience the ancient 'energy' she felt the builders fused into the environment with their love for their work. Other visitors came to the island for a conversation or a prayer request, seeking a community of Christians to help with a specific time of need, and I heard about such visits from some of the regulars who had encountered them. Several interviewees reported conversations with troubled sex-gamers, for example, visiting the site to ask advice on some particular task they had been ordered to perform.

The third and final category was less common, but very influential in Second Life religion. I encountered a handful of people visiting the Cathedral looking for a virtual space to carry out what they perceived to be a calling to mission or evangelism, to preach, lead, create, teach or reach the 'unsaved', pursuing a missional identity which is highly valued but sometimes difficult to achieve in 'real-world' Christian spaces. In some cases, these individuals were ordained offline and were looking for additional opportunities for more experimental ministry. Others had tried to achieve official approval as leaders from their local churches but had not succeeded, and they had entered Second Life to find a less-regulated sphere within which to exercise their talents and establish their authority. Community response to these self-appointed missionaries tended to be somewhat mixed. Some were highly regarded for their contributions to community relationships, and indeed most churches and Christian groups I encountered were founded by someone who had joined Second Life just to perform that task. Others endlessly moved on from one church to another as they tried again and again to achieve positions of authority for which established church leaders considered them unsuited.

Conclusion

The Cathedral of Second Life shows distinctive features not found in the other churches we have discussed, but it also engages with many of the same themes as well. The Cathedral combined the familiar look of Church of Fools with the liturgy of i-church, and aspired to the denominational identity of i-church as well. The majority of the congregation was made up of Christians who also attended local churches, just as in the other examples we have considered, but also included a minority of former churchgoers. The Cathedral is also different from other churches, however, in part because of its surroundings: Second Life is a world with its own cultures, customs and practices, and any group must adapt to accept or resist that context. In this strikingly beautiful architectural space, a gathering of Anglican Christians came into regular contact with other users of Second Life who wished to pray with them, make fun of them, teach them and occasionally, perhaps, join them.

This is a unique, different yet still very recognisable kind of online religion. We can summarise some of the major similarities and differences using the seven key categories identified in Chapter 4:

1. Scale. Second Life religion faces a serious limitation of scale. The world restricts the number of avatars who can gather in the same place at the same time, depending on the fee paid by the landowner of that area. Even below this limit, gatherings can become slow and laggy if too many people are present, particularly if their hair and clothing are complicated. The Cathedral was rarely full enough to reach its limit, but these structural restrictions help to shape the kinds of religion that could potentially emerge in a virtual world.

2. Local Churchgoing. The majority of congregation members were also connected to local churches, and some were also attending other churches online or in Second Life as well. Mark Brown emphasised missionary outreach to new worlds, but the actual community functioned much more as a social network for Anglicans. On the other hand, the Cathedral did claim that at least a few members attended church nowhere else, and I met a few visitors (like Rachel and Stephen) who did not consider themselves Christian at all.

3. Community. Regular members described strong friendships, mutual support and a sense of belonging, and this was emphasised (as a reality or at least an ideal to strive for) by almost everyone I spoke to. This understanding of community is similar to the other churches I have described. Less usually, however, Epiphany also attracted a regular stream of new visitors, including missionaries, trolls, role-players, lovers of virtual architecture and people looking for a quiet place to pray.

4. Ritual and Spiritual Experience. Second Life ritual could include gestures and animations, but the Cathedral preferred text. Services focused on written exchanges of liturgy, responses and prayers and could also include audio or typed sermons. These sermons were broad and uncontroversial, encouraging the audience rather than setting boundaries on doctrine. Solitary and group prayers were popular, and the environment and gestures of Second Life were deployed in prayer as marks of sacred space and as aids to focused concentration.

5. Familiarity. Like Church of Fools, the Cathedral relied on traditional and easily understood architectural forms. It also adapted Anglican forms of liturgy, like i-church. As we shall see in the conclusion, some of this realism has been relaxed over time: the island's buildings are still Gothic or Tudor in style today, but they have less elaborate designs. Realistic visual details have been sacrificed to reduce lag and make the space easier to move around.

6. Internal Control. At the time of my research, the Cathedral was led by Mark Brown, who visited at least once every week to run the Sunday service. Brown was assisted by a team of more regular attenders, and these were chosen rather than appointed by community vote. The Cathedral did encounter occasional trolls and troublemakers, and these were generally tolerated unless they began disrupting events.

7. External Funding and Oversight. A Second Life church needs space, and that means paying rent, but the Cathedral was able to rely on member donations for these costs. Mark Brown pursued relations with the wider Anglican Communion, however, after initially deciding to create the Cathedral without any official endorsement. The Cathedral began conversations with Anglican bishops, and Brown was eventually ordained as an Anglican priest. The Cathedral continued to present itself as Anglican, but no formal relationship was ever created. We will discuss the recent progress of this ambition in the conclusion.

Note

1 This information was delivered by private communication; the published report gives no indication of survey size.

References

Bennetsen, H., 2006. Augmentation vs immersion. *SL Creativity*, 7 December. [blog] Available at: <https://web.archive.org/web/20120505073956/http://slcreativity.org/wiki/index.php?title=Augmentation_vs_Immersion> [Accessed 1 September 2016]

Bennett, J., 2012. *Aquinas on the Web? Doing Theology in an Internet Age.* London: Bloomsbury T&T Clark.

Brown, M., 2008. Christian mission to a virtual world. [online] Available at: <https://issuu.com/mbrownsky/docs/virtualmission> [Accessed 1 September 2016]

Hansen, L., 2009. What happened to second life? *BBC News Magazine*, 20 November. [online] Available at: <http://news.bbc.co.uk/2/mobile/uk_news/magazine/8367957.stm> [Accessed 1 September 2016]

Howell, J., 2013. Whatever happened to Second Life? *BBC News*, 21 June. [online video] Available at: <http://www.bbc.com/news/business-23000809> [Accessed 1 September 2016]

Linden, Z., 2009. Second life residents logged nearly 400 million hours in 2008, growing 61% over 2007. *Second Life*, 15 January. [blog] Available at: <https://web.archive.org/web/20090117035550/http://blog.secondlife.com/2009/01/15/q42008/> [Accessed 1 September 2016]

Miczek, N., 2008. Online rituals in virtual worlds: Christian online services between dynamics and stability. *Online: Heidelberg Journal of Religions on the Internet* 3(1), pp. 144–173.

Nunes, M., 2006. *Cyberspaces of Everyday Life.* Minneapolis: University of Minnesota Press.

Spencer-Hall, A., forthcoming. *Medieval Saints and Modern Screens: Divine Visions as Cinematic Experience.* Amsterdam: Amsterdam University Press.

8   Church Online at LifeChurch.tv

I woke up one morning and googled some stuff about church and some stuff about God, because I needed something different, I was starting to search again, and I came across Church Online, and it was about 3 o'clock in the morning, and I cracked a beer open and I see this chat thing going on, and I see there's live music playing to the left, and I just sat and listened to it and it was beautiful, it was really beautiful, really engaging, and I went over at the end and I logged on and I kept saying to myself what on earth am I doing, I'm sharing with people on some chat thing, these could be anybody, and I started to talk with [the campus pastor]. I felt as if I was breaking down [. . .] I finished the beer and went to bed, and I know people say this but I woke up the next morning and I was a different guy.

—William (Gruenewald 2009)

Right now we're reaching tens of thousands, by next year I believe it will be hundreds of thousands, and before long I honestly believe it will be millions and millions of people.

—Craig Groeschel, senior pastor, LifeChurch.tv, 2009

Unlike every other church studied in this book, this one is connected to a physical location. 'Church Online' is not an independent online community but the online ministry of a single large church founded in the United States in 1996. By the end of my ethnographic research in 2009, LifeChurch.tv— the '.tv' was part of the name of the church, not just its website address— had 13 different physical locations or 'campuses', 8 in Oklahoma and 1 each in Arizona, Florida, New York, Tennessee and Texas. The church changed its name to Life.Church in 2015 and has continued to expand, operating 26 campuses in 2016 across the US.

LifeChurch is a multisite ministry, offering one church service (called an 'Experience') across all its many locations. Senior Pastor Craig Groeschel speaks from his base in Oklahoma City, standing on stage beneath three giant video screens. Every other campus is almost identical, except that Pastor Craig is not actually there. Cameras record his words, and a technical team broadcasts these live to the other campuses, where the same giant screens show him pacing the stage and speaking to his audience. Each campus has its own worship band, campus pastor, small groups, children's and youth ministries and mission projects.

LifeChurch has much in common with the 'New Paradigm' churches discussed by Donald Miller (1997), and with the 'Appropriators' he identified a decade late in collaboration with Richard Flory (2008). Both categories are characterised by the appropriation of elements of style and organization from secular culture. According to Miller and Flory, such churches adapt their environments and practices to reject whatever might be alienating in their dress, words, music, worship or lifestyles while emphasizing the personal, life-changing challenge of their religious message. Sermons focus on relationship with God, not doctrinal conformity. The senior pastor sets out a clear vision for the church but gives great autonomy to lay leaders. Small group fellowship is strongly encouraged. All of these features can be found in LifeChurch, which has attracted much attention for its innovations— particularly its use of the digital media (Fast Company 2011).

'Church Online' brings the LifeChurch campus model to the Internet, broadcasting music and messages through a website that offers a constellation of interactive communication options. We see here a very different kind of online church from those discussed before. Church Online is more centrally controlled, less relational and more evangelistic than my other case studies. The video broadcast is the focus of activity and discussion, there are no forums or private messages and the chatroom is supervised and only open at specific times. Church Online is also much larger: according to statistics shared with me by a staff member, 980 Experiences were held online in 2009, assisted by 175 volunteers, and the total number of different computers connecting to Experiences during the year rose to over 1.2 million.

Church Online represents an alternative possibility for online church-building, rooted in and expanding the influence of powerful local churches to a global religious stage. Preaching online is becoming one of the expected activities of high-profile church leaders, at least in the United States, and their compelling messages are now supported by sophisticated, well-funded teams of web developers and online community managers. 'Online campuses' are now offered by scores of other large churches across the United States (see Chapter 1 and Conclusion). Large churches have long sought to expand their public profile and share the story of their success through books, music, conferences, radio and television shows. Through digital media they can communicate more material, in more diverse forms, more frequently and at lower cost to more people than ever before.

This chapter will begin by outlining the history of Church Online. Because Experiences are so central to Church Online, I will then discuss an example in detail. I will also describe activity away from the main website, focusing on the Second Life Campus, LifeGroups and LifeMissions. This chapter also includes details and photographs gathered during offline research: I was able to visit the offices of LifeChurch in Oklahoma in October 2008, where I interviewed members of the Church Online team in person, toured some of the physical campuses and attended as many Experiences as possible.

From 'Internet Campus' to 'Church Online'

LifeChurch began its online ministry by posting sermon videos to its website, like many other churches, but it soon began to develop more ambitious and innovative plans. As staff member Brandon Donaldson recalled to me, they 'kept getting stories' from people watching those messages online. 'We realised God was using that', he explained, and in 2006 the church decided to follow that guidance by creating some kind of community space, initially called the Internet Campus, around its online content.

This origin story is echoed in accounts from other large churches, including Christ Fellowship in Florida. According to J. Todd Mullins, Christ Fellowship expected its video stream to appeal to church members travelling away from home, but soon 'began to hear of people who were watching online from [Christ Fellowship's own] city and all around the world' (2011: 2). Some were beginning to call this experience 'church', while others used the online stream as a chance to find out more about Christ Fellowship before visiting the church in person. Christ Fellowship decided to launch their own interactive online campus in 2008.

Donaldson had worked for LifeChurch as a youth pastor before leaving to take a master's degree in computer science. In his own words, he combined 'the heart of a pastor' with the technical skills and experience needed to 'talk the language' with web developers. He was invited back to LifeChurch to become the first Internet Campus pastor, managing the project, speaking to his online congregation as part of each Experience, engaging in pastoral work one-on-one with some of those visiting the site and delivering video and blog messages through the week.

When it was first launched, the LifeChurch Internet Campus reproduced almost every aspect of the LifeChurch system online. Visitors were able to watch one of two worship channels recorded at local campuses, watch Groeschel's message of the week and join online small groups and mission trips. Strikingly, the Internet Campus initially offered no synchronous communication between visitors during the Experience and very limited options for conversation at other times. Donaldson suggested in our interview that the 24-hour connectivity and user-generated content of the Internet could be 'scary to churches', and that forum discussions were too difficult to moderate and direct. Instead, the Internet Campus invited viewers to enter a set of small chatrooms afterwards instead. This was intended to replace the social interaction that visitors to a local campus might find in the lobby area after an event, without risking to much disruption.

The next iteration of the campus chat system added 'Friends in Your Row', a function that allowed visitors to invite a few friends to talk to them during Experiences, just as they might whisper to the person next to them in a physical church. An email address was needed for each friend, ensuring that conversations were limited to those who already knew one another. This function allowed Internet Campus regulars to invite their friends to church and talk to them during the service, without encouraging open conversations that might distract attention from the video stream.

When I first interviewed Donaldson, he explained the careful adherence of the Internet Campus to offline ideas in theological terms: 'we don't want to do anything outside what you're already doing, God.' This statement combines conservative caution with a striking epistemological confidence. For Donaldson, LifeChurch's growth was undeniable evidence that God was already at work there, blessing the structures and programs that the church has developed—a significant difference from the other churches considered in this book, which were created by, funded by or associated with churches characterised by numerical decline. At the Anglican Cathedral of Second Life, for example, Mark Brown framed his work as a contrast to the failings of older Christian institutions that were no longer 'at the cutting edge'.

Over time, LifeChurch has moved away from copying its successful offline model in favour of more context-driven engagement with the unique potential of the Internet, signalled by a change of name in 2009 from 'Internet Campus' to 'Church Online'. LifeChurch was ready 'to grow to that next level' of scale and commitment, Donaldson said, and needed to find new models to achieve that aim. Church Online featured a much more active blog, continual proliferation of Experience times, and appropriation of a whole range of online tools and social networks. Church Online dispensed with Friends in Your Row and placed an open chatroom, no registration necessary, directly alongside the Experience broadcast window.

This willingness to change reflect LifeChurch's pragmatic attitude to media. Donaldson referred to the Internet as a 'tool', and explained that LifeChurch tried to take that tool and ask, 'How can we use this for the glory of God?' This concept of 'tools' was a recurring theme in interviews with staff and volunteers, referring to strategies, media and even people that could be used to achieve core mission aims. This perception of the Internet as 'tool' is a striking contrast from the other churches I have studied, where the Internet was more likely to be conceptualised as a place to be entered or a culture to be engaged with. A 'tool' is used for a purpose, and its value lies only in how successful it is at achieving that end. This tool-discourse was identified by Heidi Campbell as one of the classic features of the Christian e-vangelism movement, used to encourage the development of concrete techniques, strategies and training programs (2010: 139).

Digital sociologist Sam Han has recently written about the kinds of communality emerging in Church Online, using LifeChurch as his case study. For Han, 'the church lobby, traditionally where the fellowship occurs, and the church sanctuary, traditionally where worship occurs, are both "remediated", that is, paid homage to, rivalled, and refashioned in new media'

(2016: 78). In particular, he believes, the church lobby and the sanctuary are being digitally combined: 'the phenomenon of online Christianity is pushing religious experience and religious community . . . closer together by facilitating certain modes of connectivity and communality intrinsic to digital media.' Instead of a traditional bounded community, LifeChurch is now facilitating a kind of 'proxemic' sociality constituted by shared moments of feeling and ephemeral contact. Spiritual experience, prayer and teaching circulate within the same platforms and networks as social interaction (2016: 88).

For Han, the design of Church Online is a clear example of this 'collapsing' of religious experience into community (2016: 88). The chat window is accessible alongside the sermon broadcast, and typed prayers and responses to the preacher are interspersed with off-topic discussions. Han considers this design an attempt 'to reorient the hierarchy of values found in traditional liturgy' (2016: 81) by making chat the 'structural equal' of the preaching. Indeed, given the relative sizes of the chat window and video window, it seems that 'the chat . . . is as, if not more, important than the streamed sermon'.

Han and I have studied LifeChurch at different times, and his observations relate to a more recent stage of Church Online's activity. It is likely that at least some of the differences in our observations are due to actual changes in platform design and group culture over time. However, the account and interviews discussed in this section do complicate Han's interpretation. Han suggests that the church 'seems rather amenable' (2016: 88) to the kind of communality he identifies, but LifeChurch actually refused to offer chat during Experiences for several years. Even when the chat window was opened, as we shall see in the next section of this chapter, moderators and chat participants took care to protect the status of the preaching window as the primary focus of attention. At the same time, the church tried to promote long-term social interaction in house groups and online groups, rather like i-church's pastoral groups. 'Proxemic' sociality may be a fair description of at least some forms of online networking today, but LifeChurch has not always considered that kind of community particularly desirable.

'Behind the Curtain': An Experience at Church Online

We can explore the major features of worship at Church Online through a detailed description of one Experience hosted on August 9 at 1730 (UK time). Focusing on one event will allow us to discuss how a broadcast is constructed and consider some of the responses posted by viewers in the chatroom. Experiences are central for Church Online and form the only point of contact with LifeChurch for a high proportion of visitors, so this section will be lengthy and detailed, interspersing descriptions with analysis of key patterns and themes and quotes from interviews and other sources. The specific Experience I have chosen to describe discussed the goals and vision of Church Online, so I will also use this section to introduce more of the ideas and aims that underlie this online ministry.

In mid-2009, Church Online hosted ten Experiences each Sunday and 27 at other times during the week. Only one Experience, on Saturday evening, offered an actual live feed, with the remainder throughout the week repeating that one recording. Most content was automated, but certain tasks, like starting the video feed, were carried out manually. Trained Experience teams were formed for this task, each comprising an 'Experience Captain' and a group of volunteers to welcome and pray with visitors. Anyone who wanted to propose a new time to add to the weekly schedule could volunteer to become the next Captain.

The Experience described here was the first of a new series, 'Behind the Curtain', a three-week set of events describing the vision underlying the digital ministries of LifeChurch.tv and introducing a new fund-raising website, 'Digital Missions'. Experiences fall into series of three or four weeks, themed around some issue from the Bible or contemporary life: finance, self-confidence, sex, fear, bad habits, and so on (for a complete archive, see http://www.life.church/watch/archive/). A particular highlight of each church year is 'At the Movies', a series using Hollywood films to introduce issues of faith. Each series is heavily promoted in the preceding weeks and illustrated with elaborate and visually striking posters and graphics. In the trailer video created for 'Behind the Curtain', a series of animated figures run, hammer and engineer their way through a giant machine landscape, symbolising the hidden work the message series will uncover.

On the viewer's screen in 2009, the Church Online website was divided into two roughly equal halves (Fig. 8.1). The video broadcast appeared on the left-hand side. On the right, the viewer could toggle between a series of tabs. These tabs include a chat window, a global map marking the location of each computer connection and a set of talk notes to annotate and share by email. Volunteers frequently reminded viewers that anyone unduly distracted by the conversations in the chat window could hide it: 'remember if the chat becomes distracting you can click on the video to watch in full screen'.

Chat was easy to join during my research, requiring no log-in or registration. The visitor simply typed in whatever name he or she wished to use during that session and could easily select another for his or her next visit. To encourage international conversations, LifeChurch.tv launched a 45-language translation tool called babelwith.me in 2009 and integrated it into the chatroom (Parr 2009).

Beneath the video window, seven buttons offered connections to social network sites, including Facebook, MySpace and Twitter. Messages published through these buttons could be fed directly into the main chat stream to show who had posted it, what they had said and how many followers had received it. A prescribed message suggestion was available. This feature encouraged visitors to invite their friends and allowed viewers to see that invitations were being sent, providing a visual reminder of the success of the church at appropriating technology for its evangelistic goals.

Fifteen minutes after the start of the Experience on August 9, the Map tab showed connections from North and South America, Europe, Africa and Asia. The United States was represented, of course, but also the United Kingdom, Russia, India, China, Argentina, Brazil, Egypt, South Africa and 17 other countries. A screenshot of the Map tab from a different Experience is shown in Fig. 8.1.

The Experience on August 9 began, as always, with contemporary Christian music. Prior to the launch of Church Online, the Internet Campus offered two different worship streams for viewers to choose from, but reducing this to one option ensured that all those commenting in the chat space were responding to the same words, music and visuals. Streams were occasionally recorded specifically for Church Online, but it was more common to replay worship performed at one of the local campuses. On this occasion, those watching in the chatroom responded warmly:

> listen to the words of this song. Let the truth of it wash over you.
> he gets deep into his songs
> He has amazing lyrics
> Listen to how God loves us!
> Let this song wash over you—this is a powerful message from God's heart to ours.

The space beneath the video window offered a range of other interaction options, as well as the social media buttons mentioned above. The viewer could read the title of the song, its original singer and the album from which

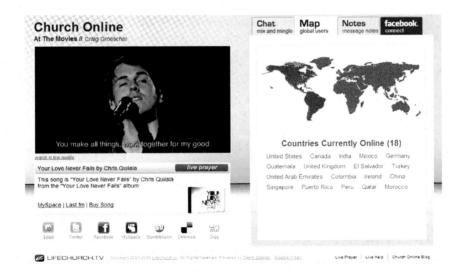

Figure 8.1 The Map tab at Church Online, 2009.

it comes, click a link to buy their own copy from Amazon, or use MySpace and Last.fm to find more music by the artist.

Some of my interviewees were indifferent to these worship sessions, focusing instead on Groeschel's preaching. One disliked the style and much preferred listening to country music. Others were more enthusiastic. Anthony, a young man from Wales who also attended a local Pentecostal church, explained 'it feels exactly the same as being in a church . . . after a while you don't even see the monitor . . . it's just the worship leader taking you into the presence of God.' 'I tend to sing a lot', he confessed, waking up his parents, and if there were a little more space around his computer desk he would love to get up and dance.

The musical segment lasted fifteen minutes and was followed by a series of video segments. In one of these, Brandon Donaldson introduced the customary 'offering' or request for donations through a story of online success. Two volunteers, he claimed, had recently used their Facebook statuses to advertise a LifeChurch experience. A homeless man they did not know somehow stumbled across that message, followed it to LifeChurch and asked for prayer. By chance, he was allocated to the very volunteer whose status message he had seen, and he later emailed her to declare that his life had been utterly changed by their encounter. 'God is on the move!', Donaldson insisted, claiming that stories like this were clear proof of God's work through LifeChurch.

'Live Prayer' was one of the interactive options offered beneath the video window, singled out by a red box. Clicking on this button sent the viewer to a form, into which he or she must enter a name and some details about the help they require, and this form was forwarded immediately to one of a number of volunteers standing by with access to one-to-one chat software. This system was identical to that used by some customer service websites and enabled anyone seeking prayer to enter a private conversation with someone authorised and supported by LifeChurch.

Chat contributors at the Experience on the 9th frequently directed viewers to the Live Prayer button. Contributors posted general warnings and advice—'This song brings up a lot of feelings and emotions, if you need prayer, click the live prayer button under the video'—or responses to specific individuals. 'Hi.I really need a prayer!!!!', posted one visitor. 'click on the live prayer button under the video', a volunteer quickly replied, 'we would love to pray with you.' When one poster announced that she wanted to die and 'go home', two contributors repeatedly directed her away from the public space: 'click on live prayer and someone would love to talk to you one on one', ' . . . I hope you'll go to live prayer and let someone pray with you'.

These instructions suggest that the public space of the chat window was considered an inappropriate place for prayer. The fragmented nature of chat conversation may be a factor influencing this pressure toward private communication, which does not parallel anything I have observed in the other churches I studied. Posts in the main chat window could attract a dozen unconnected responses or none at all. In the private prayer chatroom, an approved church representative could coordinate a more sustained, focused conversation.

This insistence on privacy was not universal, and other contributors resisted to pressure to use the private function by posting supportive comments, theological reflections and their email addresses. One, for example, wrote, 'Taking one's life only hurts those left behind . . . think how yor mother might feel. God never moves so you must be moving around too fast for him to keep up with you. Slow down, take some time and listen hard for His words—he led you to this chat line so that is a start.'

On rare occasions, the chatroom could also be used to share words of prophecy. At another Experience, for example, a visitor wrote '[name], I do not know what is wrong, but God told me to tell you, "I'm here with you, I love you and you are very precious to me."' I did not often see this kind of charismatic activity, but other participants in the chat room accepted it without protest.

After the video interlude came the sermon. The head pastor, Craig Groeschel, now appeared centre screen looking directly into the camera. He wore a casual, open-necked shirt with cufflinks, smart jacket and jeans, with a hands-free microphone clipped to his ear. Only two camera angles were used during the broadcast, either full-length or half-length shots of the pastor. He welcomed his listeners, including all categories of his audience:

> Welcome today to all of our campuses, all of our Network Churches, we love you guys, and with us now at Church Online, we're so glad to have you with us, and I am super glad to be back teaching today . . . I really feel a deep passion to help engage our whole church to understand all the different resources that are available for us to do ministry, and I pray that you'll get a passion and a deeper understanding of what is possible.

'Network Churches' are located around the world, using free LifeChurch resources and video teaching to organise ministries loosely connected to LifeChurch.tv.

Reading Luke 24:45–47, while the verses appeared as subtitles on the screen, Pastor Craig explained that 'Scripture says, "Jesus opened [the disciples'] minds so that they could understand the Scripture."' That Bible verse was about to come true again: 'that's exactly what's going to happen to some of you today, your minds are going to be opened to spiritual truth.' That spiritual truth would be a call to radical mission. Many churches around the world do not even preach 'to their own neighbourhoods', Groeschel claims, but 'this must change!' From now on, 'we must do anything short of sin to reach people for Christ'. This series would showcase some of the tools and strategies LifeChurch had been developing to achieve that goal: 'I want to really tell you what's going on in my heart, what's going on in my life, and where I believe God is taking us as a church.'

This introduction, lasting four minutes, demonstrates key aspects of Pastor Craig's preaching style. Certain structural elements are very consistent in his preaching, including his relaxed-yet-smart style of dress and the restricted range of camera shots. Groeschel takes care to speak straight to camera, establishing eye contact with the viewer—just enough, never too much—to reinforce key messages and maintain a sense of direct personal address. Cameras are sited near the centre of the auditorium, allowing Groeschel to shift his gaze from congregation to viewer in a relaxed and natural way, and shots of the audience are never shown. The overall effect that LifeChurch strives for is one of near-transparency, the illusion of presence and direct communication; every viewer in every campus must feel as though Groeschel speaks directly to him or her.

This contrasts strikingly with Christian television preaching, where shots of audience reactions are common. Here, there is to be no division between those physically present and those watching from afar, no sense that those watching the broadcast are separate from the 'real' audience. I interviewed the LifeChurch innovations pastor, Bobby Gruenewald, in Oklahoma, and he emphasised the importance of this strategy:

> we don't take shots of the crowd, which in a television ministry context is what you always do, because in television you want to show people that you're a big church and lots of people care, but in a video teaching context you're not trying to remind people that the video's in a different place, you're trying to suspend disbelief that this is happening somewhere else and you create this concept that this is happening right where you're at.

As one of the churchgoers I met in Oklahoma explained, any shot of the audience would give a sense that 'you're watching someone else's church'. In fact, he claimed, video teaching was much more effective than a face-to-face message. In a crowd it is easy to lose concentration and hide from the preacher's challenge, but every viewer of the broadcast could see Groeschel's face clearly, as if he were talking directly to him or her and looking into his or her eyes.

Like most of Groeschel's preaching, this message included anecdotes taken from Groeschel's own ministry. These stories were anonymous and often humorous, but still intensely personal, and were accompanied by promises to reveal honest truths about his own 'heart' and life. Donald Miller identified this as one of the common features of 'New Paradigm' churches: 'pastors tend to be understated, humble, and self-revealing' (1997: 20). Helje Kringelbotn Sødal has applied concepts from classical rhetoric to analyse the success of Joel Osteen, and also draws attention to his use of personal examples from his own life. According to Sødal, these stories serve to persuade, advise and rouse emotions, 'to bind Osteen's huge congregation together by including everyone in a common history centred on Osteen's family' and to 'give identity to a church which has a short history' (Sødal 2010).

These features of Groeschel's preaching were highlighted time and again in my interviews. Bridget, for example, praised 'the blatant honesty' of the LifeChurch preaching, claiming Groeschel 'doesn't pull any punches' when showing how much God demands we change our lives. Christina in Austria explained by email that a good church must be 'real, relevant and relatable':

> [A real pastor] is himself all the time, above all when teaching. [Relevance] means practical teaching that is useful for my day-to-day life and that doesn't just speak about evangelism, missions or spiritual gifts. [Relatability] pertains to teaching as well as people. Pastor and congregation should teach and act in a way that helps Christians and non-Christians alike relate to them.
> (Addressing current issues might help, as might modern worship and using video and Internet.)

According to Christina 'a church like that is impossible to find in Austria, both in real life and online', but LifeChurch suited her perfectly.

Groeschel's introduction also shows something of the attitude of LifeChurch to leadership. The ideal LifeChurch member is imagined as highly committed and engaged with personal Christian mission work but not engaged at all with shaping church vision and strategy. It was up to the pastor to explain to the congregation where God is taking the whole church.

Continuing his message, Groeschel attacked those who demand 'a church that meets my needs', but insisted on the importance of adaptation. 'The Church's message never changes', he proclaimed, 'but its methods must change'. Change is vital because 'the way people relate is changing by the second', particularly through technology. Groeschel's conclusion was sombre:

> To reach people today we must change the way we do things, or we're going to lose an entire generation. That's why, here's one of the key behind the scenes thoughts that we talk about all the time, and I want us all to embrace this—if you're taking notes, write this down, it's so important—here it is: to reach people that no one is reaching, you have to do things that no one is doing.

The vision of LifeChurch is often conveyed through the repetition of memorable slogans like this. Some of these sayings became embedded in church discourse, and were repeated back to me in interviews by staff, volunteers and church participants. As Sødal argues, repetition of messages can 'lead to recognition and the feeling of being an insider' (2010).

Groeschel's call to action reflects another key technique of LifeChurch preaching. The main purpose of each talk is not the study of the Bible for its own sake but the presentation of a challenge to the lives and thinking of the audience. Each sermon does include a small number of short, simple passages and key words from the Bible, but these serve to demonstrate the scriptural foundation for a message that is direct and personal. This challenge is conveyed rhetorically through a range of tools and strategies, including camerawork—Groeschel takes care to gaze straight to camera when delivering key points—and a constant shifting of tone. Moments of high tension and demand are introduced and followed by light-hearted and often self-deprecating stories, illustrations and digressions, lowering the tension to restore a comfortable atmosphere. The sharp shifts from laughter back to intense seriousness reinforce the impact of each personal challenge.

Groeschel now introduced three LifeChurch projects that 'will be controversial for a little while', but will eventually become 'some of the best ways to reach people'. 'We will do new things to reach new people', he declared, 'and if that offends you please go someplace else.'

Groeschel is not afraid to encourage his congregation to leave, and any controversial comment he makes will often be introduced by recognition of its difficulty—acknowledging that many in the congregation will struggle with this concept, reminding them that other excellent churches may teach them differently, and suggesting they go elsewhere if they disapprove. This kind of statement reinforces the image of the church as unified and decisive, frames obedience to Groeschel's personal authority as one of the key markers of church identity, and encourages audience members to see their continued participation as an active and courageous decision. At the same time, we can also interpret this challenge as a gesture of inclusiveness. By acknowledging the presence of people who will dislike the teaching, Groeschel implicitly admits that LifeChurch is diverse.

All three projects are digital. The first is YouVersion, a Bible website, social network and mobile app designed by LifeChurch (Hutchings 2015). YouVersion is 'a great place to interact with God's word online', and also makes it easy to keep a Bible text to hand at all times. 'I'm not spiritual enough to carry this text around with me all the time', Groeschel confessed self-deprecatingly, 'but I am practical enough to keep hold of my phone.' Just as importantly, 'I want you to see this as a great tool' for witnessing. Anyone spotted using an iPhone should be encouraged to download the YouVersion application. Groeschel claimed he had started conversations with strangers all over the world and never had his offer declined. Note again the prevalence of the language of tools and techniques in LifeChurch discourse about technology.

In chat, some users responded to these revelations with great enthusiasm. '<<holding up hands in thankfulness for our ability to contact the world>>', wrote one. 'That is incredible indeed', wrote another, 'God's word becoming available to everyone'. When Groeschel described the opportunities offered by YouVersion, one viewer typed, 'I have not done that yet . . . I MUST GET THIS on my phone!! [. . .] LOVE IT'. Another quickly encouraged her: 'You should [. . .] it's an amazing app [. . .] I use it all the time'.

The second project was LifeChurch.tv's online sermon archive, offering 'free messages to anyone with the Internet.' Sermons are powerful, Groeschel assured his audience: 'there is something that happens when the truth of God is taught, I don't know how and I don't know why, but the truth of God changes lives'. 'We made an aggressive decision a few years ago that we would not sell God's teaching', so all messages are available free online. In a pre-recorded video, a Church Online viewer declared that 'making those resources available free online does incredible things'. He had personally shared messages with 'over 100 people', and thanked LifeChurch for helping him 'do and be church' while travelling.

Again, chat contributors responded enthusiastically. 'This church is really doind some amazing stuff', one wrote. 'This is how God is working in the world', posted another. The concept of offering free messages online received particularly warm comment: 'Word of God changes lives..Amen'; 'The truth of God is not for sell here [. . .] It's FREE!!!'. One viewer shared her own experiences: 'The first one I watched when I was lost was Satan's Sex Ed, lol [. . .] couldn't believe they talked about sex in church, lol'.

The third project, Pastor Craig warned, will be 'despised by many people today and massively accepted by people in the future': Church Online. 'Right now we're reaching tens of thousands, by next year I believe it will be hundreds of thousands, and before long I honestly believe it will be millions and millions of people.' He gazed into the camera to address those viewers directly. 'I want to welcome you in the name of the Lord Jesus Christ', who said that wherever two or three are gathered he would be there with them:

> Even though you are at places all over the world right now, you are gathered together in the name of Christ, and I know that he is with you, and I believe that he is going to speak to you, and by faith I know that you are going to be different.

Like YouVersion and the message archive, Church Online can be a witnessing tool, enabling believers to share a digital resource with anyone they meet. Groeschel also encouraged his audience to join Church Online as volunteers: 'many of you, you need to see this as your primary ministry, that you're a Church Online evangelist'. Chat contributors repeat this appeal: 'We need tech nerds, social butterflies, administrators, and prayer warriors. Whatever your gift is we have a place for you. Join us.'

Many of my interviewees routinely attended the same recorded Experience several times each week to work as volunteers. Anthony, for example, attended Church Online at 9:00 a.m., went to his local church at 11:00 a.m., went back to Church Online mid-afternoon, and then went to his local church again at 6:30 p.m. In the mornings, he explained, he was too busy welcoming people to the chatroom to actually listen to what Groeschel was saying. Others claimed that Groeschel's messages were so rich and valuable that they gained new insights with each repeat.

This chapter opened with a long quotation from a story told through Church Online's blog, illustrating one example of apparently successful digital evangelism. According to William, he 'woke up one morning and googled some stuff about church and some stuff about God', and discovered Church Online. 'I woke up the next morning', he concluded, 'and I was a different guy.'

Of course, not everyone is as enthusiastic about rediscovering church as William. LifeChurch has also adopted more active strategies, Groeschel explained, including buying adverts on search engines:

> The problem is, we've found that not many people were googling Church Online—but we did find that a lot of people were googling things like 'naked ladies' [laughter from the congregation]. So if you're googling for naked ladies while church is online, an ad will pop up saying 'Looking for naked ladies? Why don't you try Church Online?' [laughter, applause]. And you say, does anybody actually click through? You would not believe what happens when people are about to go to something, and, oh man, church, maybe this is God, maybe this is . . . [laughter].

The pastor read out an email the church had received from a man who confesses he was 'lost':

> I was looking at some girls dancing on YouTube and about to go to a porn site when your ad popped up. I never made it to that other site because I was drawn to LifeChurch instead. I know God was drawing me. Thank you.'

The audience cheered. 'To reach people no one is reaching', Pastor Craig repeated, 'you've got to do things no one is doing.'

This story received a warm response from chat contributors:

- searching naked ladies. . . . try church online! LOL
- woohoooooooo!
- Love that
- that's hilarious

One theme of chatroom conversation throughout the Experience may not be unrelated to this strategy. 'anyone interested in sexy chat?', asked one contributor; 'i want to see sex', typed another. Church staff tried to reply encouragingly, responding to the first 'no [username], i'm not, but thanks for asking!', and to the second, 'you will not see that, but I encourage you to stay', and 'that isn't here, but you are welcome to stay in this conversation about God's love and what community with followers of Jesus looks like'. Other viewers sought to silence and evict these contributors: 'you need to leave', 'You are out of line', 'why would you say that?'

In one case, a visitor, S, explained that he was a 'true hindu' from India who considered himself a Christian, but then began to ask another visitor for her phone number. 'ADMIN BAN S', a visitor, R, typed. 'R church online is for people like s', replied one of the church leaders. LifeChurch.tv may have decided to invite those searching for online pornography to join Church Online, but not all viewers appreciate the contributions of those who take up the offer.

Groeschel told a final story to illustrate yet another potential impact of Church Online:

> We got an email from a 13-year old boy from Malaysia, a Muslim who had been coming to Church Online secretly, and he committed his life to Christ and he was asking us for some resources that could help him, but we had to mail somewhere secretly or he could be kicked out of his family or something worse.

This tale lead to an announcement. The Malaysian boy asked, 'Can I get this for free?' And Groeschel's answer 'is yes, that's how we do it, we give all this away for free [. . .] It's free to him, but it's not free to us'. 'Because so many people are excited about this', the church has established a new online giving option. 'No hard pitch', Pastor Craig assured his audience, but 'some of you are going to want to give above your normal giving to a place called Digital Missions'. This kind of optional giving is expected in addition to the normal tithe (10 percent of income), not as a way to redistribute giving to a new cause.

Comments about tithing are relatively rare in LifeChurch, generally restricted to one fundraising series per year, but the expectation is a key point to bear in mind when considering the success of Church Online. Financial resources are needed to employ teams of pastors, digital strategists and technical support workers and the hardware, software and bandwidth they rely on. That said, Groeschel took care to show how cost-effective online ministry can be, in keeping with the discourse of tools and techniques encountered above:

> When we reach someone, we call them 'digital touches', just our language. If someone downloads a message, that's one digital touch. If someone comes to Church Online, that's one digital touch. [. . .] A year ago last month we had 362,000 digital touches at only 32 cents each— that includes our whole staff that's devoted to this, all the start-up costs and such. Then one year later, just a month ago, that number increased to over 880 000, 888 000 digital touches, and the cost went down to 8 cents. And here's what's going to happen: we're going to continue to reach more people and the costs are going to continue to go down. And some of you may catch the vision for this and you're going to want to dive in and use your gifts, use your skills, and give to this. And I'll tell you right now, we're not going to be a church like churches used to be, we're going to change, we're going to push the limits, and I promise

you we're going to do anything short of sin to reach people who do not know Christ. The number of people in need is at an all-time high, and this is not just an opportunity, it's a responsibility.

Prayer and sex talk are not the only activities discouraged in public chat. Some contributors sought debate and discussion during the message, and these were directed to other channels by volunteers and other visitors. One self-described atheist posted a series of unconnected questions and statements. Others responded with enquiries—'have you been reborn?'—web links, private email addresses for further conversation, and eventually discouragement. This poster—who seemed to write flawless English—claimed he or she had only studied religion in Italian and Spanish and couldn't understand terms like 'being born again', an interesting example of the opportunities and challenges posed by the global ambitions of LifeChurch. When the atheist poster asked 'So, what is your opinion about the Dead Sea manuscripts?', Brandon Donaldson finally intervened. A brief conversation ensued, scattered over unrelated intervening posts. A here is Donaldson, B the atheist poster, C a volunteer, and D a visitor:

A: B this is not the place write me at [email address]. I love the conversation
B: Brandon, why isn't this the place?
B: I mean, that's the purpose of having a chat, right?
C: B—e-mail [Donaldson's email address] and he would love to talk to you about your questions.
A: This chat is built around this video message to the left. It is to help us engage further with the content there
D: B, it's really to keep on track with the teaching going on
D: But B, if you want to keep in touch, I invite you to follow me on Twitter
D: I'm @ [. . .] I'd like to keep in touch

Sam Han has argued that the presence of moderators in Church Online 'does not influence the discussion very much. Their main task is to minimize trolls, he believes, and 'there is very little "moderating" of the discussion in that sense' (2016: 79). My own observations suggest a more complicated picture. In the example above, Donaldson intervenes repeatedly to guide and shape discussion, establish norms of behaviour and redirect inappropriate lines of conversation. In the earlier example of sex-themed conversation ('anyone interested in sexy chat?'), it was the other chat participants who intervened most strongly to demand expulsion, while the chat moderators themselves gently rebuked both sides and tried to redirect discussion back to the video stream. The moderators of the chatroom took the most active role in all interaction, welcoming newcomers, sharing information about the church and generally ensuring that lively discussion was going on. These volunteers played a crucial role in guiding and maintaining the atmosphere of the chat window, not just in defence against trolls.

The main message lasted half an hour and ended with a shift into a time of prayer. Pastor Craig invited his audience to commit to evangelism, and then closed his eyes, raised his arms and started to pray: 'Give us a heart and a passion for those who don't know your son Jesus'. As viewers prayed around the different campuses, they were instructed to think of someone far from God and work out how to reach them:

> Can you get them a free Bible? Can you refer them to a message? Can you say, 'Hey, I know you'll never go to church, but would you mind meeting me at Church Online? Totally safe, no way you can be endangered. Would you do this with me?''

This was the first of two sets of prayers, a pattern repeated in every Experience. As usual, the first related to that message and the second was a kind of altar call.

Each prayer at a LifeChurch campus involves audience participation through the raising of hands, and this was reproduced online. A specific phrase was highlighted from Groeschel's prayer and posted below the main video window, accompanied by a small silhouette. When the viewer rolled their cursor across the image, the figure moved, shifting from a simple head and shoulders to a dramatically raised arm. In this screenshot (Fig. 8.2), 17 people have announced that they 'give their life' to Jesus. In LifeChurch internal discourse these clicks were referred to as 'salvations', and their total number (according to one staff member I interviewed) rose from 4000 in 2008 to 8600 in 2009.

In the early months of the Internet Campus, the first set of prayers was delivered by Craig Groeschel and the second set by Brandon Donaldson. This mirrored the practice of each local campus, where the campus pastor comes on-stage to deliver the call to decision in person. The immediacy of this personal address is central to the delivery of the prayer. At physical campuses, volunteers line the aisles, look out for raised hands and bring these to the attention of the campus pastor, who then publicly acknowledges them—I can see one hand raised at the front, two on the left at the back and so on. By assigning the decision prayer to Donaldson, the same practice could be pursued online, with each electronic 'hand raised' acknowledged personally, and this call to Christ could come from the same person who spent time talking with the Internet Campus visitors in their chatroom.

By the time of the Experience described here, in mid-2009, this division of labour had ceased. Church Online no longer followed every detail of the Campus system so closely and had changed in other ways too. The vastly increased numbers of Experiences were now manned around the clock by teams of volunteers, with Donaldson appearing only at a few, and it made less sense to suppose that each viewer would have a more personal relationship with Donaldson than Groeschel. One recorded prayer was, perhaps, as good as another. Groeschel's own prayers were broadcast to Church Online, and Donaldson contributed a brief video after the Experience to congratulate new believers.

Figure 8.2 : The 'Salvation' button at Church Online, 2009.

At this time, LifeChurch encouraged anyone who made a 'commitment to Christ' to fill out a 'Communication Card' reporting his or her decision to the church, including a space for 'your story' and a box to check to give permission for that story to be shared anonymously. Anyone who completed a card with their name and address received a free pack called the 'What's Next Kit', including a study Bible, carry case and CDs of messages. Over 1,500 follow-up packages were mailed in 2009 to people who had registered a 'salvation'.

The chat window responded to the decision prayer with great enthusiasm, posting streams of messages praising God, congratulating new believers and declaring faith:

- Call on his name today!
- SURRENDER to Him in love
- i surrender completyly to you

- Heavenly Father, I am a sinner, I need a savior, Save me . . . my life now belongs to you.
- Amen..Welcome to God's family!!!!!!!!!!
- Congratulations to those of you who are committing to Christ right now. This is the most important decision of your life! The Bible says angels in heaven celebrate when just 1 person commits to Christ. Awesome!!
- If you just surrendered your life to the One Jesus, request your What's Next Kit. Link under video,http://Internet.lifechurch.tv/whats-next/ or in the top right corner where it says What's Next.
- Thank you Jesus for drawing these people to You

Notably, none of the 17 who 'raised a hand' discussed their decision in the chat window. Only two postings could be interpreted as reporting some kind of new commitment or conversion, the third and fourth quoted above, and it is far from clear what kind of spiritual decision these statements actually represent.

The whole Experience lasted exactly one hour. This precise duration was carefully planned and executed, requiring perfect timing by every contributor in each of the many campuses to ensure that each component started and ended at the right times and the service flowed flawlessly between on-stage, recorded and live broadcast elements. The decision to fix an Experience at exactly one hour was intentional: as a staff member in Oklahoma explained to me, Americans are accustomed to television shows lasting one hour and might baulk at anything longer.

The event closed with a call-and-response. 'Whoever finds God', Brandon Donaldson declared, 'finds life!', and this key LifeChurch slogan was repeated by many in the chatroom. The video screen cut to show the LifeChurch logo, while a clip of the song 'God of the City' by Chris Tomlin played. 'Greater things are yet to come', sang Tomlin, 'and greater things are still to be done, in this city'.

The community continued to speak to one another for half an hour, discussing their favourite Christian songs and books and sharing theological advice. 'I'm going to be an author', one declared, 'and I want to make a fantasy novel about God. Is there anything that would be blasphemous about putting God in a fictional book?'. Some viewers typed praise for LifeChurch—'Thank God for Lifechurch.tv and the community of believers!'; 'the great thing about church online is that you see people from ALL walks of life'. Others bid farewell, sometimes giving insights into their offline lives as they did so: 'well Im on my way now to server at my Pysical Church . . . I love you all and God bless you all!' At the end of the half-hour, the chatroom closed, without warning; any conversations were cut off, the private prayer lines were no longer available, and communication ceased until the next Experience.

Certain themes were missing from this chatroom discussion, even after the Experience ended. There was also very little conversation relating to offline lives or non-Christian themes and almost no use of humour or play.

Chat covered diverse topics, as quotes above have shown, but most comments responded to the streamed content and participants focused almost exclusively on Christian, devotional communication. They prayed, praised God, congratulated LifeChurch, shared their enthusiasm for the content and engaged in some level of conversation with some of the small minority who seek to ask questions about faith. Attempts at off-topic conversation were quickly quashed.

In the Experiences I attended, there was almost no recognition by visitors of one another. Indeed, at this Experience no visitor posted a comment suggesting that they remember any other visitor from a previous week, despite the very frequent expressions of 'love' for the 'community' and great affection for LifeChurch. To some extent this was a function of the Experience time. The Experience I have described here was one of the busiest of the week, and may therefore be expected to show a particularly high fluctuation in members and volume of chat postings. Smaller Experiences do offer greater opportunities to build recognition. Still, the general point remains valid: Church Online Experiences were not, according to my observations, successful places for generating long-term acquaintances or friendships, apart from connections with and between the volunteers who serve there. We will return to this point below, particularly in our discussion of LifeGroups.

LifeChurch in Second Life

LifeChurch has also created its own space in Second Life, 'Experience Island', launched in 2007 (LifeChurch 2008). In our conversation in Oklahoma, Brandon Donaldson welcomed the virtual world as 'an opportunity to go into a community': 'that's a place where we can actually go to where they are and say well, you've created this world, here's a church, and be able to reach those people that are out there.' Donaldson observed that 'many people use Second Life for things that are not what I would say are healthy, like pornography'—'we want to be that other option, that light, in what we might consider the darkness.' This understanding of the virtual world as a place to be entered echoes theologian Douglas Estes' discussion of Second Life as 'an unreached people group' (2009: 29) waiting for the creation of new churches, or Simon Jenkins' description of the Internet as 'a new town' where 'no one has thought to build a church' (Doney 2004). LifeChurch's evangelistic discourse primarily frames the Internet as a tool, as we have seen, but this is a clear example of the alternative frame identified by Heidi Campbell: the Internet as 'mission field' (2010: 139).

For LifeChurch attenders, Experience Island (Fig. 8.3) would have looked very familiar. According to Donaldson, the design '*is* the Stillwater Oklahoma Campus', exactly reproducing one of LifeChurch's physical locations. The logic here was twofold: 'we wanted to be a campus', a place people would visit to attend Experiences, but also 'it's a great way for people to take a look at a campus' and 'really experience' what visiting LifeChurch was like. Design work was outsourced to a professional company, but volunteers were encouraged to add more creative touches as needed. I visited Stillwater in 2008 and include photographs here to demonstrate the similarity; note the golf cart on the right-hand side of the Stillwater photo (Fig. 8.4), one of several used to ferry the congregation from their cars to the church door.

The attention to detail was striking and went far beyond what might have been required or useful in-world. A visitor in Second Life walked through a lobby area to an auditorium (Fig. 8.5) lined with rows of seats that vastly outnumbered the actual in-world congregation. The Experience was

Figure 8.3 The Second Life Campus, Experience Island, 2008.

Figure 8.4 The Stillwater Campus, Oklahoma, 2008.

Figure 8.5 An Experience at the Second Life campus, 2008.

displayed on three large screens, copying the layout of Stillwater but bringing no in-world benefit—after all, a visitor could zoom in to view whichever screen he or she chose. Note the fairy-clown-fisherman avatar at the bottom right—despite its realistic and conventional architecture, Experience Island did not object to unusual avatar design. Most visitors, however, were more conventionally attired.

Each side of the hall was lined with small tables modelled on those used in local campuses to offer bread and juice for self-administered communion, but these could not be consumed or animated.

Adjoining the lobby, the visitor could find an office—containing an automated avatar responsible for logging traffic—and set of classrooms for children's ministry (Fig. 8.6). This area was also faithfully reproduced from the Stillwater campus, right down to the signs in the hallways and the special LifeChurch wallpaper, even though it could serve no useful function in a world that does not permit under-18s to register.

LifeChurch had not developed any material designed to appeal specifically to Second Life users. According to Donaldson, 'that's not something we feel called to do'—particularly given the small numbers of people attracted each week, which he estimated at around 50 per weekend. LifeChurch couldn't be all things to all people, Donaldson explained, so 'we try to create an environment where God can do what only He can'. LifeChurch had seen that God uses the one-hour Experience format, 'so we try to push that to as many places as we can.' Here again a technological experiment is described in terms of continuity with established success, motivated by confidence in discerning God's approval.

Figure 8.6 The children's ministry corridor at the Stillwater Campus, Oklahoma (left) and at the Second Life campus (right), both 2008.

Figure 8.7 Advertising at the Second Life campus, 2008

Experience Island was monitored by Dylan, a volunteer. Part of Dylan's task was the development of tools and advertising to distribute around Second Life, and here we do see some original and culture-specific material. Dylan offered me a large sword and sheath and a set of controls to animate it, created to advertise a series entitled 'Warrior'. 'At the Movies' was advertised with free movie-star avatars, and freebie clothing decorated with Life-Church logos was on offer in the lobby. The billboard shown here displays an advert for the island, with the slogan 'Prayer in your Underwear'—note also the red sports car parked precariously on the church roof.

Small pavilions on the island advertised the anti-pornography group XXXchurch.com and mysecret.tv, an online confessions project run by Life-Church. Churchgoers might have been in their underwear, but their avatars certainly were not. Donaldson explained these spaces as a 'strategic' response to the guilt felt by some of those in Second Life: 'For those that are looking for help and come to the church, they can find it right there on the island.'

I interviewed seven visitors to Experience Island, including Dylan, and heard various accounts of its appeal. One English visitor, Paula, spoke dismissively of the actual building—'it's like a cinema', she told me, 'how boring!'—and described the island as 'a venue to meet people'. We encountered Paula already as a visitor to the Anglican Cathedral of Second Life, which she described as 'beautiful' and visually 'inspired'. In contrast, Florence showed little concern for architecture—'we could meet anywhere and accomplish the same thing'—but claimed the builders of the Second Life Campus 'did a wonderful job with it [. . .] it does make the church look more "legit"'. Paula and Florence clearly had different expectations of what virtual architecture should try to achieve, or what a 'real' church should look like, but this idea of legitimacy-through-conservatism was echoed across all of my case studies.

Several of my interviewees preferred the island to the Church Online website, because it let them see others watching with them. 'It felt more like "real church" to me', Florence explained, 'I think it feels more like a community.' After discovering Second Life, Florence 'wasn't at all interested in watching on the web site any more.'

Despite this reference to community, one striking feature of Experience Island was its emptiness. Visitors to the Anglican Cathedral engaged one another in conversation after events and at unplanned times throughout the week, but visitors to LifeChurch.tv throughout the period of my observations left the island as soon as services ended. I did discover avatars there on several occasions outside Experience times, but these were often drawn to the space precisely because they knew it would be empty. On one occasion I discovered two women conversing on the roof. They politely talked to me for a few minutes, before explaining that they were trying to discuss the end of their romantic affair and sending me on my way. When I asked Dylan if visitors came to the island to socialise, he seemed unconcerned:

> occasionally, but not much
> for the most part people just come to watch the experience
> [. . .]
> this is a lot more like a real life life church
> ppl meet ppl here and then go somewhere else to do things

For many of my interviewees, like Paula, Experience Island was just one destination in their in-world peregrinations. Gloria, a Swedish-American woman, combined multiple church affiliations to satisfy different aspects of her spirituality:

> lifechurch teaches me to grow in my Christian faith
> and noway church [a Swedish Lutheran church]
> gives me tradition

Gloria also visited other churches in Second Life to find peaceful places for solitary prayer. For participants like Gloria, friendship and companionship were not reasons to attend Experience Island. Reluctance to linger after services reflected their satisfying attachments elsewhere in and out of the virtual world.

Robert Geraci is highly critical of LifeChurch's efforts with Experience Island, arguing that the church 'does not appear to have seen that Second Life is a place, and not merely a tool' (Geraci 2014: 142). The empty island, with its cavernous worship hall and boring branded T-shirts, represents 'a misuse of Second Life's resources' (Geraci 2014: 142), ignoring what really makes Second Life work. Geraci argues that LifeChurch sees its online community as 'subservient to its conventional, physical one' (Geraci 2014: 141), and therefore ignores the opportunity to cultivate new communities of belonging inside the virtual world.

These criticisms are not entirely fair, as we shall see in the following section: a few small LifeChurch community groups did emerge in Second Life, and some more imaginative items were created in-world by enthusiastic volunteers. The real problem of LifeChurch in Second Life, however, was more fundamental. LifeChurch attracts tens of thousands of congregants to its physical campuses every week, while hundreds of thousands watch online, and this scale is made possible by centralised production of high-quality resources. Second Life is a distinctive environment for small gatherings and conversations, and it doesn't support the kind of standardised mass engagement that LifeChurch pursues. Experience Island was never going to work, either as an engagement with Second Life culture or as an expansion of LifeChurch—although it did, for a time, win some positive media coverage (e.g., Teague 2007).

LifeGroups and Watch Parties

The lack of relationship-building activity observed at the Church Online website and in Second Life is offset to some degree by the presence of small groups offering opportunities for contact outside the Experiences. The structure and style of these 'LifeGroups' is enormously diverse, but those I have visited, and the members I interviewed, offer some insights into their activity and culture.

For Brandon Donaldson, LifeGroups are an essential response to ines-capable facts about human existence. 'We're built for relationships', he explained, 'we weren't built to lead a Christian life alone'. I interviewed George, Church Online's LifeGroups and missions pastor, in 2009, and he described small groups as a response to the biblical precedent set by Jesus and the early church. The crowds at Church Online make it easy to 'come and go' without intimate fellowship, but this is unbiblical and ineffective:

> you cannot do Christianity as an individual . . . for creating spiritual transformation I think small groups are more effective than Experi-ences. So my goal would be to see more people engaging in our small groups than in our Experiences [. . .]
>
> LifeGroups [are] where you're going to develop friendships, its where you're going to develop community, it's where you're going to receive encouragement, it's where you get some accountability, and have, in biblical community you're going to have the Word of God, it's going to saturate your life, everything's going to be exposed with it in that kind of a group [. . .]
>
> I would hesitate to see people move further away from any type of commitment, you know, come post on this forum whenever you feel like it. I'd like to see us go the other way and let's start by perhaps meet-ing in a large group setting, then let's come to a small group, then let's email, let's text, let's speak on the phone [. . .] I would look for tools that create greater engagement instead of a loose operating system.

This official emphasis on the centrality of LifeGroups was shared by other interviewees. Jodie argued that 'just attending the Internet Campus on the weekends would not be good', because 'I really believe that the LifeGroup is everything . . . it's where you build community' and are held accountable. For Ken, a LifeGroup leader, Experiences brought people in to hear the gos-pel, but 'we don't believe anything really significant happens' unless people get into groups. 'By connecting with each other', Ken claimed, 'we connect with God.'

Almost all of my interviewees were part of LifeGroups, simply because small, stable groups with regular members proved to be my most successful source of contacts. A minority were not LifeGroup participants, however, and they offered interesting explanations for their resistance to the small group philosophy.

For some, the role of a LifeGroup was already filled in their everyday lives. Lester cited a 15-year friendship group: 'we have a kind of LifeGroup with each other'. Others argued that online LifeGroups could never achieve real fellowship. Mary and Bridget were flatmates in Dublin. For Bridget, online friendship was not meaningful. 'If we're going to do LifeGroups', she explained, 'we're going to have to do physical LifeGroups', and none existed in Dublin. A similar view was expressed by Christina in Austria in the emails we exchanged, with a different rationale:

> I haven't joined a LifeGroup. The only possible LifeGroup would be an online group, which I don't think is a very effective way of doing small-group. There may be a core of committed members, but at the same time there are too many strangers (one-time attendees) just dropping by and listening in. That kind of prevents more deep-going conversations. Don't know, I think smallgroup is best done offline and really meeting up face to face, with people staying from beginning to end.

One interesting feature of several LifeChurch conversations was a disconnection between 'community', which was highly valued, and 'friendship', which was not. Christina came to LifeChurch after finding that many church websites had 'no live online communities', and she valued the chance to connect with people she considered to be like herself: 'I enjoy the community of people [at LifeChurch] who are my age—I'm 30—and who also use modern technology'. For Christina, the key is that 'people are ACTUALLY THERE. It's this virtual place where they meet, but the way they participate online is real: they sing, listen, take notes, talk to each other, etc. With their minds, people are at the same place at the same time.' There is no mention here of the quality of relationships between these people, only of the fact that they are communicating together and sharing an experience. When I asked if she had made friends at LifeChurch, she replied 'No, I haven't started to make friends there, and it isn't important to me. It's a process that takes time, and one that is usually based on sharing a certain life situation, helping each other, similar interests, etc. . . . doing life together, I guess.' The difference here between LifeChurch and the other churches considered in this book is striking.

Those who did join LifeGroups could choose from many themes, audiences and media. Church Online offers text and video chatrooms for Life-Groups, and some use these weekly. Text and video material is provided each week, but groups can choose to use these as they wish or not at all. Leaders have great freedom over the style and theme of the groups, and volunteers are encouraged to lead groups of their own. During my visit to Oklahoma in 2008, the LifeGroups pastor claimed that some 40 groups were meeting online and another 25 face-to-face. This might have added up to a total number of participants in the low hundreds, at most—only a small percentage of the total number said to be viewing Experiences at Church Online at that time.

Rebecca moved from Oklahoma to London with her family to pursue mission work using LifeChurch resources, and subsequently spent time travelling in Eastern Europe to encourage churches there to set up their own 'online campuses'. She also worked as Captain for several Experiences aimed at the GMT time zone, and led a LifeGroup called 'Global Posse'. Posse meetings were held after the 10:00 a.m. GMT Sunday Experience, usually in a text chatroom but sometimes using video. Each meeting started with social conversation, then discussed questions composed by LifeChurch to explore the week's message and closes with prayers. Posse membership was very fluid, with a regular core of three or four and another three or four newcomers each week.

A more stable and relational group was described by Pamela. Her group, 'Friends of the Family', met in a web-cam and text chatroom and communicated through the week via an email list, exchanging several prayer requests each day. Pamela originally wanted to get more 'plugged in' to LifeChurch and to meet a range of new people, and the couple leading her LifeGroup were so supportive of her personal problems and disability that they 'started drawing me in even more'. 'They're family', she explained. The members are all open with one another, to the point of harshness when required, and Pamela considered the leaders especially gifted at such judgement: 'it's like God's given them the exact right words'. These close relationships helped keep her focused and accountable, and included conversations on MSN and email and one opportunity to travel to meet some of the group face-to-face. Pamela had no other friends in LifeChurch at all. The benefits Pamela claimed from her group were powerful and wide-ranging. She had become more positive, 'more outgoing', willing to talk online but also in face-to-face situations. 'I'm not trying to stay in my shy little corner'; the 'healing' God had done in the group was 'part of God's will in showing me that it's OK to open up.'

Other groups focused on a specific theme. Ken ran two groups at once and composed his own curriculum for each. One was intended for new believers and lasted six months, after which members were encouraged to move on to other groups; the series attracted 'a large crowd', he claimed, with around ten people remaining by the end. The other was 'kind of an exclusive group', with six members, intended for people 'who *really* want to study Scripture' and not for the 'weak at heart'.

Groups also met in Second Life, and I met two leaders active there in late 2008. Florence and her real-life husband, also her Second Life partner, ran a group in their house. An array of seating around a video screen allowed participants to watch LifeChurch videos, comment on the questions, and end with prayers.

Noah's LifeGroup (Fig. 8.8) was less conventional in design, meeting at a 'church in the clouds' high above the ground. Four wooden pews were arranged in a square, circled by a ring of large images and video screens. The screens were used by Noah himself to watch the weekly message, streaming from Church Online.

Noah claimed to have gathered up to 20 people at a time to his group, but preferred '5 or 6 true devoters'. He used his group for 'putting people on the

Figure 8.8 Church in the Clouds, a LifeGroup meeting space, 2008

right path and straight', specifically by rejecting in-world sex and relation-ships, but his teachings were not always popular:

> i had one come one time
> told me i spent too much time talking about how people need to be careful in sl
> I told her I really don;t do it enough
> that if you look around sl, you can see i am losing
> and she even agreed.

Noah created his own study material, using messages for inspiration and speaking 'frequently' to staff, but visited Experience Island only rarely and expressed disappointment with the lack of community interaction he saw there.

Florence first bought land in Second Life when a regular LifeChurch attender suggested he would like to start his own LifeGroup and needed a venue. Unfortunately, 'he came 2–3 times and taught the group . . . and just disappeared. And that is how I learned to lead a LifeGroup ;-)'. Leading the group proved 'fun, rewarding, hard, disappointing . . . probably not so different from any RL bible study'. It was rewarding to see people grow, and to feel herself growing in confidence, but hard 'seeing so many people come and go . . . I just haven't seen the stability in our group that I would like, and which I think would be easier to maintain in an RL group.' Noah shared the same complaint, and connected it to his own insistence on truth and virtue:

> I let them know they need to grow
> a lot of times, they dont want to hear me

so i get some that come a time or two
tell me they really like the message
but then they never come back

Sin was a major theme in both interviews, echoing Donaldson's desire for LifeChurch to be the 'light' in the 'darkness' of Second Life. As Florence explained:

> I've [. . .] befriended people who have come to our church and group . . . spent a lot of time building a relationship with them, and then have seen them get involved with some very questionable things on SL . . . and that has been hard for me as well.

These 'questionable things' included 'things like Gor [a domination-themed subculture based on a series of science fiction novels], the really nasty combat sims, strip clubs and the whole sex thing on SL [. . .] SL makes it so easy for people to get involved with the wrong things'.

Online sin was also a constant theme throughout my conversations with Noah:

most of SL is crap
most of sl is a lot of sinning
a lot of lust
even the so-called Christians
I see them all the time
they get hurt
I tell them they need a closer relationship with God
they feel better
then they jump right back into sin :(
it hurts a lot
I know I can feel some of God's pain
but this is how people are
and all we can do is try to help
and if e can't, just move on

Conversations at the Anglican Cathedral also touched on this concern, but it was a much less prominent theme there.

Not all LifeGroups meet online. Using Church Online as a focal point and source of resources, some individuals persuade friends and neighbours to join 'Watch Parties', gathering with them in person to watch Experiences online. As George explained in Oklahoma, 'some say, I don't want a LifeGroup online, I want to engage with my co-workers or people in my neighbourhood or an already existing circle of friends. So we lead through that as well.'

We have encountered one of these offline teams already: Mary and Bridget, the flatmates from Dublin quoted above. These friends decided to invite acquaintances to their flat to watch episodes of the flagship annual series 'At the Movies' and had hosted two such gatherings by the time of our interview. They spoke to people at work, church and a social club they have joined, and organised their computer network to show the Experience on their large flat-screen television. They echoed the movie theme with popcorn, pizza and sweets, and discussed the message afterwards. Three people came to their first meeting, and two to the second. Some who attended were Christians, but others were not. According to Bridget, 'they all so far have really enjoyed it.' LifeChurch offered a perfect chance to show that churches can be modern, young and relevant.

Martin, a Church Online volunteer, had been planting churches in Spain for over a year before our 2009 interview, trying to present 'a modern and relevant Christianity in the 21st century.' Martin decided to use the 'Watch Party' model to host a monthly English-language event called 'Breakfast Church':

> We invite existing contacts to our home to share a full cooked breakfast and then watch a broadcast from LifeChurch, usually the live Sunday morning broadcast, but we have also used downloaded sessions from Open Source at Lifechurch.tv.

Participants were encouraged to sing along with the worship bands, to help offer 'an introduction to church and "church type" behaviour', and 'the style of worship and the talks fits well with our mission objective to reach out to young people and young families.' An average of ten people attended at the time of our conversation, including one or two with no previous church experience; the remainder come from the small congregation of Martin's church plant.

LifeMissions

As we have seen, much of LifeChurch's online activity is motivated by and justified in terms of proselytism, outreach and conversion. Online resources await those who seek them out, Google adverts target those looking for pornography, churchgoers are instructed to invite their friends and anyone watching an Experience online can register their new commitment to Jesus. One of the most active forms of LifeChurch evangelism is the 'LifeMission', and digital versions of mission trips were regularly promoted by Church Online during my ethnographic research. None of the interviewees I spoke to had taken part in a LifeChurch mission, so the accounts here are drawn from the LifeChurch blog and interviews with staff.

By 2009, Church Online had launched a number of online evangelistic projects. According to George, one key strategy has been to develop resources that churchgoers can promote to their own contacts:

One of the things that we identified early on was to leverage people's place in their social networks [. . .] Something that we say is, 'Make Your Space His Space.' So we've created tags, we've created banners, we've created badges, we've done video that people can embed, to reach out and share the name of Jesus and LifeChurch, use it as marketing, sort of viral marketing for LifeChurch.tv.

Church Online has also scheduled short-term evangelistic events, encouraging churchgoers to engage their online networks with prayer and conversation at particular times. In May 2009 (LifeChurch 2009) and April 2010 (LifeChurch 2010), 'Online Micro-Missions' encouraged participants to spend an hour sending personal prayers to as many of their Twitter followers and Facebook friends as possible. MicroMission participants were encouraged to take part as groups, using a private chatroom to pray together beforehand, support one another during the event and share stories afterwards.

Some initiatives have tried to inspire work in the individual's local area, using online tools and resources to publicise events and share success stories. George offered an example:

We've done an event called Revolutionary Love [. . .] it was kind of a random acts of kindness, where you would do something for someone and you would either have a talk or you would just leave a card saying why you scraped the ice off their windshield or why you bought their Starbucks or why you raked their yard or bought their meal at a restaurant, and it was just to show the love of Christ in very tangible ways, and where the web came in, obviously people signed up and we notified people but then we asked people to come back and post their stories, and we felt that that inspired other people to go out and do the same.

Other missions have been aimed at specific categories of people. My arrival in Oklahoma coincided with the launch of a 'Military Mission', and Church Online visitors were encouraged to participate by sending mail 'to tell a veteran or a soldier thank you for serving', posting prayers online or sending out care packages. Some, George hoped, would be willing 'to actually start a support group, one of our small groups, a life group, targeted specifically at our soldiers and their spouses.' Another mission initiative was organised independently by a truck driver, who printed out cards and copied messages and left them at truck stops to advertise Church Online.

Conclusion

The style of online churchgoing developed by LifeChurch is quite different from that pursued in the other churches we have considered. Church Online is larger and more hierarchical and shows no interest in liturgical styles of worship. Preaching and music are more central to Experiences than times of open prayer. The congregation does not encourage the kinds of debate and questioning that other churches considered essential, and friendship is not generally a priority. If we return again to the seven themes we have discussed at the end of each case study, we can see that all of them emerge in significantly different ways in Church Online.

1. Scale. Experiences at Church Online far exceed the other churches described in this book, both in frequency and in size of audience. Church Online relies on centralised production of high-quality video resources, including the messages of a popular preacher and new music from skilled performers, and new Experiences can be launched just by repeating the same content with new chatroom hosts. Viewers do not expect to be involved in consensus-based decision-making or to make friends across the whole community. Paid advertising raises the profile of the church and avoids reliance on media coverage. These are all significant advantages for an organisation that is looking to grow quickly, avoiding many of the limitations that restrict the potential size of the other churches we have considered.

2. Local Churchgoing. No visitor survey was published by Church Online, but once again the vast majority of those I encountered were or had been regular churchgoers. Most Experiences included chatroom contributions challenging LifeChurch views, but these received little if any support. Other contributors sought to silence, convince or convert such posters, strongly suggesting that the great majority of participants are already committed to the LifeChurch style of Christianity.

    At the same time, there were some interesting exceptions. Several of my interviewees from different online churches said that they only attended online, but they attributed this decision to disability, geographical remoteness or a negative experience in a local church. Christina from Austria was almost unique among my interviewees in admitting that she attended an online church simply because she preferred it: she was looking for preaching, and Church Online offered the best.

3. Community. A sense of community was important to visitors at Church Online, but in a different form from that so highly valued elsewhere. Worshipping alongside other people seemed to be key for my interviewees, rather than debating new ideas or forming close friendships. Church Online was not designed for open discussion, and while some found friends in LifeGroups, many insisted they had other priorities.

4. Ritual and Spiritual Experience. Some praised the worship music, others were indifferent, but the main spiritual benefits cited in interviews came from the preaching of Craig Groeschel. Preaching delivered a focused, clear, authoritative, challenging message that set the vision and tone for the whole church. Church Online's emphasis on teaching and focus on making new disciples were quite different from the other

churches studied, where more discursive, meditative, participatory and often ritualised kinds of spiritual experience were preferred.

5. Familiarity. Continuity was again key to site and worship design, but for different reasons. LifeChurch represents an evangelical Christian tradition in which religious symbolism is deliberately downplayed and styles of architecture, dress and music respond to contemporary secular fashions. Nonetheless, the structures and styles of LifeChurch were still reproduced carefully online. Those patterns were seen as techniques that had been proven effective, and must therefore have received divine approval. This reliance on familiarity began to change with the move from Internet Campus to Church Online, but the basic model remained similar.

6. Internal Control. Discipline was a major concern, with debate and dissent in the chatroom quickly silenced. The church platform offered limited opportunities for interaction, particularly in the early versions of the Internet Campus. Trusted volunteers guided chat discussion and operated private prayer channels, while other participants often stepped in if anyone failed to follow chatroom norms. At the same time, the level of delegation to these volunteers was high: anyone could lead a LifeGroup, for example, using freely available teaching resources.

7. External Funding and Oversight. No other group studied showed such a strong connection to a particular local church, or such lavish resources. The other four churches were maintained through generous commitment from volunteer designers and operated with a considerable degree of independence from their funders or denominations. At Church Online, on the other hand, dedicated staff could commit time and finances to original, complex, sophisticated design work and community management, fully integrated into the overall strategy of the LifeChurch organisation.

References

Campbell, H., 2010. *When Religion Meets New Media*. London: Routledge.

Doney, M., 2004. Computer church. *Church Times*, 14 May.

Estes, D., 2009. *SimChurch: Being the Church in the Virtual World*. Grand Rapids: Zondervan.

Fast Company, 2011. Most creative people 2011: 97. Bobby Gruenewald. *Fast Company*, 18 May. [online] Available at: <https://www.fastcompany.com/3018502/most-creative-people-2011/97-bobby-gruenewald> [Accessed 1 September 2016]

Flory, R. and Miller, D., 2008. *Finding Faith: The Spiritual Quest of the Post-Boomer Generation*. London: Rutgers University Press.

Geraci, R., 2014. *Virtually Sacred: Myth and Meaning in World of Warcraft and Second Life*. Oxford: Oxford University Press.

Gruenewald, B., 2009. Why church online? *Swerve*. [blog] Available at: <https://web.archive.org/web/20090816165242/http://swerve.lifechurch.tv/2009/08/13/why-church-online/> [Accessed 02 September 2016]

Han, S., 2016. *Technologies of Religion: Spheres of the Sacred in a Post-secular Modernity*. London: Routledge.

Hutchings, T., 2015. E-reading and the Christian Bible. *Studies in Religion/Sciences Religieuses* 44(4), pp. 423–440.

LifeChurch, 2008. LifeChurch.tv second life campus tour, 5 February. [online video] Available at: <https://www.youtube.com/watch?v=1MB4Gwg0k_U> [Accessed 1 September 2016]

———, 2009. Online micro-mission opportunity. *Church Online*, 28 April. [blog] Available at: < https://web.archive.org/web/20100610111328/http://Internet. lifechurch.tv/2009/04/online-micro-mission-opportunity/> [Accessed 1 September 2016]

———, 2010. Easter online mission opportunity. *Church Online*, 24 March. [blog] Available at: <https://web.archive.org/web/20120501032852/http://Internet. lifechurch.tv/2010/03/easter-online-mission-opportunity/> [Accessed 1 September 2016]

Miller, D., 1997. *Reinventing American Protestantism: Christianity in the New Millennium*. London: University of California Press.

Mullins, T., 2011. Online Church: A biblical community. *DMin. Liberty Baptist Theological Seminary*. [online] Available at: <http://digitalcommons.liberty.edu/ cgi/viewcontent.cgi?article=1467&context=doctoral> [Accessed 31 August 2016]

Parr, B., 2009. HOW TO: Chat in real-time in 45 languages. *Mashable*, 21 June. [online] Available at: <http://mashable.com/2009/06/21/babelwith-me/> [Accessed 31 August 2016]

Sødal, H., 2010. "Victor, not victim": Joel Osteen's rhetoric of hope. *Journal of Contemporary Religion* 25(1), pp. 37–50.

Teague, D., 2007. Give me that online religion: Virtual religious services are gaining in popularity. *NBC News*, 21 May. [online] Available at: <http://www.nbcnews. com/id/18789168/ns/nbc_nightly_news_with_brian_williams/t/give-me-online-religion/#.V8hUHWVlui4> [Accessed 31 August 2016]

Wilson, G., 2004. In cyberspace, can anyone hear you pray? *BBC News Online Magazine*, 12 May. [online] Available at: <http://news.bbc.co.uk/1/hi/magazine/ 3706897.stm> [Accessed 1 September 2016]

9 Creating Church Online
Media Design and Media Logic

So far, we have considered our five online churches holistically, using an ethnographic approach to represent something of the norms and practices of each group and the experiences of their members. We have identified degrees of continuity and change in styles of worship, visual and architectural forms and structures of religious authority, heard from group founders about their aims and intentions, and reflected on what participants say about their own experiences and their motivations for joining these groups.

In this chapter, we will use these case studies to make sense of the role of religious institutions in the design and adoption of technology. We will test the merits of two well-known approaches: the religious-social shaping of technology or RSST (Campbell 2010), which emphasises the agency of religious designers, and the institutional approach to the mediatization of religion (Hjarvard 2008), which emphasises conformity to a pre-established 'logic' of the media.

These theories are strikingly different in their implications, and each needs some adjustment to suit the particular context of online churches. At the end of this chapter, I will suggest that we can profitably combine these two approaches to construct a new model of 'mediatized religious design' (MRD), focusing on how group values and media logics are constructed and contested discursively in the creation of an online church. Church leaders struggle to decide which aspects of their traditions should shape a new technology, to discern the themes that will prove most appealing to their target audience and to identify a 'logic' for successful media communication. New perceptions of community values and media logics emerge through engagements with technology, and those engagements can often be hotly debated.

The Religious-Social Shaping of Technology

In each of our five case studies, we saw that founders tried to create a new online space that would enable them to meet certain of the goals of their affiliated denomination or sponsor church (such as evangelism, re-engagement with society or experimental exploration of the possibilities of online media). All five projects hoped to achieve these ends by creating a kind of online community of prayer, worship and conversation. In each case, the church that eventually took shape was not quite what its founders had had in mind.

The social shaping of technology (SST) is an area of research that focuses on the processes through which groups design, use and interpret technology, and it offers a great deal of insight for the study of how online religion is constructed. Heidi Campbell has pioneered its application to the field of digital religion, and we will focus on her approach here. Campbell describes SST as the study of 'how and why a community of users responds to a technology in a certain way', including 'what values or beliefs influence this negotiation' (Campbell 2010: 58). The key insight of SST research is that 'technology is negotiable' (Campbell 2010: 50): users evaluate a new technology, identify opportunities and seek to resist aspects that they consider dangerous, and this leads to innovations in design, new strategies for use and the emergence of a new rhetoric to construct an appropriate place for the technology within the routines of group life. A technology therefore comes to have meaning only within a specific social context, and it can have different meanings and impacts for different users in different locations.

Campbell argues that these basic insights must be developed further to help understand the specific technological practices of religious communities, in which 'unique' constraints are imposed by 'spiritual, moral, and theological codes of practice' (Campbell 2010: 59). To make sense of a religious community's engagement with technology, SST researchers need 'a deeper awareness of the role history and tradition play' in the negotiation process, understanding that technologies are imagined and used 'in light of a religious community's beliefs, moral codes, and historical tradition of engagement with other forms of media technology' (Campbell 2010: 59). To encourage this awareness, Campbell has proposed a four-stage model called the 'religious-social shaping of technology' (RSST), and this approach has been extensively used and discussed among scholars of digital religion (e.g., Lundby 2012).

The first stage of the RSST model, 'History and Tradition', focuses on the historical origins of a community's attitudes to media. Text is particularly important, Campbell argues, because 'decisions made regarding texts . . . often serve as a sort of template for future negotiation with other media' (Campbell 2010: 60). The second stage, 'Core Beliefs and Patterns', considers 'how religious communities live out their core social values in the contemporary context' (Campbell 2010: 60). The third stage is the 'Negotiation Process' through which communities 'draw on their history, tradition, and their core beliefs' to evaluate a new technology (Campbell 2010: 61). The community must decide if old norms still apply, or if some features of a new technology raise new challenges. Some aspects of the technology may have to be adapted to better suit the needs and values of the group. The distribution of authority within the community is key during this process, determining 'who has the right to govern media decision-making and be involved in innovation'. The fourth and final stage of Campbell's model is 'Communal Framing and Discourse', in which the community seeks to justify its approach to the new technology, to reaffirm its traditions and to create boundaries for acceptable use.

In our conversations, the founders and leaders of online churches frequently referred to the history, ideas and values of their Christian traditions. In Mark Brown's account of the design of the Anglican Cathedral, for example, he stressed the need to create something 'very clearly Christian, an icon, a symbol of Christianity.' Brown's intent was to produce a space that audiences would recognise, while the LifeChurch Internet Campus pastor described the familiarity of his online platform as an act of obedience: 'we don't want to do anything outside what you're already doing, God.' In his sermons and media writings, Richard Thomas spoke extensively of the Benedictine ideals of i-church, its commitment to an Anglican understanding of mission and its location within the diocese of Oxford. Campbell's model of RSST reminds us to take these claims seriously, analysing these churches as technologies produced in very specific ideological and social contexts.

On the other hand, the model also needs some adjustment. For example, Campbell argues that religious leaders evaluate a new technology by 'contextualising it within a larger history of the community in relation to media and technology appropriation' (Campbell 2010: 65). This can be true for some technologies in some traditions—I have applied the RSST model in other research to analyse digital Bible publishing among American evangelical Christians, for example (Hutchings 2015)—but in these five case studies, references to older media traditions were actually quite rare. St Pixels has featured on the British television programme 'Songs of Praise', but I saw no evidence that any church was explicitly drawing on television and radio broadcasting as a model for its online activities. In interviews with staff members at Church Online, TV evangelism was mentioned only as an example of what not to do. Debates about online communion were commonplace across the five case studies, but I saw very few signs of interest in or even awareness of the debates that once raged around radio and television sacraments.

For participants in these online churches, more relevant historical comparisons were found in parish ministry, church-planting, experimental communities and the history of missionary projects. As Campbell points out, Christian discourses about the Internet often identify digital media as a 'mission field' (2010: 137; see Chapter 2), a place that must be claimed for Christ by heroic acts of evangelism. This kind of language was prominent across all case studies, but other understandings of mission also featured: Richard Thomas, for example, framed i-church's online ministry as part of the Church of England's mission to the whole of society. I-church and St Pixels both formed links with the Fresh Expressions movement of local church initiatives, on the basis of a shared approach to community experimentation.

The 'History and Tradition' stage of Campbell's RSST is clearly important, but these religious technologies draw on a much wider range of precedents than decisions about texts.

The concept of 'community' is very important in Campbell's account of RSST, and this also requires some closer examination. For Campbell, a religious community is 'a network of social relationships, connected through a set of communal life practices' (2010: 8) and a shared history. This kind of community is distinctive, with clear institutional and structural boundaries, and it shares a common story, ideology and theology, supported by 'distinctive patterns of practice and circulating discourse' (2010: 9). The religious-social shaping of technology is a model for technology development at the level of this kind of community.

Campbell actually uses one of the churches discussed in this book (the Anglican Cathedral of Second Life) as a case study for her argument (2010: 123–127), but online churches do not seem to fit neatly with this definition of 'community'. When my interviewees spoke about community, they were not necessarily referring to a network of social relationships linked by a common story and a shared theology. In St Pixels, the shared story of the group was important and social relationships were crucial, but members shared a common theology only in the very broadest sense. The intense theological debates on the group's forums were a particular attraction for some members (and less attractive for others). Participants in the online campus of LifeChurch also praised the 'community', and they did seem to share a common theology to a much greater degree, but in this case only a few had invested in personal relationships. The LifeChurch online community was united by a carefully enforced repertoire of shared emotions and shared language, not by a shared social network. Participants were committed to a story of future growth and success rather than shared memories. In both of these churches, we see only some aspects of what Campbell refers to as 'community'.

We must also recognise the internal complexity of religious communities. The RSST model tends to see technology production as the work of 'the community' as a unified whole, but we must remember the different contributions and often rivalries that actually constitute that process. The distribution of decision-making authority within a group is not static; it must be regularly renegotiated, and technology design can be a catalyst for that process. Established bureaucracies and leaders tend to be slow to respond to unexpected opportunities, and this can leave space for those on the margins of a group to attempt to seize the initiative through the development of new media and technology projects. Conversely, once the value of a new technology has been recognised, established leaders can draw on their symbolic and financial resources to defuse the destabilising potential of that technology by integrating it (and its users) back into the structure and activity of the group. The religious-social shaping of technology is pushed forward by specific pioneers, leaders and supporters and opposed by particular critical voices within the community, and individuals can take up and set aside different roles in this process over time. Different camps can emerge within a community, promoting different visions of how technology should be shaped and used.

The internal politics of the technology-shaping process can include acts of dissent, resistance and silencing and intensely emotive conflict. We have seen evidence of conflict throughout this book, from the trolling of Church of Fools—generated, at least in part, by different expectations of social norms within the virtual space—to the multiple leadership crises experienced by i-church. Campbell uses the Anglican Cathedral of Second Life as one of her examples, but presents a relatively homogenous picture of the group's attitude to leadership. This group actually endured intense and long-lasting internal disagreements over authority, and these were described to me very differently by different participants. When one leader resigned, her contributions to the Cathedral landscape suddenly disappeared (as described in Chapter 7)—but was that her own act of vandalism, or an attempt by the remaining leaders to 'exorcise' her? Interviewees volunteered both interpretations. A complete account of the social shaping of religious technologies must include space for these moments of conflict and acts of violence, which can significantly influence how community members relate to one another and to their technology. Campbell's language of 'negotiation' suggests that religious communities produce technology through harmonious collaboration in pursuit of common goals, but at times that process becomes something rather less consensual.

These discussions of history, community and negotiation bring us to the final and most important issue to be considered here. In Campbell's model, 'communal framing and discourse' is the fourth stage of the social shaping of technology, in which the group decides how to speak about the technology it has produced. We must remember, however, that discourse is not separate from the other stages of the process. When Richard Thomas spoke of i-church as part of the Anglican mission to the whole of society, for example, he summoned a discourse that was simultaneously part of the history that motivated the project (stage one), a claim about contemporary community values (stage two), an explanation of church design decisions (stage three) and part of the communal framing that explained how the project should be understood (stage four).

If every stage of the social shaping of technology in religious communities relies on discursive constructions, then we need a more dynamic model. Historic and contemporary values, beliefs and practices can only be identified as 'core' discursively and competitively: different actors throughout the technology-shaping process attempt to claim one aspect or another as nonnegotiable, and other actors may disagree. Leaders and followers may have quite different understandings of what 'really matters' about their community. The idea of 'core'-ness is strategically valuable, because it helps to rally (or deflect) support for particular projects and to defuse (or provoke) criticism. The understanding of a group as a 'community' is itself also produced through competing discourses, in which boundaries are drawn, norms established and membership contested. The representation of a group as a 'community' (or not) and particular values as 'core' (or not) are essential parts of the 'communal framing' process, for both supporters and critics, and feed back into future iterations of technology design.

The values identified as 'core' shift over time according to the needs of particular interactions. For example, several of the online church projects discussed in this book initially emphasised the 'core' importance of long-term stable commitment and developed technologies to support that kind of belonging (like the i-church pastoral groups or the first LifeChurch chatrooms). As the churches developed, participants proved to be more interested in other practices (like prayer), and stability was accordingly downplayed in official church discourse. In the Avatar Wars of Church of Fools, an intense dispute broke out over the replacement of the small images used to identify each member's profile. For church leaders, these images were trivial, but for some members image choice was a key part of their online identity. Leaders were forced to reconsider their perception of the core values of the community. It is often only through processes of negotiation and change that participants come to realise and articulate which aspects of their community are most important to them.

This approach also has methodological implications. We cannot study the religious-social shaping process merely by interviewing a community leader or designer, because they can only offer one construction of the history and meaning of the technology. The account of the design process offered in such an interview is likely to sound a lot like Campbell's RSST model, because it is politically advantageous for project leaders to reassure their sponsors and critics that their new technology is nothing more than a continuation of timeless group values. We can use leadership interviews to analyse how a project is framed and promoted, but this will not show us how project goals have changed over time, or if the leaders' vision met with resistance. To gain a nuanced understanding of how a technology is shaped over time, we need to observe that shaping process directly, participating in the community in search of evidence to contextualise the narratives offered in expert interviews. In other words, we need ethnography.

Campbell's four-stage model of the religious-social shaping of technology makes a valuable contribution to our study of digital religion, by reminding us to consider religious communities as active critics, constructors and adopters of technology, motivated at least in part by the distinctive priorities of their own traditions. In this discussion, I have drawn on my case studies of online churches to suggest some areas in which the model needs adaptation. We need a more recursive, iterative, heterogenous understanding of the process of technological development in religious contexts, with more room for resistance, conflict and competing visions. As we have seen, religious leaders, designers and technology users can have quite different values, needs, ambitions and interests, and the social shaping of religious technology emerges through the collision of all their different projects.

Our discussion so far has focused on the religious community itself, as a self-contained unit engaged in producing new technology, and we have already seen that this focus can be useful. However, we cannot fully understand technology development by studying a religious community in isolation. We must also consider the inherent limitations and affordances of the technology itself, and the engagement of the community with norms that have already developed around that technology. Religious communities have considerable freedom to shape technology through the RSST process, but that freedom is not unlimited. We need a counter-theory, an approach that can complement this focus on the agency of religious actors and enhance our understanding of the wider relationship between religion and digital media.

The Mediatization of Religion

We can find a helpful candidate for that counter-theory in the concept of 'mediatization', which we will apply here to analyse the encounter between a communicator and the inherent 'logic' of the medium they are trying to use. Rather than emphasising agency, mediatization emphasises the subordination of institutions—including religion—to requirements of communication that are imposed by media systems themselves. Debates over the definition and usefulness of the concept of mediatization are extensive (see Finnemann 2011 for a summary of different variants, and see Lövheim 2014 for a survey of the debate as applied to the study of religion), but this institution-focused approach makes a very useful contribution to our discussion in this chapter. The institutional approach to mediatization helps to identify some of the factors that guide church leaders and designers, beyond their own ideas about their core values and practices, and it is therefore a useful complement to the RSST approach introduced above.

According to Stig Hjarvard, 'religion is increasingly being subsumed under the logic of the media' (2008: 11). He describes a process that operates on two levels: the media confront religious institutions from the outside, and they become part of institutions from the inside. Media companies like newspapers, radio stations and television broadcasters function as independent institutions, with their own interests to pursue. These media institutions structure how information is accessed and communicated, adopt symbols and concepts from religious traditions to use in their own storytelling and represent religion through the genres of popular culture. As older social institutions like 'family, school and church' have gradually lost their authority, 'the media have to some extent taken over their role as providers of information and moral orientation [and] have become society's most important storyteller about society itself' (2008: 13).

At the same time, mediatization also operates within institutions, as a part of their daily communicative activity. Religious organisations publish their own newspapers, sponsor radio stations, coordinate their activities by email, create public Facebook pages and so on. Hjarvard sees religious media like these as 'less mediatized' than the representations of religion in journalism or television dramas, because religious organisations can exercise more control over their own media (2012: 30). Nonetheless, even when a religious institution owns its means of communication it must still adapt to the logic of the media. 'Religious media come to be judged by the same standards as other media', Hjarvard points out, 'including their ability to use technology and genres in an appropriate and interesting way' (2012: 31). This creates opportunities for new communicators with media talent and resources to gain attention and challenge more established authorities.

Peter Fischer-Nielsen makes a similar distinction in his study of the digital mediatization of the Church of Denmark. The Internet becomes a new communicative context, in which Danish people can find religious information without needing to pay any attention to traditional institutions, and Fischer-Nielsen describes this process as 'the mediatization of religion' (2012: 45). This kind of mediatization takes place within 'a media-saturated environment', as Knut Lundby argues, in which 'various media provide a horizon for the communication and interaction between individuals, part of which is about religion' (Lundby 2013: 199). There is nothing new about mediation, of course, but Lundby uses these concepts of saturation and horizons to distinguish mediatization today from earlier historical periods in which media were more restricted in access and more closely embedded in specific social contexts.

The Church of Denmark has also begun using digital media extensively for its own communication and internal organisation. As Hjarvard argues, the media becomes an independent social institution, but at the same time, it also becomes part of other institutions. Fischer-Nielsen describes this as a separate process, 'the mediatization of church' (2012: 45), which includes the efforts of the denomination and its pastors to reorganise their communication, gain new access to information and ideas and reestablish their social authority. The state church generates its own 'mediatized world' (Hepp and Krotz 2014), which only sometimes intersects with the other worlds that make up the media-saturated environment of Danish society.

Hjarvard has used the crisis over cartoons of Mohammed that erupted in Denmark in 2006 as one example of the significance of mediatization for religious institutions. As Hjarvard points out, the conflict was 'not primarily controlled by religious actors', but rather 'instigated and structed by a series of media dynamics', including the initiative shown by particular journalists, the wider framing of Islam in the news media at that time, 'popular mobilization through various mobile and digital media', and so on (2012: 21). This was 'a *mediatized conflict*', because 'the media became partly constitutive of the ways in which this clash over public representations of religion was played out.' Religious institutions can use their own media to promote their own perspectives and interpretations, but—at least in the Danish context— these efforts attract much less public attention.

In Stig Hjarvard's formulation, the process of mediatization operates antagonistically. The (secular) media gains power at the expense of religious institutions. Journalists and broadcasters begin to define what religion is and what parts of religion are most important, and the public increasingly encounters religious symbols and identities only through news coverage, movies, novels, TV shows and games. When religion is 'subsumed' under the logic of the media (2008: 11), religious institutions lose some of their authority.

This understanding has been challenged, particularly outside the highly secularised societies of northern Europe with their historic state churches, and it is worth noting three particularly relevant critiques. First, some religious traditions are much more compatible with 'media logics' than others. When Evangelical Christians developed a print culture in the 19th century, for example, 'religious actors and beliefs played an active part in the development of these media forms' (Lövheim 2014: 554). The production and circulation of tracts did not represent a loss of control:

> [they] did not need to incorporate the logic of print media or give up control of the communication of the sacred to secular media producers, because much of the modus operandi of these new media practices were already integrated with their beliefs about the religious message.
> (Lövheim 2014: 554)

In the same way, when LifeChurch uses Church Online to broadcast the sermons of Craig Groeschel, they must adapt to the requirements of cameras and screens—but those requirements have already been absorbed into LifeChurch culture. Congregations at all LifeChurch sites can watch Groeschel on a screen, whether they are online or visiting a local campus.

Second, even if some degree of change is needed, achieving conformity with media logic can still seem highly attractive to religious institutions. Andreas Hepp and Viktoria Krönert have analysed the branding of the Pope by the Catholic Church at World Youth Day to demonstrate that religious organisations can use the frameworks of media culture in an attempt to reinforce their own values, identities and forms of belonging (2010: 274). When the Methodist and Anglican Churches invested in the launch of Church of Fools and i-church, they understood that they were supporting new kinds of community, but that opportunity to experiment with new social formations was a major aspect of the projects' appeal. The relationship between religion and media in these examples is more complex than some forms of the mediatization thesis might suggest.

The third critique to be considered is the most fundamental. Is the idea of 'media logic' really helpful in digital contexts? The concept has a long history in media studies, but it was first developed for the study of mass media. In the late 1970s, David Altheide and Robert Snow argued that the media had become 'the dominant institutions in contemporary [American] society'

(1979: 9) and 'the dominant force to which other institutions conform' (1979: 15). The media operated according to 'a particular logic of its own', they argued, and they defined this 'media logic' as 'the process through which media present and transmit information' (1979: 10). Through the demands of media logic, the different institutions of society had been absorbed into a shared 'media culture', characterised by two key characteristics: an expectation of rational efficiency in communication, which must be accurate, up-to-date and relevant to the audience; and a demand that every form of media must be entertaining. Altheide and Snow identify religion as an example of this media logic in action, noting that Christian leaders had 'adopted a television entertainment perspective to reach the people' (1979: 11).

There are some immediate parallels here to the case studies we have considered, because the online churches discussed in this book did show great interest in seizing media attention. The press releases produced by Church of Fools emphasised the quirkiest aspects of the project and its satanic adversaries, and received worldwide coverage. Mark Brown emphasised the need to 'create buzz' with the design and name of the Anglican Cathedral, and attracted interest both inside and beyond Second Life. In both cases, we see a Christian group adapting to media logic by trying to produce the kinds of visuals and narratives that journalists want to write about, just as Altheide and Snow argued.

Identifying a 'logic' to digital media is not quite so straightforward. Online, content can be produced, circulated, accessed and edited by independent users, without the involvement of traditional media companies. Religious institutions can construct their own media channels and platforms, and online communities can develop their own unique cultures. The idea of 'media logic' implies something linear and rigid, and some have argued that the phrase is therefore inappropriate for describing online networks. According to Finnemann, for example, we should replace language of 'logic' with a more flexible discussion of 'cultural grammar' (2011: 83), understanding digital media as a set of constraints, affordances and biases that can be deployed in different ways. According to Nick Couldry, mediatization is now best understood as 'a meta-process that emerges from the continuous, cumulative circulation and embedding of media contents across everyday social action, rather than as a reproductive logic or recipe already lodged somehow with media contents themselves' (2013: 3).

The creators of online churches do have to reckon with constraints, affordances and biases, and we can briefly consider what this reckoning might involve. Church-builders need to understand the Internet on four different levels, as infrastructure, platforms, formats and data, and on each level there are rules to learn, expectations to satisfy and commercial companies to engage with.

The infrastructural level concerns the materiality of digital media, including the affordances of the particular devices that audiences will be using.

Online churches are accessed through cameras, keyboards, microphones, wireless Internet connections, tablets, smartphones and so on, and this collection of technologies structures what can be communicated or received, by whom and in what context.

The second level addresses the platform through which media content circulates. If a church chooses to create a Facebook page, they must abide by the often-changing rules and regulations imposed by Facebook, adapt their communication to fit the possibilities that Facebook offers and tolerate the algorithms through which Facebook selects which content to show to which users. A church can choose to build their own website instead, to evade these limitations, but any platform they create will still have its own set of affordances.

The format level addresses the expectations and interests of the audience. Digital communication is evaluated by users accustomed to particular genres and styles, just like any other form of communication. Readers of a Christian blog already know what they expect a blog to be like, and people who visit a Christian video-sharing website will almost certainly be familiar with YouTube. To attract an audience, an online church must learn how to adapt its message to satisfy these expectations. Of course, format preferences may be distinctive to the particular group the communicator wishes to reach, and a style that plays well to one audience may be rejected by another. Format calculations rely in part on evaluations of the culture and interests of potential congregants, but also on understandings of what it takes to be successful in digital environments.

The data level recognises that online content can be circulated, tracked, measured and analysed. If material can potentially travel into new networks, then the new church must either learn what kinds of content are most likely to be shared or develop rules to prevent this from happening. The church can also gain access to unprecedented data about the spiritual practices of its members, and in some cases that data may also be recorded and analysed by commercial companies and government organisations. Church-builders must work out what data exists and how that data could be used, make decisions about how to analyse their own members, and decide how much those members need to know about their data security.

This simple categorization is not exhaustive, but it is already clear that it will be difficult to identify a single linear media logic at work across all of these levels. There are constraints, affordances and rules at work in digital media, but they vary from device to device and platform to platform. Nonetheless, I will argue here that the language of 'logic' still has its advantages. Church designers are faced with a complex and uncertain situation, in which the exact details of platform design, algorithms and data analysis practices are often inaccessible and the preferences of online audiences can be unpredictable. In response, they must develop their own theories of digital success, and these stories about media can be understood as constructions of media logic.

Instead of looking for a fixed, universal logic that is inherent within digital media and media industries, we can therefore analyse the discourses about media that circulate through institutions. As Marcus Moberg has argued in his very helpful study of the 'technologization of discourse' in the Church of Finland, media logics can be understood as particular sets of ideas about what institutions need to do in order to use digital media effectively, discourses that call on organisations 'to adapt and conform to new technological realities' (Moberg forthcoming). Such ideas are always provisional, open to disagreement and adjustment, and an institution's perceptions of the logic of digital media can change over time.

Constructions of digital media logic recur throughout discussions of online church, including press releases, reports, sermons and my own interviews with church leaders. In some cases, the founders and leadership teams of online churches were confident that they had grasped the right way to use digital media. In other cases, interviewees emphasised their unfamiliarity with the logic of the new medium, describing their church project as an experiment. The language of experiment is of course ambiguous, working to emphasise the bravery of the project or the miraculous nature of its success against the odds, while also minimising the embarrassment caused if expectations are not met. These two modes of confident or experimental speech could sometimes be combined: Simon Jenkins, for example, describes Church of Fools as an attempt 'to try translating church into the medium of the net . . . to find out if online church is a viable way to "do church"' (2008: 99), but he also boasts that worship teams 'quickly learned what worked for online church', as if only one kind of liturgy can really succeed in a virtual environment (2008: 108–109). Jenkins is not just reporting what worked for a particular audience or a particular environment, or what a particular group of leaders felt able to manage, or what the values of a particular tradition demanded. He is making a universal claim about what works online—the logic of the medium.

'Media logic' is not just a set of affordances and processes but also a discourse, an argument about how to use media effectively, and it is made concrete as a set of propositions about the kind of communication that a specific medium requires. The 'mediatization of the church' (Fischer-Nielsen 2012), the integration of digital media into the everyday workings of Christian organisations, is heavily influenced by the circulation of discourses about what the 'logic' of digital media might be. Ideas about how to be successful online as a Christian organisation are promoted by an advice industry that includes popular books, magazines, conferences, websites, social media channels and consultancy work.

Mediatization theory helpfully reminds us that even religiously controlled media must meet technical requirements and audience expectations in order to communicate effectively and compete for attention. Communicators must acknowledge the affordances of their infrastructure and their chosen platform, the expectations of their audience and the future uses of the data they are producing. In practice, this means developing an understanding of what it takes to be successful online, and this understanding is always open to challenge in the face of new ideas, experiences and user feedback. Online churches are operated by religious groups for religious purposes, in line with Heidi Campbell's model of RSST, but their independent agency is still constrained and their understanding of those constraints is always incomplete.

Mediatized Design: Combining the Two Approaches

The religious-social shaping of technology (RSST) and mediatization theory both address parts of the relationship between religious institutions and the technologies they use. RSST focuses on the role of group history and values in the process of creating a technology, emphasising the agency of religious communities as critics and designers. The institutional approach to mediatization emphasises the limits of that agency, focusing on the demands imposed on religious communication by the 'logic' of the media. In each case, I have argued that we need to pay attention to religious discourse, remembering that ideas about 'core values' and 'media logic' are only ever temporary and partial constructions. In the final part of this chapter, we will try combining these two approaches in search of a more complete model of the process of religious design.

The Anglican Cathedral of Second Life is a particularly relevant case for us to consider, because—as noted above—Heidi Campbell uses it as one of her examples of the religious-social shaping of technology (2010: 123–127). Campbell's account focuses on the relationship between the Cathedral and the Anglican bishops of Guildford (UK) and Wellington (New Zealand), particularly the decisions in 2007 and 2008 to ordain Mark Brown in the diocese of Wellington and to set up committees to discuss management and systems of oversight for the Cathedral. According to Campbell, these efforts to connect the online church into offline ecclesial structures shows that 'new technologies used for religious purposes might require the reconfiguration of the relationship between the technology and the community' (2010: 124). Both technology and religion must change in the process: 'the virtual world of Second Life has been adapted so that certain traditional religious practices can take place inside' (2010: 124), but in doing so 'the Internet provides the Anglican Church a new opportunity to reflect on its traditional boundaries and forms of ministry' (2010: 125).

This account of the Cathedral's potential and significance is supported by interviews with Mark Brown himself, rather than conversations with other church members or with representatives of the wider Anglican Communion. Brown can be a compelling advocate for his vision of online ministry, as we saw in Chapter 7, but many of the possibilities he mentions to Campbell, like full-time paid staff and a bishop of Second Life (2010: 125–6), were never very plausible. Campbell's argument that new technologies might 'require' religious change (2010: 124) could be seen as a claim about the media logic of Second Life, but we have to understand this logic as part of a discourse being constructed by Brown and intended for a public audience. By framing his vision for the future of online ministry in terms of techno-logical inevitability and global transformation, Brown positions himself as a pioneer and his critics as those left behind by history.

If we return to my own interviews with Mark Brown, we can see that his accounts of the construction of a traditional-looking cathedral in a virtual world are more complex than the original four-stage model of RSST might lead us to expect. He does reflect on the values and practices of his com-munity, by referring to the historic values of Anglicanism, but he also criti-cises that tradition ('they don't have a reputation for being early adopters'), shares his ideas about the interests of a contemporary audience and explains his own understanding of the logic of digital media. Brown was not just building a church for Anglicans, but trying to attract a wider congregation by appealing to what he thought they might be interested in and what he thought would work in a virtual environment.

For example, Brown explained the ancient-looking architecture of the Cathedral by arguing that 'the mystery of the Middle Ages' is 'kind of in at the moment', as part of postmodernity's 'fascination with tradition.' At the same time, he argued, contemporary society is drawn to 'synchronous com-munication.' The Cathedral was therefore designed to satisfy both of these desires, combining new, 'cutting edge' technology with ancient style. This is an attempt to create something that would satisfy an imagined audience's expectations of Anglicanism; the historical accuracy of the construction, its relevance to Anglican values and indeed whether or not Brown himself was interested in 'medieval' spirituality were all beside the point.

Brown also explained the design in terms of his own understanding of journalism and digital media. The traditional design was a chance to attract media attention by creating something newsworthy—a classic example of the conformity of religion to mass media logic, as noted above. However, Brown also argued that the familiarity of the design 'grounds what is actu-ally a fairly amorphous experience' and 'tricks people into believing that actually it's a real cathedral', helping them to forget the strangeness of going to church online. This is Brown's own construction of the digital 'media logic' of Second Life, a claim that a particular kind of environment must be constructed to support particular kinds of experiences.

Mark Brown envisaged the Cathedral as simultaneously traditional, post-modern and digital. It was to be recognisably Anglican, appealing to con-temporary audiences and at home in a virtual world, and Brown did not see any contradiction between these ambitions. This level of comfort with media logic was not universal, however, and some church leaders claimed that the values of their religious tradition were directly opposed to the logic of digital media.

Richard Thomas claimed that the monastic connections of i-church would 'give it "bottom", a solidity that many Internet communities lack' (Thomas

2004). Contemporary society expected individual autonomy, but i-church was going to demand real commitment from its congregation. Thomas expected i-church's emphasis on long-term stability to be quite different from the norms of wider Internet culture, deliberately rejecting the demands of media logic. LifeChurch staff and volunteers shared even more negative perceptions of digital culture, particularly in Second Life. As one pastor put it, 'we want to be . . . light, in what we might consider the darkness' of virtual sin. If 'media logic' includes attention to the formats and genres that audiences expect, then this was a defiant refusal of—and indeed an attempt to cure—the logic of the Internet.

To make sense of these examples, we need to combine the two approaches discussed in this chapter. When an individual or institution creates an online church, the development process is shaped by the founder's understanding of group history and core practices, their understanding of the values of the intended audience and also their vision of the logic of the medium. Based on these understandings, the founders try to develop a discourse about the church and its potential significance, and different versions of this discourse are shared with other members of the design team, the congregation, co-religionists outside the church, mainstream journalists, academic researchers and other audiences. Those discourses have political significance, framing the activity, value and future development of the church in ways that support the founders' goals. They are also open to challenge, and rival understandings often emerge within and beyond the online congregation—sometimes motivated by the failure of audiences to respond as enthusiastically as predicted. Over time, the leaders and members of the church will continue to refine their perceptions of core values and media logic, using their own experiences of success and disappointment to evolve new discourses that will feed back into future iterations of church design.

Campbell's original model of the religious-social shaping of technology included only four 'core areas': history and tradition; core beliefs and patterns; the negotiation process; communal framing and discourse (2010: 60–61). We can broaden the range of historical precedents considered in the first area without assuming that previous decisions about media will be uniquely influential. We can divide the second area into two, to differentiate between the values of the designer's own community and those of the intended audience(s). We also need to add a new area, to reflect understandings of the logic of digital media. At every stage, we must emphasise the importance of perception, representation and resistance, remembering whose perspective we have access to, who they are trying to convince, what is at stake and what alternative perceptions might be available, and we can adjust the final two categories to reflect this new awareness.

These adjustments leave us with the following six-part model:

1. History and precedent;
2. Community values and practices;

3. Audience values and practices;
4. Media logic;
5. Negotiation and conflict;
6. Communal framing and debate.

We can call this model the *mediatized* religious-social shaping of technology—or to keep the acronym short, Mediatized Religious Design (MRD). Emphasising *mediatization* (M) reminds us of the importance of discourses about media logic, highlighting *religion* (R) incorporates the existing insights provided by Heidi Campbell's original RSST approach, and including *design* (D) focuses attention on the actual production of technologies for religious purposes.

The MRD approach identifies six different aspects of the design and creation of online churches, encouraging us to analyse them as technologies produced or sponsored by particular entrepreneurs and organisations hoping to achieve particular aims. We can use this approach to follow changes in discourse over time, looking for evidence of failure, disappointment or resistant counter-discourses and seeing how the intersection between rival ideas generates new designs and new framings.

Analysing the production of online churches addresses only one small part of their activity, culture and significance. MRD may prove to be a helpful way to analyse what institutions and entrepreneurs are trying to achieve online, but it tells us very little about what online churches mean for the actual people who visit them. Few of the online churches discussed in this book ended up developing quite as their original founders had predicted, and individual churchgoers often developed their own unique understandings of what the church was, why it mattered to them and what part it should play in their lives. To make sense of this, we need to move on from design to consider online churches from the perspective of their users. This will be our task in the next chapter.

References

Altheide, D. and Snow, R., 1979. *Media Logic.* London: Sage.
Campbell, H., 2010. *When Religion Meets New Media.* London: Routledge.
Couldry, N., 2013. *Mediatization and the Future of Field Theory.* Communicative Figurations Working Paper 3. Bremen: ZeMKI. [pdf] Available at: <http://www.kommunikative-figurationen.de/fileadmin/redak_kofi/Arbeitspapiere/CoFi_EWP_No-3_Couldry.pdf> [Accessed 1 September 2016]
Finnemann, N., 2011. Mediatization theory and digital media. *Communications* 36(1), pp. 67–79.
Fischer-Nielsen, P., 2012. The Internet mediatization of religion and church. In: Hjarvard, S. and Lövheim, M., eds. *Mediatization and Religion: Nordic Perspectives.* Gothenburg: Nordicom. pp. 45–62.
Hepp, A. and Krotz, F., eds., 2014. *Mediatized Worlds: Culture and Society in a Media Age.* Basingstoke: Palgrave Macmillan.

————, and Krönert, V., 2010. Religious media events: The Catholic "World Youth Day" as an example of the mediatization and individualization of religion. In: Couldry, N., Hepp, A. and Krotz, F., eds. *Media Events in a Global Age*. London: Routledge. pp. 265–282.

Hjarvard, S., 2008. The mediatization of religion: A theory of the media as agents of religious change. *Northern Lights: Film & Media Studies Yearbook* 6(1), pp. 9–26.

————, 2012. Three forms of mediatized religion: Changing the public face of religion. In: Hjarvard, S. and Lövheim, M., eds. *Mediatization and Religion: Nordic Perspectives*. Gothenburg: Nordicom. pp. 21–44.

Hutchings, T., 2015. "The smartest way to study the Word": Protestant and Catholic approaches to the digital Bible. In: Bosch, M., Micó, J. and Carbonell, J., eds. *Negotiating Religious Visibility in Digital Media*. Barcelona: Blanquerna Observatory on Religion, Media and Culture. pp. 57–68.

Jenkins, S., 2008. Rituals and pixels: Experiments in an online church. *Online: Heidelberg Journal of Religions on the Internet* 3(1), pp. 95–115.

Lövheim, M., 2014. Mediatization and religion. In: Lundby, K., ed. *Mediatization of Communication*. Berlin: De Gruyter. pp. 547–570.

Lundby, K., 2012. Theoretical frameworks for approaching religion and new media. In: Campbell, H., ed. 2012. *Digital Religion: Understanding Religious Practice in New Media Worlds*. London: Routledge. pp. 225–237.

————, 2013. Media and transformations of religion. In: Lundby, K., ed. *Religion across Media: From Early Antiquity to Late Modernity*. Bern: Peter Lang. pp. 185–202.

Moberg, M., forthcoming. Mediatization and the technologization of discourse: Exploring official discourse on the Internet and informaiton and communications technology within the Evagelical Lutheran Church of Finland. *New Media & Society*. Available at: <http://journals.sagepub.com/doi/full/10.1177/146144481 6663701>[Accessed 9 January 2017]

Thomas, R., 2004. Why Internet church? *Thinking Anglicans*, 5 March. [online] Available at: <http://www.thinkinganglicans.org.uk/archives/000499.html> [Accessed 1 September 2016]

10 Being Church Online
Networks and Existential Terrains

In 2002, Caroline Haythornthwaite and Barry Wellman accused the previous decade of Internet studies of 'the fundamental sin of particularism, thinking of the Internet as a lived experience distinct from the rest of life' (2002: 5). It was still too common, they argued, for users to be considered as if 'immersed in online worlds unto themselves, separate from everyday life' and from the processes and dynamics active in wider society.

Discussion of the online church has been—and sometimes still is—plagued by this 'fundamental sin'. As we saw in Chapter 2, Christian critics have tended to evaluate online churchgoing as an alternative to local church attendance, to be held accountable to a common set of requirements and ideals. All of my case studies demonstrate that this is a misreading of the situation. We can only understand what any church means for its participants if we understand religiosity as a diverse portfolio of local and mediated practices and connections. Churchgoers seek out the resources and networks they need at each moment by drawing on a wide range of online and offline contacts, groups, communication channels, media resources and activities. Chapter 9 looked at the work of the builders of online churches, but we also need to analyse the integration of these churches into other spheres of belonging and activity.

Stewart Hoover, Nabil Echchaibi and their colleagues at the Center for Media, Religion, and Culture at the University of Colorado (Boulder) have sought to develop a concept of 'third spaces' for the study of digital religion. We will consider third spaces in more detail in the second half of this chapter, but it is helpful at this stage to draw on their idea of 'in-betweenness'. As Echchaibi has written, 'religious meaning is generated and religious practice is performed at the borderlines of a complex ecosystem of media ensembles and hybrid spaces' (Echchaibi 2014). Scholars need 'to visualize the mobility of everyday religion and explore the dynamic ways in which contemporary subjects imagine, produce and navigate new religious and spiritual places', and that means looking closely at spaces that exist in-between our established categories—including 'between private and public, between institution and individual, between authority and individual autonomy', and more.

For an example of this embeddedness and in-betweenness, we can consider the body. As we saw in Chapter 1, critics from the 1990s to the present day have claimed that online churches appeal to those who wish to escape from the responsibilities and limitations of their material bodies into a separate and disembodied 'cyberspace'. Online communities have been accused of heresy, as a modern-day revival of the ancient anti-body theologies debated in early Christianity. In fact, however, a flight from the body into cyberspace is not what we see in these case studies. On the contrary, the body is a key component of religious life online, which exists in-between ' "embodiment" and "virtuality" ' (Hoover and Echchaibi 2014: 12).

The body of the churchgoer is integrated into the life of online communities in multiple ways (Hutchings 2014). In some cases, the body becomes directly visible or audible in group communication through photographs, video broadcasts and phone links. Even where this level of shared embodiment was not possible, many of the online church participants I spoke to still involved their bodies in solitary online worship. Participants sang aloud and gestured with their hands and then talked about these practices in typed conversation. Anthony, a Church Online regular based in the UK, sang at his computer in his bedroom but tried not to wake his sleeping parents, and his unwilling self-restraint demonstrates the embeddedness of online activity in mundane, everyday, physical realities of access, location and context.

The body and its limitations also entered conversation, becoming a key topic in social chatroom interactions, diary-style blog posts and prayer requests—a good example of the flexible, ever-moving borderline between private and public. Heidi Campbell offers prayer as an example of the connection between online and offline in the email-based communities she studied, arguing that 'sharing real prayer needs enables members to become more aware of the lives of others, and consequently more invested in them' (Campbell 2005: 132). Prayer was a very popular activity in all five of the online churches we have discussed, in different forms, and discussions of the body and its material troubles were unsurprisingly common in prayer requests. In some cases, personal needs were answered in material forms through posted gifts or home visits, a practice Campbell also observed (Campbell 2005: 132).

In the previous chapter, we looked at online churches as technologies, designed by religious groups, institutions or entrepreneurs to reflect their understanding of their own religious values, the interests of their audience and the logic of their media. That approach is helpful, but we must also consider online churches from the perspective of their congregations. These churches are not just created technologies: they are also focal points of sociability that are accessed in specific material contexts, as part of the rituals of everyday life, connected into wider networks and protected by carefully-positioned boundaries.

In the first half of this chapter, we will see that participants visit these churches as part of their everyday religious and social activity, one resource among many others. Each congregant constructs his or her own personal set of social contacts, information sources and activity spaces, online and offline, and the significance of an online church for that participant can only be understood within this wider context. We will apply theories of the network society (Rainie and Wellman 2012) to encourage attention to this social and religious connectedness.

At the same time, we must be careful not to overstate the blurring of online and offline worlds. The second half of this chapter will explore isolation and separateness, demonstrating that online congregants also find ways to maintain boundaries around their activity, keeping their church hidden from the gaze of friends and family. We will consider the possibility that isolation can be politically transformative, as argued by the 'third spaces' theory developed at CMRC (Hoover and Echchaibi 2014). We will also argue that the separateness of online spaces can support a search for existential security in the face of intense personal vulnerability, as argued by Amanda Lagerkvist and her colleagues on the Existential Terrains project at the University of Stockholm (Lagerkvist 2016). Online church participants ensure that their activities and environments are both networked and bounded, locating their churches within everyday life and also in separate, private spaces, and this chapter brings together three quite different theories to ensure that neither dimension is overlooked.

Online Churches as Networked Religion

According to sociologists Lee Rainie and Barry Wellman, recent centuries in the West were marked by a shift in social organisation, leading to a decline in the significance of large bureaucracies and close-knit communities and the emergence of a new kind of 'network society'. 'Small, densely-knit groups like families, villages, and small organizations have receded in recent generations', they argue, and 'a different social order has emerged around social networks', in which individuals 'have more room to maneuver and more capacity to act on their own' (Rainie and Wellman 2012: 8–9). 'The new media is the new neighbourhood' (Rainie and Wellman 2012: 13), and most people's most important contacts are now maintained online over long distances. This network society transforms economics, politics and sociality, becoming what Rainie and Wellman have called the 'new social operating system' (Rainie and Wellman 2012: 7). Traditional communities are stable social groups with clear borders, but now—as Wellman argued in his earlier work—'boundaries are permeable, interactions are with diverse others, connections switch between multiple networks, and hierarchies can be flatter and more recursive' (Wellman 2001: 227). Social connections in this network society are characterised by 'networked individualism', in which *'personal communities* . . . supply the essentials of community separately to each individual: support, sociability, information, social identities, and a sense of belonging' (Wellman 2001: 227, italics original).

This shift took place in gradual stages, each entangled with the emergence of new technologies of communication and transport like the train, the car and the telephone. The Internet did not cause this change, but theorists of the network society argue that digital technologies did intensify it. According to Manuel Castells, the Internet makes it easier and more efficient for social actors to choose when, where and how they communicate and who they connect with, and these affordances are ideally suited to networking:

> the Internet is not just a tool, it is an essential medium for the network society to unfold its logic. This is a clear case of co-evolution between technology and society . . . The network is the message, and the Internet is the messenger.
>
> (Castells 2001: xxxi)

This emphasis on networks has significant implications for our understanding of online communities, including the churches discussed in this book. As Castells points out, belonging to an online community does not necessarily require a high level or long duration of commitment, and Internet communities 'rarely build lasting, personal relationships' (2001: 129). Instead, people develop 'portfolios of sociability' by 'investing differentially, at different points in time, in a number of networks with low entry barriers and low opportunity costs,' and this leads to 'extreme flexibility in the expression of sociability, as individuals construct and reconstruct their forms of social interaction' (2001: 132). From this perspective, the distinctive cultures and intense relationships found within online churches might not be their most important features. We should focus our attention instead on the wider networks of connections that these churches are part of, and examine their significance for users as temporary sources of sociability.

The novelty of social networks should not be exaggerated, of course. Religious belief and practice have always been complex and changeable, constructed from a diverse range of sources and authorities. Meredith McGuire argues that official and popular beliefs and practices are used 'in combination or separately, overlapping in layers, serially or simultaneously, hybridized and sometimes completely transformed', and that such fluid appropriation typifies 'nearly every sector of the religious population' (2008: 67):

> An individual's religion could include an elaborate combination of, say, a denominational tradition [. . .], the preaching of a nondenominational church leader and the particular congregational practices of a nondenominational church, beliefs and practices learned from television or radio evangelists, practices related to objects sold at Christian gift shops, and more.
>
> (2008: 95)

This range of accessible sources and channels of information and encouragement is broadened by new media, further reducing reliance on geographical communities and intensifying the changes and shifts discussed above, but it is by no means new for individuals to curate their religious identities, practices and commitments using diverse elements gleaned from many sources. Even centuries ago, 'individuals' religious practices may have been far more diverse and complex, eclectic, and malleable than we have realized' (McGuire 2008: 17).

Nonetheless, even a partial shift of significance from local communities to personalized social networks will have significant consequences for religious lives. Wellman argues that a more networked society can allow people to find new freedom for individual autonomy and agency, while also leaving them in 'an insecure milieu where no one fully knows anyone' (2001: 234). A particular social environment has 'decreased control over inhabitants' behaviour', but it also has 'decreased commitment . . . to its inhabitants' well-being'. According to Rainie and Wellman, one implication is a need to actively cultivate connections: people 'must devote more time and energy to practicing the art of networking than their ancestors did', because 'they can no longer passively let the village take care of them and control them' (2012: 9). Personal alliances must be forged, maintained and activated at the right moment to access the right kind of support.

To understand our case studies, we need to consider the location of online churches within the social and religious networks of their members. Participants visit online churches to search for particular kinds of social and religious resources, experiences and connections, as part of their everyday routines or—in some cases—in response to particular moments of need. We will consider the social connectedness of the online church first.

Each Internet user is linked into a pattern of weak and strong ties, including family members, work colleagues and friends, and these connections are activated and maintained through online communication as well as face-to-face and other forms of mediated contact. Some online churchgoers allowed parts of their social networks to connect, encouraging their families and friends to participate in their church activities. During my research at St Pixels, for example, four mothers participated online with their daughters, several married couples were active and at least three new romances began between community members during my research (one leading to a marriage). Other spouses and younger children attended the regular face-to-face gatherings.

This harmonious blending of social worlds was not universal, of course, and even in St Pixels it was much more common for participants in online activities not to involve their families. In some cases, online churches were forced to compete against other network commitments. Families could resent the encroachment of computer-mediated connections into the home, and it could be difficult to make time for prayer services and forum debates in a participant's daily routine. Some users during my research period gave up or scaled back their Internet activities to spend more time nurturing their face-to-face connections. Even if two family members did share the same online church, involvement was usually more intensive for one party than the other. The less active partner would be aware of the other's online life, more or less warmly appreciative of it and willing to log in and participate at least occasionally. I interviewed one such light user in 2007 at a gathering in Manchester. Her husband visited St Pixels constantly—it has 'taken over his life', she confessed—and she was willing to acknowledge the validity of online church, defend it to others and visit occasionally for worship, but for her the website simply 'didn't seem important'. Like many other family members of St Pixels regulars, she routinely attended face-to-face gatherings with her husband and children but spent very little time at St Pixels online.

Facebook gained in significance for online churchgoers during the course of my research, because it offered two opportunities: the chance to interact outside the formal space of the church, and a way to integrate their church into their wider online social networks. In each of the churches studied, at least some of the users I encountered quickly added me on Facebook as a personal contact. St Pixels members were particularly enthusiastic about Facebook, and the community set up St Pixels groups and embraced some of the more popular Facebook games. A constant cycle of Facebook competitions, challenges and exchanges of assistance emerged, and members' progress was much discussed within the community. In 2012, St Pixels decided to shift its live worship services from its chatroom to a Facebook app, and this continued to operate until late 2015. This development occurred after the end of my ethnographic research, but it will be discussed further in the final chapter of this book. LifeChurch also operated a very active Facebook page, although Church Online itself at that stage did not, and several online LifeGroups set up their own Facebook groups during my research.

Online churchgoing is embedded in the social networks of participants, but it is also just one part of their religious lives, almost always combined with a range of other Christian activities. Some of this connectedness takes place within the landscape of online churches, where congregations forge connections with each other, building up informal networks of conversation and sometimes migration. We have encountered a number of examples, particularly in our discussions of Second Life. Paula visited the Anglican Cathedral and LifeChurch's Experience Island, and she was also an active member of a number of other in-world churches. Gloria spoke of attending different churches to access different resources: LifeChurch 'teaches me to grow in my Christian faith', she said, while a Lutheran church 'gives me tradition'. Participants also sometimes moved between the Anglican Cathedral, i-church and St Pixels, three groups that shared a common denominational background, worship style and approach to theology. Pam Smith, for example, has written about her own activity in Church of Fools before becoming the pastor of i-church (Smith 2015). The network theorists discussed above described overlapping and fluid switching between community commitments as a key aspect of social life in a network society, and this was certainly the case for at least some participants in these online churches.

Christian commentators have frequently expressed concern about increased autonomy and mobility online (see Chapter 2). In a networked society, individual churchgoers have greater freedom to leave a community that does not satisfy their expectations, and that freedom was seen as a problem in several of the case studies in this book. In our study of Life-Church's Church Online, for example, we met Noah, the unhappy leader of a Bible study group in Second Life. The virtual world was mostly 'sinning', Noah said in our interview, but the sinners were not interested in his message of moral reform: 'I let them know they need to grow', but then 'they never come back'. Even the apparently sincere, devoted leader of Florence's study group proved flexible in his interests: 'he came 2–3 times and taught the group . . . and just disappeared.'

In theologian Douglas Estes' book *SimChurch*, 'discipline' features prominently as one of the major challenges faced by online churches. Estes lists discipline as one of the marks of a real church (2009: 50), citing the theology of Calvin, but he acknowledges how difficult this would be to impose online. Estes uses the example of modesty: it seems clear to him that a church in a virtual world must stop visitors from dressing their avatars inappropriately, but 'what will prevent those churchgoers from picking another scantily clad avatar and next week attending a different virtual church?' (2009: 186). As a proposed solution, Estes calls for greater emphasis on checking the identities of churchgoers and greater cooperation between churches, to ensure that punishments cannot be so lightly evaded.

Some online churchgoers do leave after a negative encounter, looking for a better experience elsewhere—exactly the kind of mobility that Douglas Estes was afraid of. At the Anglican Cathedral, the gardens of an unnamed member of the leadership team were deleted (by herself or by her opponents, according to different sources) after her acrimonious departure. At St Pixels, one individual declared his intent to leave the church in a fiery and highly critical blog post, only to relent after commenters begged him to stay. In some cases, these highly emotional acts of resignation or expulsion were followed by a move to another online church, where the exiled individual hoped to find or create a more ideal social and religious environment.

Unlike Estes, many of my interviewees saw personal freedom as one of the greatest strengths of online churchgoing, offering a safer way to reconnect with Christian community after offline hurts and disappointments. Martha and Lucy both joined i-church after negative experiences of unwelcoming local churches. Online, they could find people they actually wanted to talk to and pray with, while avoiding the kinds of argument they found unpleasant or tedious. Martha's online freedom was balanced by her social obligations, her commitment to friends in i-church 'who would kill me if I left'—a very different kind of limitation than the hierarchically imposed church discipline called for by Estes.

Critics have assumed that online religious activity will replace local participation, as we saw in Chapter 2, but academic studies have repeatedly argued that this is rarely the case. In Heidi Campbell's study of Christian email groups, for example, the 'overarching claim made by members' was that 'online community was a supplement to, not a substitute for, offline church involvement' (2005: 161). Resources and encouragement found online strengthened commitment to local involvement for some, and provided many with particular kinds of resources—like a connection to global Christian issues—that they were not able to access in their local congregations (2005: 164).

My own observations and interviews also show that most online churchgoers are attending a local church as well, and this general trend is supported by the membership surveys conducted by Church of Fools, St Pixels, i-church and the Anglican Cathedral of Second Life. A 2004 poll of Church of Fools visitors suggested that 61 percent of 2400 respondents regularly attended a local church, not including those who visited only for major festivals like Christmas. St Pixels' 2008 survey reported that only 7 percent—8 respondents—never attended a local church. More than two-thirds of respondents considered that St Pixels could be a valid replacement for offline churchgoing, but very few of them had actually made that decision. In 2006, just over 65 percent of the 110 respondents to i-church's survey attended a local church at least 'sometimes'. Only 25 percent described i-church as 'my main church', almost identical to the number who said the same of St Pixels. At the Anglican Cathedral of Second Life in 2008, almost 85 percent of 79 respondents attended a local church. These surveys did not phrase their questions in the same way, but they do all agree that online churchgoers are likely to attend a local church as well.

No survey data was available for the congregation of Church Online, but the individuals I spoke to there also tended to combine their online activity with some form of local churchgoing. Some attended a local LifeChurch campus and then watched the Experience again online at home, either to serve as a volunteer or to revisit the pastor's preaching. Anthony in Wales attended his local Pentecostal church twice each Sunday and watched Experiences online in between.

While most online churchgoers attend a local church, a significant proportion do not do so very often—and this has been noticed less frequently in research on digital religion. At St Pixels, for example, almost 60 percent of respondents were attending a local church less than twice each month, and in i-church only 50 percent described their attendance as regular. I found almost no evidence that these churches were attracting attention from people who did not already consider themselves Christian, beyond occasional rumours and testimonials of conversion and, of course, attacks from trolls. Instead, my observations and the membership surveys suggest that almost every member had attended a local church regularly in the past. It seems that a considerable number of those who join online churches are people who have left or partially disengaged from local church communities.

I did encounter some people who chose not to attend a local church because they thought online churches suited them better. Christina, for example, insisted that no church in Austria could provide the kind of relevant, relatable preaching she found at Church Online. This is just what critics of online church have always predicted, but stories like this made up only a tiny minority of the people I spoke to. More commonly, individuals like Martha or Lucy spoke of negative experiences with local churches, and had stopped attending some years before discovering online community.

For many others, participation in local churches was severely constrained by illness or disability. Heather's online engagement in i-church was motivated by a number of factors, including an injury that confined her to a wheelchair and made it painful to sit still, the lack of any local churches that appealed to her theologically and the failure of those local churches to respond helpfully to her enquiries. She was able to type lying down, with her computer on a special sloping rest, and from that position she led online services several times each week. Esme, similarly, spoke of online churches as 'a boon' in a time of serious illness, 'something I have waited and prayed for', because of the opportunity to worship, discuss and learn from her own home.

The decision to attend church online instead of locally could also be temporary. Rob found that moving jobs left him without time for church and then fell ill for three months. Rob was already a member of St Pixels, but now slowly became aware that 'this was *my* church', where all his pastoral needs could be met. This dependence proved to be short-lived: on returning to health he found a local church to attend, although he did remain involved with St Pixels. Pam Smith became involved in online Christian discussions 'while caring for an ill relative', because their global membership allowed her to find conversations even if she was awake at night (2015: 12). Other interviewees shared similar stories of intense but short-term commitment, caused by a time of illness, moving to a new town or switching churches. Their online community provided the spiritual support, stability and fellowship that they needed during those times of isolation, but did not become a permanent replacement for local churchgoing.

For most online churchgoers, online groups are an additional resource in long-standing religious networks that also include at least occasional visits to a local church. Just as theorists of the network society have predicted, people maintain connections to different social groups at different times to access different kinds of resources. Online churchgoing can offer the excitement of participating in a new experimental community, the chance to join theological debates, access to inspirational preaching or late-night prayer sessions. For Pam Smith, online conversations became 'an important part of my Christian formation' because of their honesty and diversity: forums 'offered critiques of contemporary Christianity that I wasn't hearing in my own church, both from Christians and non-Christians' (2015: 12).

In its 2008 user survey, St Pixels asked respondents to compare online and offline church with respect to a range of values, and the features in which St Pixels performed better included diversity, tolerance of difference, accessibility, 'allowing me to be myself' and 'potential for making friends'.

On the other hand, more than a third of respondents in the St Pixels membership survey reported greater 'opportunities to get involved' in a local church, and a quarter felt they were able to 'trust other members' more in a face-to-face context—suggesting that, for some people at least, the chance to be themselves also meant the fear that others might be pretending to be someone else.

Church Online frequently emphasised its imaginative missionary outreach activities and shared testimonies of the converted as evidence of success, while founders of each of the other churches studied in this book used imagery of the mission field as part of the justification for their online work. In my own experience, however, encounters with individuals who had discovered new Christian faith online were extremely rare: almost every member of these online churches had current or past experience of attending a local church. There are certainly people who are unable to attend a local church because of illness or disability, or who left because of negative experiences. However, the majority of online churchgoers continue to attend a local church at least occasionally, even among the sizeable minority who considered their online community to be their main church. Participants accessed their online churches as one resource in their wider religious networks.

Online Churches as Third Spaces

According to Edward Castronova, 'the allegedly "virtual" is blending so smoothly into the allegedly "real" as to make the distinction increasingly difficult to see.' Users 'have begun to see no line whatsoever between their online activities and their offline activities', he argues, rejecting the online-offline distinction as a handicap to their understanding (2005: 148). More recently, as we saw in Chapter 3, Christine Hine has described the Internet as 'embedded, embodied, and everyday', suggesting that it has now receded from our awareness to become part of the infrastructure of daily life (2015: 46). For many users of digital technology there is no such thing as 'cyberspace' or the 'virtual'; new media are simply one component of ordinary existence.

So far in this chapter, we have considered online churches as components in wider networks, integrated into the embodied, social and religious lives of their congregations. Such an approach is consistent with this infrastructural, everyday approach to digital media, and has received some support from the founders of online churches. Richard Thomas, for example, argued in his homily for the Dedication Service for i-church that cyberspace 'does not exist, and the Church should not be promoting it as if it did' (2004). Instead, he claimed, we build relationships through the Internet 'with real people who live in real places and live real lives.'

This blended, networked approach is important, but it can also be misleading. As Tom Boellstorff points out in his anthropological study of Second Life, the distinction between different online and offline contexts can be crucial. Boellstorff argues that 'the binarism of virtual and actual is an experientially salient aspect of online culture' (2008: 19), something that users really do perceive and care about, and the distinction is therefore a valuable tool when used ethnographically rather than ontologically. That is certainly the case when it comes to online churches: the willingness of a churchgoer to dress up as a dragon, make fun of the pastor and share their innermost thoughts is founded at least in part on the sense that this online community is separate from the networks of everyday life. Because it is separate, an online church can become a space in which activities and ideas that would not be encouraged in a local church can be safely pursued.

This doubleness—integration into the religious and social networks of everyday life, but also separateness from those networks—is key to Hoover and Echchaibi's concept of 'third spaces'. Third spaces can be 'generative positions from which important personal, social, and cultural work can be done' (Hoover and Echchaibi 2014: 13), and digital media makes these third spaces possible by facilitating action 'in between' received categories, locations and registers. Digital religion can be found between categories like 'authority' and 'autonomy', or 'individual' and 'community' (Hoover and Echchaibi 2014: 12), and that fluidity encourages 'a reflexive consciousness of location, place, project, and technology' (Hoover and Echchaibi 2014: 13). In a digital third space, participants must play an active part in building the norms, environments and networks they want to engage with.

Through these creative and often playful practices, 'formal and unitary structures of religious knowledge and practice become the object of both revision and transformation' (Hoover and Echchaibi 2014: 17). Digital interactions are not always transformative, of course, but Hoover and Echchaibi insist that participants in a digital third space have at least the chance to reimagine the received categories of religious identity, sociality, practice and experience. The 'religious' itself is also being reimagined: 'Social actors are using the digital precisely to work against the dominant, unitary views of religion. They are not bound by that definition, and are in fact actively subverting it' (Hoover and Echchaibi 2014: 23).

Hoover and Echchaibi's ideas of in-betweenness, fluidity and generative practice are helpful for the study of online churches. As we have seen, the churches discussed in this book operate in-between traditional institutions and autonomous online community: they are all related to established religious institutions, but they also exist—to differing degrees—beyond the direct control of those institutions. Even Church Online, which broadcasts directly from LifeChurch's physical campuses, affords a degree of independence to its volunteer chat hosts and LifeGroup leaders. All five churches have promised some form of transformative impact, as a new kind of digital outreach to society but also in some cases (most notably i-church and the Cathedral) as an experimental challenge to the denomination they represent. Churchgoers are often attracted to this transformative inbetweenness: most members argued that these online groups were really church, and yet they were also something different, available for participation in a different way. As we have seen, members often combine online and local church attendance, looking for different resources and experiences in different places, and online participation can fluctuate in intensity over time as needs alter.

Hoover and Echchaibi argue that third spaces rely on a kind of shared fiction:

> People act "as-if" these were bounded contexts of discourse and interaction. They act "as-if" they were communities of shared experience and sentiment. They act "as-if" they were contexts of public discourse and public deliberation.
>
> (Hoover and Echchaibi 2014: 13)

We saw this 'as-if-ness' at work in some of the more utopian, euphoric accounts I received in my interviews. Martha, Lucy and Esme spoke of the amazing warmth and welcome of i-church, the feeling of togetherness with the like-minded and the friends who would never let them go, but that does not mean they were unaware of the moments of tension or disagreement that occur in any online community. They were, we could suggest, speaking the genre of as-if, sharing their vision for the perfect online community they were trying to build together. The intensity of disgust we encountered in some other interviews, like Noah's account of the sinfulness of Second Life, can be understood as another kind of as-if-ness, a fictional construction of depravity that served to emphasise the urgency and disappointment of his own mission work.

The value of third spaces as places of meaning-making and transformation depends, in part, on their separateness from the established fields of everyday life. Third spaces are 'fluidly bounded', and these boundaries are 'subject to a constant process of negotiation' (Hoover and Echchaibi: 20), but they are still crucially important. A third space 'unsettles the singularity of dominant power narratives and opens up new avenues of identification and enunciation' (Hoover and Echchaibi 2014: 18), but only by remaining on the margins, away from the gaze of those invested in perpetuating those narratives. As Echchaibi puts it, such spaces must remain 'strategically peripheral', deliberately on the edge, 'as they imagine creative ways of thinking about faith and spirituality while resisting entrenched frames of social power and nested structures of religious authority' (Echchaibi 2014).

The concept of third spaces adds nuance to discussions of networked religion by reminding us of the importance of boundaries, limits and strategic invisibility. The decision not to connect one network to another can be highly significant. However, the desire to be separate is not always part of a strategic and creative quest for political transformation. For an alternative, more personal and ambivalent understanding of the boundedness of online churches, we turn now to a different theoretical approach: the idea of digital media as an existential terrain.

Vulnerability and Digital Existence

As the third spaces approach demonstrates, online cultures can only be fully understood if we attend not only to their reproduction of and integration into everyday routines, locations, networks and practices but also to their separation from those 'ordinary' realities. In some cases, as we have seen, online churchgoing becomes a shared activity, into which participants invite their spouses, parents, children and friends. In other cases, however, quite the opposite seems to be the case: online churchgoing can also be valued as an escape, a safe space to express thoughts away from the disciplinary gaze of the local church, family or friends. Some participants dismiss the boundary between the online church and the social and religious networks beyond it, but for others that boundary is the foundation and guarantee of any value the online church can offer them.

Understanding this kind of boundary work requires a move beyond the norms and networks of online communities to explore the felt vulnerabilities of the individual churchgoer. This kind of approach is long overdue in the field of digital religion, which has tended to focus on online cultures and practices and their relation to institutions instead of attending to the ambivalent experiences and concerns of users themselves.

The current debate around 'third spaces', for example, draws on language of creativity, resistance and marginality that is part of a long-standing theme in the study of digital religion. Researchers have long tried to find evidence that the Internet is in some sense transformative, empowering individuals to challenge their traditions and institutions. To contest this focus on the revolutionary, recent studies have tended to emphasise continuities between online activities and wider religious institutions, demonstrating the familiarity of online rituals, the use of online media to support existing structures of religious authority and the role played by those authorities in the design of new technologies (see Chapters 2 and 9). What can be overlooked in these arguments about transformation and continuity is the actual experience of users themselves, which can be much less one-dimensional.

Amanda Lagerkvist has recently pioneered an existential approach to media, focusing on vulnerability as part of a call for a return to the human in media studies (2016). For Lagerkvist, the ubiquity of digital technologies in contemporary life means that 'classic existential issues have become more and more entwined with our digital lives'—including 'our sense of time, memory, space, selfhood, sociality and death' (2016: 2). We are not just users of carefully designed and thoughtfully domesticated technologies, or nodes in mediated social networks: citing Heidegger, Lagerkvist argues that we are '*thrown* into our digital human existence, where the ambivalent and massive task awaiting us is to seize our vulnerable situatedness, while navigating through sometimes unknown waters.' This state of thrownness 'implies being faced with a world where we are precariously situated in a particular place, at a particular historical moment, and among a particular crowd with the inescapable task of tackling our world around us and making it meaningful.'

For Lagerkvist, making sense of 'the existential terrains of connectivity' means paying attention to both the mundane and the extraordinary aspects of digital life (2016: 2). Digital media may be embedded, embodied and everyday (Hine 2015), but that is not the whole story. There are also moments when 'our thrownness is principally felt, and our security is shaken' (Lagerkvist 2016: 3), times of crisis that leave us uncertain, vulnerable and scrambling to find meaning. 'Media are indeed tools of everyday existence', Lagerkvist acknowledges, 'but they are at the same time momentous and life-defining' (Lagerkvist 2016: 4). To understand digital media and their role in society, we must remember that each person 'is a struggling, suffering, and relational human being' (Lagerkvist 2016: 6) engaged in an impossible 'quest for *existential security*' (Lagerkvist 2016: 7, italics original).

The human search for meaning is closely linked to religion and spirituality, but Lagerkvist points out that '*existence precedes religion*' (Lagerkvist 2016: 4, italics original). Religious symbols, structures and practices can be resources in the quest for existential security, but they are not the only resources available. Lagerkvist calls instead for new attention to the classic existential themes of selfhood, time and death to explore how experiences and expressions of vulnerability are changing in digitally networked societies (Lagerkvist 2016: 8). For example, one aspect of this new terrain has been the emergence of a digital afterlife, in which the dead remain present online through the persistence of their Facebook pages, blogs and other digital traces. Faced with the existential shock of loss, survivors build online memorials, share their memories through videos and photographs, join online support groups, and often use digital technologies to maintain a kind of relationship by sending messages to the deceased. These practices, according to Lagerkvist, reflect 'the gist of social media practices of our time: selves in constant connectivity even with the ultimate others—the dead' (Lagerkvist 2016: 9). Our digital existence generates new uncertainties, including the danger of unexpected encounters with digital traces of the dead, but also new ways to come to terms with disaster.

This existential approach to media offers opportunities for the study of online churches. Most of the theoretical approaches discussed so far in the last two chapters—the religious-social shaping of technology, mediatization, the network society—emphasise the integration of digital religion into the structures of institutions and the patterns of everyday lives. The idea of transformative 'third spaces' comes closer to what Lagerkvist terms 'momentous media' (Lagerkvist 2016: 11), but an existential approach demands more attention to experiences of vulnerability, ambivalence and uncertainty, and to the role those experiences play in the development of practices, norms and boundaries that seek to reinforce a sense of security.

We already noted the significance of death at the start of this book, in our brief summary of the history of online churches. Death and grief have often been used both as a prompt to ritual innovation and as a demonstration of the shared values and close relationships of online communities. David Lochhead (1997) and Annelise Sessa (1989) both included responses to disaster in their accounts of the early stages of online Christian activity, and these stories function in their narratives as evidence of sincerity. According to Lochhead, for example, a memorial service for those who died in the Challenger space shuttle 'demonstrated the power of the computer medium to unite a community in a time of crisis beyond the limits of geography or denomination' (1997: 52). We know that online communities are real, according to these stories, because their grief is real.

More recently, Mark Howe used the story of the death of a member of St Pixels as one of the first anecdotes in his brief booklet about online churches. 'T' was an active participant, according to Howe, until 'suddenly, he stopped logging in' (2007: 5). Other community members knew his real name and where he lived, and they eventually discovered from local news reports that T had died after a traffic accident. His funeral service had already taken place. Members of the St Pixels community contacted T's family and asked for permission to host an online memorial service, and family members agreed to attend. At the memorial, 'T's virtual friends gathered in the sanctuary to share their stories about T and to pay their last respects' (2007: 5). Howe argues that this online event was more appropriate and more significant, in some ways, than the funeral itself: T had no connection to the chapel in which his funeral was held, but the chatroom sanctuary was a familiar and meaningful space in which he had spent a great deal of time, filled with people 'who knew and cared about' him (2007: 5).

For Howe, this funeral event demonstrates that 'the words "real" and "virtual" fail to capture the way in which online church relates to real life—and death' (2007: 5), but we can also analyse this event in other ways. T's family were unaware of his online life, and so they had not contacted St Pixels to pass on the news; if it were not for T's own decision to share his real name and location with his online friends, his fate would have remained a mystery. Members of online communities can invest in intense relationships and feel a powerful sense of belonging to the group, but those bonds remain vulnerable to the existential shock of sudden, unexplained severance. From this perspective, the decision to arrange a special online memorial event shows something common to all mourning rituals, offline or online: a desire to reaffirm the meaningfulness of the community and its relational projects by reasserting the value of what has been lost. As Lagerkvist argues, virtual mourning rituals are part of the 'collective repair work' that individuals and groups need to restore their sense of meaning (2016: 11).

Another of St Pixels' members, Ben, also died during my period of research. As we saw in Chapter 6 of this book, Ben was remembered in many ways within the ongoing life of the group. In this case, his illness was widely known and had been prayed for by friends in the community, and his family had contacted St Pixels with regular updates on his condition. His death was formally announced to the community just a few hours after 'the angels took him home' and prompted a cascade of more than 200 written responses. Many of these replies shared memories of Ben and praised his character, and respondents also shared prayers for his family and expressed their expectation of a future heavenly reunion. That hope of future meeting is a common theme of the digital afterlife, but it also reflects a long-standing popular vision of heaven as a place where family and friends gather in eternity (McDannell and Lang 1988)—an idea that became popular in 18th-century Europe and 19th-century America as a bold challenge to the more theocentric teachings of Christian theology. St Pixels members organised a memorial service for Ben, just as they did for T, but they also found other ways to remember him. Members continued his daily practice of posting a favourite hymn verse and mentioned his name whenever the bell sounded for the start of chatroom worship.

These two stories demonstrate the power of existential crisis moments to provoke ritual innovation, reassertion of relationships and renegotiation of boundaries. Both deaths were marked by online discussion, shared memories and an online memorial service, and both deaths prompted an outpouring of affection for the deceased, expressed particularly through prayers and the retelling of favourite memories. T's death forced the community of St Pixels to reach outside their website and connect with the family of the deceased, while Ben's illness forced his family to reach in to contact the community.

Death is, of course, not the only source of existential vulnerability encountered in an online church. The boundary between the church and the world outside it can itself become a focus of existential concern. Some members recognise no difference between their church friends and their wider social networks, as we have seen, but for others the value of the online group lies specifically in its separation from other contexts. The online community must never discover the identity of the user, nor must family or work colleagues discover what occurs online. This attitude of complete separation was rare, but some degree of concern for privacy and information control was a common theme among my interviewees. Most churchgoers wanted to be able to decide if, when and how the different domains of their lives would intersect.

One particularly striking example of the separation of worlds was Harriet, a member of St Pixels. Harriet designed an avatar that looked totally unlike her physical appearance, as we saw in Chapter 6: 'avatar is not like me—anon[ymity]!'. She also used a pseudonym, gave deliberately misleading information regarding her location, and showed great concern regarding the exact details of the research I was undertaking. Our interview had to be typed through a chat program, to avoid revealing a hint about her location through the area code of her telephone number. In our conversation, Harriet explained her need for privacy by describing particular local situations and individuals that she wanted to avoid to protect her own safety. She created a separate Facebook profile for her online self, using her St Pixels name and no photographs, and engaged with great enthusiasm in a variety of Facebook games. Maintaining more than one profile was theoretically banned by Facebook at that time, but creating new profiles offered a number of online churchgoers the chance to pursue their online connections without introducing different spheres of activity to the same communication space. This option was particularly popular among my Second Life interviewees, many of whom created a special profile for their avatars. Importantly, however, this separation of domains is not static and fixed. Some of Harriet's concerns diminished over time, and eventually she began attending St Pixels meets, replaced her Facebook profile with another that used her real name, and began to integrate her online church friends into her wider social network.

For many participants, the separateness of the online space also allowed room for intellectual and personal honesty. Among respondents to the 2008 St Pixels survey, for example, 49 percent claimed that the online community was better at 'allowing me to be myself', opposed to 40 percent who had no preference and only 5 percent who felt offline church was better. To a large extent, this opportunity to be oneself depends on isolation, which ensures that online disclosures do not present a danger to the individual's reputation elsewhere. Daniel, for example, attended a conservative evangelical church where he felt unable to discuss his theological questions, and he began using online forums in search of a safe space to explore new ideas. Online churches can provide a safe haven for serious debates missing from participants' local churches, but only because online pseudonymity served to keep transgressive thoughts safe from local censure. For Daniel, as for Harriet, the boundary of the online church was of existential importance. Online anonymity provided the security they needed to be open about—and, in Daniel's case, to gradually discover—who they really were.

I also encountered individuals using digital media to find new opportunities for Christian leadership, using the online space to extend or build their reputation as preachers and pastors. In some cases, established Christian leaders—like the founders of i-church or LifeChurch's Internet and Second Life Campuses—visited the Internet in search of new mission fields, creating or sponsoring online churches as an extension of their ministry. Their press releases, interviews and official statements usually pointed out that the Internet is accessed by hundreds of millions of people who never go to church or think about Christianity, and argued that creating church communities in a space where non-Christians are already so comfortable would make it easier for them to start inquiring about faith. The separateness of the Internet was crucial for these arguments, because the safety, familiarity and convenience of online environments was expected to encourage non-Christian audiences to start exploring possibilities of faith.

In other cases, individuals who had failed to attain positions of leadership in their existing church shifted their focus online, hoping that the Internet would provide new opportunities. This was not the case for all independent leaders, of course, and many had never considered leadership at all before finding roles in their online communities. For a few, however, the Internet offered them a chance to become something they felt 'called' to be, but had been unable to achieve locally: recognition as a valuable, important Christian leader. They sometimes described themselves as de-churched and spoke to me of their longing to move beyond the control of hierarchies that failed to appreciate their gifts. The separateness of the Internet would be the means for their escape.

In both cases, these would-be leaders were convinced that online environments offered something new and different that local churches could not access, but their efforts were not always successful. Institution-sponsored online projects do not always attract a sustainable audience, and—as we have seen—online churchgoers are likely to be committed local churchgoers already. Most of those hoping for a new start as online leaders were also bitterly disappointed, and reported to me that the online church was just as 'hierarchical' and 'oppressive' as any other. Online church leaders were no more encouraging about their gifts, and online audiences were no more receptive to their preaching. In some cases a cyclical story developed, with individuals progressing through different local and online churches, seeking authority and failing to find it and moving on to try again. These ministry efforts were, in part, personal identity projects, and they remind us that our study of digital religion must include room for existential experiences of disappointment, failure and self-doubt.

In several of my case studies, the separation of online from offline behind the protection of anonymity also permitted users to pursue forms of behaviour that were strongly stigmatised even in the online church, and this generated further levels of existential vulnerability. The 'sexual sin' and 'false clergy' so feared by some Christian Second Life users are good examples, and the 'griefing' pursued by hostile visitors to many online churches is another. These kinds of activities are facilitated by the distinctiveness of an online domain, where a user can engage in mediated sexual activities, roleplay as a priest or disrupt a church service with—usually—minimal negative consequences for their physical safety or their reputation.

Users who engaged in such activities could sometimes find themselves more vulnerable than they expected. Griefers could be banned, temporarily or permanently, and community members could sometimes succeed in identifying wrongdoers who thought themselves anonymous. On one occasion, for example, a member of St Pixels announced that she was dying of a terminal illness, only to be uncovered as a fraud when community members recognised her storyline. She had already performed her death on another Christian site and had made the mistake of trying to repeat her success.

Crises could also be provoked by an excessive degree of honesty. One of the first blog posts published by the Anglican Cathedral of Second Life (now deleted, but accessible through the Internet Archive) was a speculative theological argument by a member who suggested that virtual sex might not really be sinful. The writer argued that 'since no physical contact occurs, there is no question of actual (physical) adultery, or fornication' (Brown 2007), but commenters firmly and angrily disagreed. 'Wow', wrote one respondent: 'All I can say is you should be ashamed to call yourselves ministers of the Gospel while advocating and participating in adultery and homosexuality.' The comment thread was swiftly closed, and the experiment—originally intended to be the first in a series of posts exploring the theology of virtual relationships—was not continued.

In both cases, the crisis revealed the vulnerability both of the norm-breaking user and of the community itself. Fraudulent illnesses and official tolerance for theological speculation revealed, at least to some members, that their emotional and relational investment in their community was at risk. Their friends might not be who they thought they were, and their leaders might not think what they ought to think.

A more direct kind of existential threat is represented by the griefer, who openly attacks the community from outside. Church of Fools experienced by far the highest level of trolling and griefing among my case studies, but visitors to LifeChurch's Church Online sometimes disrupted the chatroom with demands for sex, and churches in Second Life could encounter quite surprising forms of abuse. On one occasion, I attended a Second Life service at an evangelical Christian church—not one of the case studies in this book—while attackers surrounded the space with vast walls of Satanic symbols and hovered outside, dressed as medieval plague doctors and waving symbol-covered banners. Congregation members typed encouragement to one another, prayed for delivery from Satan and tried to correct the security settings for their virtual environment. The preacher at this event was reading his sermon over voice chat and seemed entirely unaware of the chaotic battle unfolding around him.

This kind of assault confronts the church with an external threat to its very survival, but tended to prove much less serious for long-term community cohesion that the internal threats of deception and misbehaviour. In fact, the work of resisting an external attacker can also generate considerable energy for the community, becoming a significant and enduring source of pride and shared identity. The beleaguered congregation I observed in Second Life congratulated one another enthusiastically, declaring that Satan's interest in their downfall was proof of their spiritual accomplishments and future potential. Banning trolls from Church of Fools demanded exhausting hours of labour from volunteers, but also generated a strong sense of ownership of the space, encouraged close ties between the core community members, and forged a memorable origin story that participants were still repeating at face-to-face gatherings many years later. Some Church of Fools participants even enjoyed their encounters with trouble-makers: 'it's nice to get a troll now and then', one told me, because their antics were amusing, harmless and could lead to new conversations about faith. In both cases, hostile encounters with people trying to disrupt the church were reinterpreted as part of the church's mission and therefore, as evidence of success and a source of inspiration.

To conclude our survey of the existential aspects of online churches, we should consider one final and very different kind of experience. As Lagerkvist points out, the existential is not restricted to the work of form-ing identity and restoring meaning in times of vulnerability: it also includes 'moments of heightened sense of joy online (love, solidarity, *communitas*)' (2016: 11). Studies of digital religion have not always paid enough attention to the nature, intensity or social significance of users' actual experiences. Indeed, some early studies questioned whether online ritual could support meaningful experiences of transcendence at all (see Chapter 2). Religious experience is of course lived and everyday, patterned and structured and familiar, but it can also be unexpected and powerfully moving. We need to include those uncommon and deeply personal kinds of experience in our understanding of online religious practice and community.

Some online churchgoers have described momentous experiences of online prayer and worship. David, for example, visited the Church of Fools space to pray for at least five years after it became a single-user space, because he could still sense that this was 'a place that is holy', 'already steeped in prayer and worship'. In i-church, Heather reported that she would 'never forget' her first visit to the online chapel: 'Quietly but dramatically that evening during Compline, my messy lounge was transformed into a sanctuary. I experienced Emmanuel: God with us, sitting in front of my laptop.' At the Cathedral of Second Life, Kevin claimed that the virtual world had transformed his spiritual practice, because it had helped him 'discover the power of praying together with other people.' LifeChurch shared the testimony of William, who claimed that his first experience of online worship had changed his life: 'I felt as if I was breaking down . . . I woke up the next morning and I was a different guy.' For Anthony, the music played by the band each week guided him 'into the presence of God'. In some cases, my interviewees told me about moments of offline experience that had shaped their spirituality. At the Cathe-dral, for example, Sam recounted an extraordinary sense of connectedness that he had once experienced while praying in a local church building. That moment had only occurred once, but recapturing it had become the goal for his spiritual practice in Second Life. These heightened moments were not universal, of course, and other interviewees spoke of comfortable familiar-ity, quiet contemplation or even disappointment—but without attending to existential experiences of joy and transcendence, our study of digital religion will be incomplete.

Conclusion: The Digital and the Everyday

Online churches are not self-contained worlds, separate from the rest of online and offline activity, and they do not merely replicate what occurs elsewhere. They reproduce elements of local church activity, accept certain norms of online cultures and spread across multiple media platforms to blur into participants' wider social networks. For certain participants, at certain times, an online church becomes a part of their everyday life, shared with their family, work colleagues and Facebook friends. For other participants, an online church is a special, separate place for confidences and practices that would become valueless or even dangerous if the boundary around the church were to be breached. Participants closely guard the separation between their church and the world outside it, because privacy and anonymity are essential preconditions for unfolding aspects of their identities that can be displayed nowhere else.

As we saw in Chapter 9, the cultures and environments of online churches are designed by religious groups to suit their own understanding of their values, their audience and the logic of their media. For users, however, an online church is just one available resource, to be connected into a social and religious network that offers them a range of different options and commitments. In most cases, participants visit online churches without leaving their local churches, because local and digital resources offer different opportunities and meet different needs.

These unique and personal networks are divided by boundaries, within which churches can become transformative 'third spaces', safe places for the reconsideration of traditions and norms. They are also punctuated by moments of existential vulnerability, times of crisis in which the survival of the community or the identity of the participant seem to be threatened—and by moments of existential transcendence, which can become the foundation for a new identity.

The stories retold in my five case studies revolve around a common theme: the complex relationship between digital media and everyday life. Online churches are produced out of religious traditions and yet retain some separateness from them; they are connected into social networks, while remaining private spaces; they are familiar and reassuring, and at the same time they are existential terrains of vulnerability. Making sense of this multifaceted relationship between the church and the everyday is the key to understanding why online churches matter.

References

Boellstorff, T., 2008. *Coming of Age in Second Life: An Anthropologist Explores the Virtually Human*. Woodstock: Princeton University Press.

Brown, M., 2007. Sin in SL. *The Anglican Church in Second Life* [blog], 30 May. Available at: <https://web.archive.org/web/20071016210148/http://slangcath.wordpress.com/ 2007/05/30/sin-in-sl/> [Accessed 2 September 2016]

Campbell, H., 2005. *Exploring Religious Community Online: We Are One in the Network*. Oxford: Peter Lang.

Castells, M., 2001. *The Internet Galaxy: Reflections on the Internet, Business and Society*. Oxford: Oxford University Press.

Castronova, E., 2005. *Synthetic Worlds: The Business and Culture of Online Games.* Chicago: University of Chicago Press.

Echchaibi, N., 2014. So what is this third space of religion in the digital age? *Third Spaces* [blog], 27 May. Available at: <https://thirdspacesblog.wordpress. com/2014/05/27/so-what-is-this-third-space-of-religion-in-the-digital-age/> [Accessed 2 September 2016]

Estes, D., 2009. *SimChurch: Being the Church in the Virtual World.* Grand Rapids: Zondervan.

Haythornthwaite, C. and Wellman, B., 2002. The Internet in everyday life: An introduction. In: Wellman, B. and Haythornthwaite, C., eds. *The Internet in Everyday Life.* Oxford: Wiley-Blackwell. pp. 1–41.

Hine, C., 2015. *Ethnography for the Internet: Embedded, Embodied, and Everyday.* London: Bloomsbury.

Hoover, S. and Echchaibi, N., 2014. *Media Theory and the "third spaces of digital religion".* Boulder, CO: The Center for Media, Religion and Culture. [pdf] Available at: <https://thirdspacesblog.files.wordpress.com/2014/05/third-spaces-and-media-theory-essay-2–0.pdf>;. [Accessed 28 August 2016]

Howe, M., 2007. *Online Church? First Steps Towards Virtual Incarnation*, Grove Pastoral Series. Cambridge: Grove Books.

Hutchings, T., 2014. The dis/embodied church: Worship, new media and the body. In: Vincett, G. and Obinna, E., eds. *Christianity in the Modern World: Changes and Controversies.* Farnham: Ashgate. pp. 37–58.

Lagerkvist, A., 2016. Existential media: Toward a theorization of digital thrownness. *New Media & Society.* pp. 1–15. Available at: <http://journals.sagepub. com/doi/full/10.1177/1461444816649921>[Accessed 9 January 2017]

Lochhead, D., 1997. *Shifting Realities: Information Technology and the Church.* Geneva: WCC Publications.

McDannell, C. and Lang, B., 1988. *Heaven: A History.* New Haven: Yale University Press.

McGuire, Meredith B., 2008. *Lived Religion: Faith and Practice in Everyday Life.* Oxford: Oxford University Press.

Rainie, L. and Wellman, B., 2012. *Networked: The New Social Operating System.* Cambridge: MIT Press.

Sessa, A., 1989. A review of MS-DOS bulletin board software suitable for long-distance learning. *#ERIC Document ED353977.* [pdf] Available at: <http://eric. ed.gov/?id=ED353977> [Accessed 28 August 2016]

Smith, P., 2015. *Online Mission and Ministry: A Theological and Practical Guide.* London: SPCK.

Thomas, R., 2004. Dedication service for i-church: Homily by Revd Richard Thomas. *I-church.* [online] Available at: <http://web.archive.org/web/20040814025842/www.i-church.org/events/20040730_sd_sermontext.php> [Accessed 1 September 2016]

Wellmann, B., 2001. Physical place and cyberplace: The rise of personalized networking. *International Journal of Urban and Regional Research* 25(2), pp. 227–252.

Conclusion
What Happened to the Online Church?

Church of the Past, or Church of Tomorrow?

In 2015, *Christian Today* magazine published an article that described a visit to the Anglican Cathedral of Second Life and included interviews with leaders of the Cathedral, i-church and several other UK-based Anglican ventures. The tone of the piece was clear from its title: 'What happened to online churches?'

The author, Martyn Casserly, was returning to look at online churches six years after his last visit. His previous explorations had suggested great things to come:

> Back then, everything looked so exciting and revolutionary. People from all over the world could meet together and worship in a virtual space, free from judgment about physical appearance or the restrictions that disabilities or distance could bring. It sounded wonderful, utopian even, and the unstoppable rise of technology in everyday life suggested that it could become a movement of huge significance.
>
> (Casserly 2015)

Now, however, the leader of the Cathedral sadly admits to Casserly that community numbers have 'gone down quite significantly.' Other churches in Second Life have closed or moved to smaller, cheaper locations. Outside the virtual world, churches using websites, forums and social media are struggling to get by on tiny budgets. Wherever Casserly looks, he finds little sign of 'the dynamic, community based hive of activity that I hoped would have appeared online by now' (Casserly 2015).

Perhaps, Casserly suggests, the Internet has just left online churches behind. In a world of mobile devices, social media and quick interactions, 'the future of digital churches seems more likely to conform to that sort of open, dispersed nature of use rather than the gathered, centralised site that previously seemed so appealing' (Casserly 2015). Or perhaps, as critics have always argued, there really was something fundamentally wrong with the idea of replacing the physical gathering of the church with an online congregation. For Casserly, it remains unclear 'whether a truly online church will ever be a reality, and if it should be one'.

For a very different news story, we can turn to *The Herald*, a Scottish national newspaper. On May 17, 2016, senior news reporter Brian Donnelly broke the startling news that the Kirk was about to introduce online baptisms in a bid to boost membership. The Kirk is a common name for the Church of Scotland, the national church and part of the Protestant Presbyterian tradition. A 'landmark report' (Donnelly 2016) was due to be presented to church commissioners, proposing digital forms of baptism and 'access to the sacraments', and these plans were 'expected to attract interest at the assembly'. Donnelly's article also discussed the new Scottish initiative SanctuaryFirst, a website and app that he describes as 'the first online congregation'. Norman Smith, vice-convenor of the Mission and Discipleship Council, described these kinds of initiatives as 'forward-thinking', showing that 'the Church is not behind the times.'

The online baptism story quickly spread across newspapers in Scotland (*The Scotsman*), the UK (*The Telegraph*) and internationally (*Newsweek*). Online, however, the idea and the Church were both widely criticised by Christian blogs and social media. For Rev. David Robertson, a minister in another Scottish denomination (the Free Church) who blogs as The Wee Flea, the whole situation was a disastrous miscalculation. 'The story itself has opened up the Kirk to ridicule from secularists and saints alike', he argued, making the Church look 'foolish and desperate' (Robertson 2016). Indeed, Robertson thought, 'it reads like a spoof'. These heated debates also became part of the story, quoted and discussed in mainstream media; the Wee Flea's blog post, for example, was quoted in *Newsweek*.

Two days after the initial story broke, the Church of Scotland tried to clarify its position. In a press release posted to its website, the Church declared that it was not considering online baptism after all (Church of Scotland 2016). The original report had not even mentioned baptism, the Church pointed out, accusing the *Herald* of 'journalistic licence'. According to Norman Smith, the denomination was simply considering 'the nature of someone's relationship with the church when they do not attend in person.' 'An increasing number of our congregations are developing an online component', Smith explained, and people watching a video stream online 'already feel part of the church.' Journalists reluctantly updated their articles, and the story faded away.

These two news stories are, on the surface, complete opposites. Martin Casserly argues in *Christian Today* that the online church was a passing fad, a once-promising initiative that never really fulfilled its supporters' expectations. As interest in Second Life dwindled and the cutting edge of digital media projects moved away from community websites, the online church had been left behind. For Brian Donnelly and the *Herald*, on the other hand, Internet church is still the almost-unbelievable future, a groundbreaking attempt to 'address the needs of worshippers in a digital age' (Donnelly 2016) and attract members back to the Church of Scotland.

These two stories also show some striking similarities. Most surprisingly, all of the contributors quoted here portray online church as something new. As we saw in Chapter 1 of this book, online congregations have been in existence since the mid-1980s, and online baptisms since the 1990s. Despite this, Casserly still wonders if online churches will ever progress beyond the stage of experimentation, and Donnelly reports that the first ever online congregation has just been launched in 2016. This focus on novelty is very common in media coverage. Online churches are always and eternally new.

There are other familiar themes here, too. Casserly, Donnelly and Robertson assume that the purpose of online church is revolutionary and substitutionary, designed to replace local churchgoing and attract new audiences. Studies of online religion have repeatedly shown that most participants are already active religious practitioners in their local contexts, and all of the studies in this book have reinforced that point: church online is much more likely to be an additional resource for people who already identify as Christians and attend (or used to attend) a local church. These findings have not been incorporated into Christian discourse, and the old hopes and fears remain. Robertson's evaluation of SanctuaryFirst is scathing, accusing its founders of 'advocating that the real life physical body of Christ (his church) should just vanish into cyberspace' (2016). For Robertson, real church demands embodied, face-to-face communication, just as critics of mediated Christianity have always argued. The idea of going to church online has never achieved mainstream acceptance among Christian observers, despite the widespread adoption of a range of other digital tools, networks and platforms.

So what has really happened to the online church? My ethnographic research was conducted between 2007 and 2010, and my accounts have focused primarily on 2008 and 2009. In this conclusion, I will return to my case studies to see how they have fared over the last half-decade. Digital technologies and digital culture have changed considerably since these churches were launched, and Christian understandings of digital media have changed as well. We will consider the each of the five churches in turn, briefly describing the current state of Church of Fools and St Pixels, i-church, the Cathedral of Second Life, and LifeChurch.

Church of Fools and St Pixels

Church of Fools operated its small virtual space in 2004, before shifting to a forum-based site and eventually relaunching as St Pixels. The original virtual space was still accessible when I conducted my initial research, however, and some of my interviewees still used it as a place for private prayer (as described in Chapter 4). That space finally closed in 2016, and the churchoffools.com website is now offline.

The Church of Fools community became St Pixels in 2006, and I described the different cultures of the site's forums, blogs, chatroom and offline gatherings in Chapter 6. St Pixels remains in existence today, but has undergone several further changes. The software was updated again with new functions and new, more cartoonish avatars in 2010, after the end of my ethnographic research.

The community underwent a more dramatic shift in 2011, relocating almost entirely to Facebook. The website remained online, first as a blog and eventually as a static timeline, a monument to St Pixels' many variations (see http://www.stpixels.com). On Facebook, St Pixels created an app that could be used to host worship services and chat conversations, reproducing most of the functions of the old LIVE chatroom. One more unusual new addition was the opportunity to vote in real time, using feedback buttons to indicate if a sermon merited an 'Amen' or a 'Zzz'. Results were aggregated to produce an ever-shifting measure of audience approval.

The decision to move to Facebook received some attention in Christian media, and quotes from the leaders of the group emphasised the need to refocus the church in response to changing trends of digital culture. According to the preacher at the first Facebook service, moving into the social network meant that '600 million Facebook users now have a church in their pocket' (Sun 2011). Mark Howe argues that, 'Love it or hate it, Facebook is where people are in 2011', and so St Pixels had to be there too:

> It's easy to build irrelevant ghettos in cyberspace, or to abandon distinctives in the rush to embrace the latest online fad . . . Our Facebook application is an attempt to engage with a cultural phenomenon on its own terms while holding onto the gospel that has transformed so many cultures across the centuries.
>
> (Howe, quoted in Sun 2011)

The new app survived for four years, but the church hosted its final service on Facebook in November 2015 (Fig. 11.1). In a statement announcing the closure, the St Pixels Facebook page described the end of live online events as a sensible response to the changing expectations and interests of the digital world: 'Internet culture shifts quickly: the Internet and even Facebook are very different places today.' The Christian Church throughout history had needed to adapt to new circumstances, St Pixels pointed out, and this would be no different.

I attended the final service (Fig. 11.2), where Bible readings on the theme of time and endings were taken from Ecclesiastes 3 ('For everything there is a season'), Hebrews 13 ('Let us run with perseverance the race which is set before us') and 2 Timothy 4 ('I have fought the good fight'). A traditional hymn, 'The Church's One Foundation', reminded viewers that Christian theology promises an eternal victory for the Church, despite the troubles it may face in the meantime. Mark Howe expanded on these themes in a brief

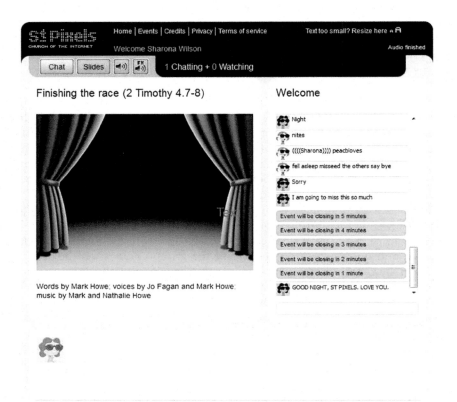

Figure 11.1 The final moments of the final service in the St Pixels Facebook app, 2015.
Image by Sharona.

sermon, emphasising that the Christian Church is bigger than any one group or platform, always changing and always under divine control:

> The season of St Pixels live services in Facebook has come to an end.
> But the thing about seasons is that they continue to cycle.
> And Jesus is still building his church.

The event was attended by 46 people, recalling the busiest moments of the old LIVE chatroom. The announcement that St Pixels was about to host its final service had prompted many of the community members to reconnect with one another, in some cases after years of absence, and provoked a new burst of energy in community activities. On the St Pixels Facebook page and in a closed private group, old members shared greetings, expressed their affection for St Pixels and for one another and returned with particular enthusiasm to the word games they had once played in the Bouncy

Castle. Participation began to fade again over time, but messages, discussions prayers and contributions to games were still being posted in the summer of 2016.

Elsewhere on social media, a few other online churches or worship communities can be found. One is d-church, a 'multimedia fresh expression of church' that was created by a UK Methodist in 2011 (Lindridge 2013). D-church organises a monthly online service on its Facebook page, posting a series of updates including prayers, images and media clips and inviting participants to comment on them. The page currently has around 900 likes, and each update posted during the monthly service tends to attract five to ten reactions. The church also runs a Twitter account and a blog. There are other examples of groups trying to coordinate prayer meetings through social media: the Virtual Abbey (@Virtual_Abbey), for example, is a Catholic-led project that has prayed the Daily Office through Twitter since 2009 and currently has almost 6500 followers, although it does not appear to refer to itself as a 'church'.

The decision to move St Pixels to Facebook was explained in terms of media logic—'Facebook is where people are', as Howe put it (Sun 2011)—but online churches are actually very rare in social media. Christians have created churches using almost every previous form of Internet media, from email lists to virtual worlds, but the rise of social network sites like Facebook has not provoked the same response. Instead, it has become much more common for local Christian churches to operate a Facebook page, and many online campuses have done the same. As we shall see below, live streaming through Facebook has also been used to broadcast Christian events, including local church services and conversations with prominent Christian leaders.

I-Church

While St Pixels has been transformed completely since 2010, i-church—at first glance—has hardly changed at all. The church remains in operation, still using the same website (i-church.org). I-church remains part of the Diocese of Oxford, and it still describes itself as 'an online Christian community based on Benedictine principles.' Pam Smith is still the priest in charge, 8 years after first taking office, and recently published a book about online ministry (Smith 2015). The church homepage (The Gatehouse) has not changed in design since 2010 (see Fig. 11.3), although some of the individual boxes that make up the page are updated periodically with new prayers and links. Worship services still take place in a chatroom, which hosts a weekly prayer service and occasional social events. Community members still work together each year to create an Advent Calendar, including daily collections of art, photography, music, prayers and reflections.

The original vision for i-church called for a private community space for the highly committed and a separate public space open to everyone. This vision took some years to achieve, but the format chosen in 2009 remains in operation today. From the Gatehouse, the visitor can reach three different areas for interaction: the Courtyard, Blogs and the Community. The Courtyard offers discussion forums for prayer and social conversation, both still active in 2016 with several new threads each month. There is also a less busy forum for theological debate. In the Blogs section, 7 have been updated in 2016; the section is currently undergoing a software update and is temporarily closed. The Community section, which I cannot access, is a private forum offering space for prayer and spiritual direction to 'core community members'. This core community is defined as those 'who are committed to the long term future of i-church and for whom i-church is an integral part of their faith journey', and anyone hoping to join them is invited to contact Pam Smith directly to make his or her case. The i-church community may be smaller than it once was, in the more chaotic years of my ethnographic research, but it remains a place for prayer and conversation.

Elsewhere in the Church of England, the i-church experiment has attracted very few imitators. The London Internet Church launched in 2007, as part of the Diocese of London, and broadcasts video prayers from the church of St Steven Wallbrook (http://londonInternetchurch. org.uk); elsewhere, as far as I have been able to discover, no diocese claims to operate an online church at all.

Instead, more recent Anglican projects have explored the potential of social media and live video streaming apps. In 2015, for example, the Church of England launched a website (http://www.justpray.uk) that collects prayers from social media and hosts short films (including a video of the Lord's Prayer that was famously banned from screening in cinemas). The denomination also encouraged churches to start broadcasting services online, promising that new apps were cheap and easy to use and would appeal to a wide range of audiences:

> It could be someone too ill to attend, a family who want to 'attend' even when on holiday or someone who just wants to know what the church is like before they make the sometimes scary step of walking into the building for the first time.
>
> (Bingham 2015)

To advertise these opportunities more widely, the Church of England collaborated with TwitterUK to create ChurchLive, a year-long project in which local churches can apply to live-stream their Sunday services using the Periscope app (Church of England 2015). This was followed in 2016 by a number of live video events on Facebook, including services and Bible studies led by Archbishop of Canterbury (ArchbishopofCanterbury.org 2016).

In 2015, the Diocese of Lichfield advertised for its first 'online pastor', and this new initiative is similar in some ways to the Diocese of Oxford's vision for i-church. In the job advert, Lichfield Diocese calls on the Church of England to 'learn to relate more effectively to the world and the experience of young people and young adults', pointing out that this new generation increasingly 'inhabits a virtual environment sustained by an array of social media applications and digital devices' (Gledhill 2015). According to the Bishop of Stafford, the online pastor initiative would be 'part of reimagining . . . what it means to be "church" in the coming years' (Gledhill 2015). The bishop promised that an online pastor would help meet the needs of 'young people' reluctant 'to sign up to endless meetings', but he also insisted that this was 'not a substitute for face-to-face contact.'

Significantly, however, no reference was made to creating an 'online church'. Success, according to the Archdeacon of Stoke on Trent, 'will look like more of our young people feeling that they are involved, connected' to each other, to the wider Church, and to God (Gledhill 2015). The Diocese of Lichfield appointed Ros Clarke to the post, and Clarke now operates a website (https://onlinepastor.org/), a Facebook group (https://www. facebook. com/groups/online pastor/), accounts on Snapchat, Twitter, Instagram and YouTube and a weekly 10-minute video discussion show (http:// www.tgimonday.show). The online pastor project is about ministry through networks, not forming a congregation.

The Anglican Cathedral of Second Life

The Anglican Cathedral of Second Life remains where it was, on a hill at the centre of Epiphany Island. The island itself has been re-landscaped several times, adding or removing valleys, rivers and gardens. All of the major buildings have been updated several times since my first visit, replacing the high-detail realism of the original design with less complicated alternatives. Figure 11.2 shows a screenshot from a video tour of the island, produced for the Cathedral in 2012, and the simplified Cathedral structure seen here is still in use in 2016. By reducing the number of components and removing ceilings, walls and stairs, these redesigns improve the functionality of the island (reducing lag and increasing ease of navigation), albeit perhaps at the cost of some of its original visual impact. Despite these changes, however, the basic visual connection with traditional Anglican architecture has been retained, and the main Cathedral building is still designed to resemble a large stone church in the Gothic style.

At the time of my initial research Mark Brown was trying to encourage new connections between the Cathedral and the Anglican Communion. Conversations began with bishops in the UK and New Zealand, and an initial face-to-face meeting in Guildford in 2008 was followed by a small event at the Lambeth Conference of Anglican bishops later the same year. Over time, the Cathedral began to develop a close relationship with the Bishop of Guildford, Christopher Hill, who participated in occasional meetings of the Leadership Team and provided a kind of episcopal oversight for the

Figure 11.2 Epiphany Island, 2012. Image by Andy Kingston (Freezing Sorbet 2012).

community. In 2011, for example, the bishop produced a document for the Cathedral to explain his position on the topic of virtual sacraments (see Chapter 2). A legal constitution was proposed in 2010 to clarify and formalise this situation, and its authors portrayed this as the next step towards some kind of official recognition of the Cathedral by the Anglican Communion. In practice, the idea of a constitution proved less popular among the congregation than expected, and the discussion continued for at least a year without concrete results (Milena 2011). Bishop Hill retired in 2013, and the Cathedral has so far been unable to find another bishop to replace him.

One of the principal leaders of the church in 2009 remains in charge in 2016, acting as 'lay pastor', although the team around her has changed almost completely. A single worship service is now offered every Sunday, down from six events each week in 2009, and there are also daily prayer meetings in the chapel and a weekly Bible study. As noted above, participation in community events has declined over time (Casserly 2015), and the Cathedral blog shows that this was already being discussed as a problem in 2011 (Milena 2011).

Second Life received intense media coverage in the early years of its existence, amid hopes that this new kind of virtual world would prove valuable for education, art, creative expression and commerce. Reports of its imminent demise have long been circulating, but there are still active religious communities in this virtual world. Second Life's own official Destination Guide lists locations that Linden Labs considers to be particularly worthy of attention, and the Guide currently includes 21 locations in the 'Spirituality and Belief' category (http://secondlife.com/destinations/belief/). Twelve describe themselves as Christian, and 10 of those advertise some form of worship in-world.

Counting exactly how many Christian spaces, groups and events there are in Second Life is very difficult. Care is needed to distinguish places that are designed for a Christian audience from role-play areas, stores and entertainment venues that include a church building as part of their aesthetic. In 2010, Robert Geraci used the Second Life search function to look for the key word 'Christian' and found 800 results (2014: 134). Repeating that search in 2016, I also found almost 800 results. Between 2011 and 2012, Stefan Gelfgren and I collaborated on a more rigorous attempt to find every Christian place in Second Life (Gelfgren and Hutchings 2014). We used the search function to look for locations that included certain keywords in their descriptions (including Jesus, church and chapel), and visited them to find out what they looked like. Some Second Life users have created their own lists of Christian spaces, so we also combed through these to look for any spaces we might have missed. In total, we identified 114 Christian locations. In 2016, the number is likely to be roughly similar: using the Second Life search function to look for locations, I found 75 results for 'Jesus', 80 for 'Christian' and 215 for 'church'. Second Life today includes spaces representing evangelical, Lutheran, Anglican, Catholic, Eastern Orthodox and Latter-Day Saint traditions of Christianity, just as it did during my ethnographic research—although, of course, the existence of a location does not necessarily mean that it attracts regular visitors.

Churches and Christian sites also continue to appear in other virtual worlds, too. A 16-year-old boy from Tacoma, Washington recently received media coverage for building a church in Roblox (www.roblox.com), a user-generated online gaming platform intended for children and teenagers. According to Duke Divinity School's Faith & Leadership blog, the 'Robloxian Christians' group has 4500 members, 15 leaders and 140 volunteer administrators (Faith & Leadership 2016). The founder created a Christian community group 'entirely on his own, asking no one for permission', and describes it as 'like a fan club for Jesus that transformed into a church' (Faith & Leadership 2016). Other virtual world projects have been created by pastors working for Christian institutions: the Church of Finland, for example, operates a space in Minecraft to teach users about Martin Luther (http://fisucraft.net/luthercraft/).

Life.Church and Church Online

My final case study, Church Online, is also still active in 2016. In fact, it seems to be growing in popularity. According to the church, more than 5 million visitors attended Experiences at Church Online in 2014 (Life.Church 2014), and 100,000 people now participate every week (George n.d.).

The current online pastor is Alan George, who was appointed in 2010 (replacing Brandon Donaldson, the online pastor we met in Chapter 8). More than 70 Experiences are now available every week, each coordinated by teams of volunteers who host the chatroom conversation and offer private prayer.

In terms of visual design and functionality, the Church Online platform (Fig. 11.3) has changed very little since the main phase of my ethnographic research concluded in 2009. The viewer is still invited to watch the Experience broadcast in a video window on the left, while chatting in a conversation window to the right and, if necessary, contacting a volunteer using a 'Live Prayer' button. Interactive options are available below the video window, offering something relevant to that moment in the Experience— perhaps inviting the viewer to click a button to purchase a song, download a free resource, or affirm a suggested declaration. On the right, the conversation window can be switched to show a number of other options, including sermon notes.

There have also been some relatively minor adjustments to this basic structure. The video window is now considerably larger, and can be expanded to full-screen. The 'map' tab (which once showed where in the world visitors were located) has been replaced by two new options: a digital Bible (powered by YouVersion, an initiative mentioned in Chapter 8), and a complete list of current Experience times (with the option to set an alert or send out an invitation to a specific event). The background colour scheme of the platform has changed from muted grey to bright red, to match the colour of the Life.Church logo.

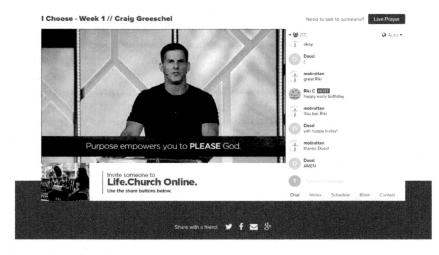

Figure 11.3 Church Online, 2016.

A more significant development for Church Online took place at the beginning of 2012, when LifeChurch chose to make its platform and support services available to other churches free of charge. Visitors to the download website (churchonlineplatform.com) are promised 'robust controls' and a 'sleek user interface', all in 'one easy-to-manage tool'. The platform 'removes the barrier of technology', in order to allow churches of any size 'to reach people for Christ through online ministry.' The platform is described as a 'community builder', but the primary imagery here is of networks, connectivity and communication: 'The world is more connected than ever. Let's connect it with Christ'. The platform launch attracted considerable attention from Christian magazines and technology bloggers, and one estimate claims that 7000 churches had registered to use the system by late 2014 (Media Fusion 2014).

As we saw in Chapter 8, Church Online also experimented with ways to expand beyond its core website. Experience Island has now vanished from Second Life, but enthusiasm for other kinds of media has only intensified. LifeGroups and Watch Parties are still encouraged, for example, and more than 150 online and offline groups intended for Church Online members are currently listed in the Life.Church database (https://lifegroups.life.church). Church Online finally launched its own Facebook group in 2016 (https://www.facebook.com/groups/LifeChurch Online/), separate from the main Facebook page of Life.Church, and this is used to share stories of ministry success, behind-the-scenes videos and free resources. A 'Social Media Street Team' was also created in 2016, led by Jason Ham in the UK, in order 'to invite people to Life.Church Online and share what God's doing in our lives' (George n.d.) 'We want to invite and share about Life.Church Online like crazy!', Alan George explains, because 'we know one invite can change a life.'

This intensified interest in social media has been shared by senior pastor Craig Groeschel, whose most recent book was titled *#Struggles: Following Jesus in a Selfie-Centred World* (Groeschel 2015). *#Struggles* promises to explain the negative consequences of social media and to guide Christians to use technology in a Christ-centred way. Given the commitment of LifeChurch to online ministry, it is particularly interesting that Groeschel has chosen to publish a critique of digital culture. Marketing for the book claims that 'the more we interact online, the more we crave face to face intimacy, but the harder it is to find'—repeating one of the oldest and most consistent Christian fears about mediated communication.

Stories of lives changed by Church Online are frequently published on the Church Online blog, often in support of calls for volunteers and financial contributions. These stories tend to emphasise international success, promoting Church Online as a global missionary initiative. In 2015, for example, a video shared the story of Ira from India, who explains that she first encountered Christianity through a television preacher and then found Church Online through a Google search (George 2015). 'There are people all over the world searching for hope every day', Alan George assured his readers, and Life.Church can be there to help them.

An ongoing crowdsourced list of Internet campuses created by DJ Chuang now includes 650 in the US and Canada and dozens more around the world (http://djchuang.com/ church-online/). In the UK, churches with online campuses include Everyday Church in London (http://everyday.online, Hailes 2015), City Life Church in Portsmouth (myclc.org.uk) and River Church in Exeter (http://www.riverchurch.tv, Walmseley 2014). The online pastor of River Church, Jason Ham, is also the leader of the Social Media Street Team of Life.Church. These lists are incomplete, of course, and we have no real idea how many churches worldwide are now running online campuses, how many are using the Church Online platform or what kinds of audiences they are managing to reach. Even so, it is clear that this kind of online broadcasting and community formation is becoming increasingly common as part of ministry activity among larger churches in the evangelical Christian tradition.

From Online Church to Church Online?

This chapter has returned to my five case studies, offering a brief update on their progress and locating them within a wider context of similar online groups. As we have seen, Church of Fools has disappeared, and St Pixels moved to Facebook and then stopped organising live events. I-church and the Anglican Cathedral of Second Life continue to operate in an almost unchanged format with a lower level of activity, although the Cathedral has updated the look of its buildings. Church Online is the exception: this part of the online ministry of LifeChurch has grown in audience and number of events since 2010, although, again, the actual design of the platform remains very similar.

In Second Life, the total number of places that identify themselves as Christian and contain churches seems to have changed relatively little since 2010, suggesting a continued interest among some users of that virtual world in defining Christian space and deploying the visual rhetoric of church architecture.

For Christian denominations, however, the cutting edge of online ministry seems to have moved on. My summary in this chapter focused on the Church of England, which once supported projects like Church of Fools, i-church, the Cathedral of Second Life and London Internet Church. Today, new Anglican initiatives are more likely to extend local church ministries through online broadcasting and social media conversations. The Church of Scotland's online baptism controversy arose over a proposal to extend participation in local congregations through digital media. My current research is based in Scandinavia, where a similar trend toward social media ministry is underway among the Lutheran state churches.

The growth area of the online church, meanwhile, has been the online campus. It is now very common for large evangelical churches around the world to offer their congregations the chance to participate in worship and teaching online, and the free Church Online Platform and live streaming apps have made that kind of ministry accessible even to the smallest of Christian groups.

In a classic article published more than 15 years ago, Chris Helland proposed a distinction between 'religion online' and 'online religion' (2000, discussed in Chapter 2). This typology divided online religious activity into two categories, separating the efforts of religious institutions to expand their presence online by providing information ('religion online') from the emergence of grassroots communities sharing new kinds of interaction and spiritual experience ('online religion'). Religious institutions soon adapted their approach to adopt more elements of community interaction, but Helland continued to argue that 'you cannot discount issues of control' (2005: 3). Institutions were primarily 'using the medium to support their hierarchical "top down" religious worldview', and preferred to restrict opportunities for free interaction through their online sites. Even if institutions began offering more opportunities for 'online religion' in future, Helland predicted, there would still be 'significant issues concerning the type of participation they will allow for and the types of communication that will occur' (2005: 13).

The first online churches (described in Chapter 1) were good examples of 'online religion', operating outside the boundaries of mainstream denominations and often offering strident critique of the perceived failings of those denominations. By the mid-00s, however, a shift had taken place. The online churches discussed in this book do not fit neatly into Helland's original typology, because they all offer some kind of online community experience and participation in religious ritual while also operating in a relationship with established religious institutions. These churches reflected a new institutional interest in the religious potential of online community. Online churches became part of the co-opting of online religion by religion online.

The developments described in this chapter represent a second shift, and we can adjust Helland's typology to make sense of what has happened. Online churches had already transcended the distinction between information about religion and participation in religion, but the tension Helland identified between grassroots independence and hierarchical control has remained significant. Over the last decade, the degree of control that Christian institutions seek to exert over their online churches has intensified considerably. We can understand this as a shift away from 'online church' (a separate community with institutional oversight) towards 'church online' (an extension of a local church or institution through digital media, focused on the voice of the leader). Denominations and churches are now more likely to use digital media as an extension of their ministries, instead of supporting the growth of independent online communities. Investment in online churches has been replaced by social media ministries and livestreams, while online campuses have exploded in number. It is this idea of extended ministry that distinguishes church online from online church.

We can explain this shift from online church to church online in a number of ways, referring back to the theories explored in Chapters 9 and 10. In Chapter 9, I proposed merging the 'religious-social shaping of technology' (Campbell 2010) with 'mediatization' (Hjarvard 2008) to produce a more nuanced model of 'mediatized religious design' that included attention to discourses of media logic and perceptions of audience expectations as well as attention to the theology, values and practices of a religious community. In Chapter 10, I emphasised the dual nature of online churches, which can be integrated into users' social networks (Rainie and Wellman 2012) or kept separate as private spaces for the exploration of new ideas (Hoover and Echchaibi 2014) or existential vulnerabilities (Lagerkvist 2016). To conclude this chapter, I will briefly indicate the value that these arguments can bring to our understanding of the shift from online church to church online.

For churches that have historically prioritised the words of the sermon, the appeal of church online is clear: the most talented preachers can now extend their voices through digital media to impact global audiences. For denominational churches that have traditionally valued the parish and congregation, this shift is more surprising. Historically, Anglicans have not expected the Archbishop of Canterbury to lead their Bible studies, and yet now he does so on Facebook. These new initiatives are typically justified by arguing that the Church needs to 'learn to relate more effectively to the world and the experience of young people and young adults' (Gledhill 2015), and can do so only by adopting the very latest trends in digital media and digital culture. As the MRD approach suggests, we need to consider perceptions of media logic and audience appeal to understand what is happening, not just the media history or core values of the religious community itself.

One possible explanation for this change emphasises the role of shared metaphor. An earlier generation of Christian pioneers imagined the Internet as a separate 'cyberspace' or 'mission field', a strange and distant world waiting to be colonized by missionaries and church-planters. Today, digital media are more likely to be seen as an integrated part of everyday life, the unremarkable infrastructure of our social networks. The language of mission fields has therefore ceased to resonate, and this change in discourse has implications for digital strategy. If social network sites are not 'places', then they do not need churches: they need communicators and content to share. A shift in discourse about media has led to a new construction of media logic, a different understanding of what must be done to use media effectively.

The continued focus on 'young people' (Gledhill 2015) in online church discourses suggests another, more pragmatic possibility. Throughout their history, online church founders and their institutional supporters have promised a missional reimagining of church that will appeal to contemporary society, particularly to enthusiastic computer users and to younger generations. For denominations with a declining and aging membership, such promises can be very appealing (see, for example, Donnelly 2016).

In practice, however, the online churches analysed in this book were much more likely to attract people who were not particularly young, not especially interested in the cutting edge of technology, and already attending a local church. These communities could be compelling for those who have ceased attending a local church, offering a safe and easy way to reengage with Christian community on their own terms, but the dream of youth revival and cultural reengagement remained elusive. Online churches never managed to win over their theological critics, either: fears of online competition, disembodied relationships and uncommitted digital consumers remain just as prevalent in 2016 as they were in 1996. It is possible that the shift from online church to church online reflects a sense that online churches failed to live up to their perceived potential. They did not attract the young, and they did not persuade the Christian majority, and so their institutional sponsors have moved on in search of something new.

As we saw in Chapter 10, however, the networked approach to digital religion is incomplete. To understand online churches, we must balance their integration into social networks against their isolation from those networks, because participants find value in the boundaries that protect their privacy as well as in open communication. If we really have seen a shift from online church to church online, then studies of 'third spaces' (Hoover and Echchaibi 2014) and the existential approach to media (Lagerkvist 2016) will have important implications for future research. Each theory emphasises the potential for digital media to provide spaces that are separate from the institutions and structures of daily life, within which individuals can critique those structures and reflect on their own vulnerability—but what happens to those spaces in the new forms of online ministry?

The online churches analysed in this book were not just extensions of Christian institutions and tools for pursuing institutional goals, but places that existed in-between institution and individual, on the margins of institutional attention, where new ideas, roles and practices could be explored and played with. Even in Church Online, the example most closely integrated into an existing religious system, we still encountered independent, sometimes anarchic spaces in LifeGroups, Watch Parties and Second Life. Online churches were integrated into users' social and religious networks, but much of their value for participants was founded on separation. These churches needed to have the option of a boundary, within which participants felt safe to explore ideas and roles that were not available to them elsewhere. That boundary could be protected by pseudonymity or passwords or simply by the ephemerality of conversations in chatrooms and virtual worlds.

In contrast, the collapse of boundaries is one of the key functions of social media. On Facebook and many other social networks, identities are known. Social media updates can build or destroy reputations, and messages are crafted to entertain the widest possible audience. For Christian institutions, this move to a more open and connected Internet offers opportunities to connect with wider audiences by training followers to perform their faith attractively. This is a key aspect of the vision behind the 'church online' approach, from LifeChurch's focus on 'invitations' to the Church of England's use of Periscope. This same shift may come at a cost for participants, undermining much of what once made digital religion worthwhile.

As the shift from online church to church online continues to gather pace, studies of Mediatized Religious Design will be needed to help track the changing visions of audience expectations and media logic that are driving the emergence of new models of online ministry. Attention to the integration of digital religion into wider social and religious networks and circulations can help us to see how these ministries become meaningful for participants, and how they fit into everyday religious lives. The third space and existential approaches to digital media, meanwhile, should encourage researchers to look more closely at the future of digital religion, to see where spaces for reflection, critique and vulnerability might remain—or might be carved out—within an online religious landscape that is becoming more public, more performative and potentially more institutional.

References

ArchbishopofCanterbury.org, 2016. Archbishop of Canterbury hosts live Bible study on Facebook. *archbishopofcanterbury.org*, 19 May. [online] Available at: <http://www.archbishopofcanterbury.org/articles.php/5719/archbishop-of-canterbury-hosts-live-bible-study-on-facebook> [Accessed 1 September 2016]

Bingham, J., 2015. Church of England to live-stream services for those who find it "scary" to sit in pews. *The Telegraph*, 1 June. [online] Available at: <http://www.telegraph.co.uk/news/religion/11643612/Church-of-England-to-live-stream-services-for-those-who-find-it-scary-to-sit-in-pews.html> [Accessed 1 September 2016]

Campbell, H., 2010. *When Religion Meets New Media*. London: Routledge.

Casserly, M., 2015. What happened to online churches? *Christian Today*, 30 May. [online] Available at: <http://www.christiantoday.com/article/what.happened.to.online.churches /54701.htm> [Accessed 1 September 2016]

Church of England, 2015. Church of England partners with Twitter to launch new "@ChurchLive" service, 8 October. [press release] Available at: <https://www.churchofengland.org/media-centre/news/2015/10/church-of-england-partners-with-twitter-to-launch-new-"@churchlive"-service.aspx> [Accessed 1 September 2016]

Church of Scotland, 2016. Church dismisses media reports of "online baptism", 19 May. [press release] Available at: <http://www.churchofscotland.org.uk/news_and_events/news/recent/church_dismisses_media_reports_of_online_baptism> [Accessed 1 September 2016]

Donnelly, B., 2016. Kirk to consider online baptisms. *Herald of Scotland*, 17 May. [online] Available at: <http://www.heraldscotland.com/news/14496669.Kirk__to_introduce_online_baptism__in_bid_to_boost_membership/> [Accessed 31 August 2016]

Faith & Leadership, 2016. Teen's online church draws young people from around the world. *Faith & Leadership*, 23 August. [blog] Available at: <https://www.faithandleadership. com/teens-online-church-draws-young-people-around-world> [Accessed 2 September 2016]

Freezing Sorbet, 2012. The Anglican Cathedral of second life (fly-by). [online video] Available at: <https://vimeo.com/user12881452/> [Accessed 31 August 2016]

Gelfgren, S. and Hutchings, T., 2014. The virtual construction of the sacred: Representation and fantasy in the architecture of Second Life churches. *Nordic Journal of Religion and Society* 27(1), pp. 59–73.

George, A., n.d. Why the street team exists. *Life.Church*. [online] Available at: <http://info.life.church/life.church-online-street-team/> [Accessed 2 September 2016]

———, 2015. Searching for Church Online. *Church Online*, 30 November. [blog] Available at: <http://churchonline.life.church/searching-for-church-online-in-india/> [Accessed 2 September 2016]

Geraci, R., 2014. *Virtually Sacred: Myth and Meaning in World of Warcraft and Second Life*. Oxford: Oxford University Press.

Gledhill, R., 2015. Church of England seeks "online pastor" to boost digital engagement. *Christian Today*, 23 January. [online] Available at: <http://www.christiantoday.com/article/church.of.england.seeks.online.pastor.to.boost.digital.engagement/46591.htm> [Accessed 2 September 2016]

Groeschel, C., 2015. *#Struggles: Following Jesus in a Selfie-Centred World*. Grand Rapids: Zondervan.

Hailes, S., 2015. I attended an online church, here's what happened. *Premier Christianity*, 4 November. [blog] Available at: <https://www.premierchristianity.com/Blog/I-attended-an-online-church-here-s-what-happened> [Accessed 2 September 2016]

Helland, C., 2000. Online-religion/religion-online and virtual communitas. In: Hadden, J. and Cowan, D., eds. *Religion on the Internet: Research Prospects and Promises*. London: JAI Press. pp. 205–224.

———, 2005. Online religion as lived religion: Methodological issues in the study of religious participation on the Internet. *Online: Heidelberg Journal of Religions on the Internet* 1(1), pp. 1–16.

Hjarvard, S., 2008. The mediatization of religion: A theory of the media as agents of religious change. *Northern Lights: Film & Media Studies Yearbook* 6(1), pp. 9–26.

Hoover, S. and Echchaibi, N., 2014. Media theory and the "third spaces of digital religion". [pdf] Boulder, Colorado: The Center for Media, Religion and Culture. Available at <https://thirdspacesblog.files.wordpress.com/2014/05/third-spaces-and-media-theory-essay-2-0.pdf> [Accessed 28 August 2016]

Lagerkvist, A., 2016. Existential media: Toward a theory of digital thrownness. *New Media & Society*, pp. 1–15. [pdf] Available at: <http://nms.sagepub.com/content/early/2016/06/10/1461444816649921.full.pdf> [Accessed 28 August 2016]

Life.Church, 2014. Celebrating 5 million with Pastor Craig. *Church Online*, 24 November. [blog] Available at: < http://churchonline.life.church/celebrating-5-million-pastor-craig> [Accessed 2 September 2016]

Lindridge, E., 2013. D-church. *Fresh Expressions*, 14 May. [online] Available at: <https://www.freshexpressions.org.uk/stories/d-church> [Accessed 2 September 2016]

Media Fusion, 2014. Media Fusion works with Church Online platform. *Media Fusion*. [online] Available at: <http://mediafusionapp.com/media-fusion-works-with-church-online-platform/> [Accessed 2 September 2016]

Milena, H., 2011. Leadership team report April and May 2011. *The Anglican Cathedral of Second Life* [blog] 24 May. Available at: <https://slangcath.wordpress.com/2011/05/24/ leadership-team-report-april-and-may-2011/> [Accessed 2 September 2016]

Rainie, L. and Wellman, B., 2012. *Networked: The New Social Operating System*. Cambridge: MIT Press.

Robertson, D., 2016. The invisible church, cyber theology and online baptism. *The Wee Flea*, 19 May. [blog] Available at: < https://theweeflea.com/2016/05/19/the-invisible-church-cyber-theology-and-online-baptism/> [Accessed 2 September 2016]

Smith, P., 2015. *Online Mission and Ministry: A Theological and Practical Guide*. London: SPCK.

Sun, E., 2011. Church in your pocket? Facebook multimedia church ready to launch. *The Christian Post*, 30 April. [online] Available at: <http://www.christianpost.com/news/church-in-your-pocket-facebook-multimedia-church-to-launch-50045/> [Accessed 2 September 2016]

Walmseley, A., 2014. Lights, camera, action! Exeter church offers Sunday service online. *Exeter Express & Echo*, 13 November. [online] Available at: <http://www.exeter expressandecho.co.uk/lights-camera-action-exeter-church-offers-sunday/story-24518843-detail/story.html> [Accessed 1 September 2016]

Index

age *see* membership surveys
Alpha Church 14
Anglican: digital projects 12, 248;
   High Church 71, 78, 155; reports on
   digital media 10, 31, 43; in Second
   Life 145, 163–4; *see also* Anglican
   Cathedral of Second Life; bishop;
   fresh expressions; i-church
Anglican Cathedral of Second Life 1–2,
   38–9, 140–67, 215–16, 249–51
architecture, virtual: in the Anglican
   Cathedral of Second Life 143–4,
   151–7, 216, 249; in Church of Fools
   69–70; familiarity and innovation in
   40–3, 205; in LifeChurch's Second
   Life Campus 187–91
atheism 75, 183
Au, W.J. 18, 60
authority: independent online
   leadership 165, 236–7, 251;
   online loss of 43–4, 255; over
   decision-making 1–2, 103–4, 106,
   119, 178; structures of oversight 96,
   98, 121, 249–50; validity 99, 162,
   178; *see also* bishop; ethnography, as
   group leader; moderators
avatar: design 72, 118–19, 157–60;
   ethnicity 120, 159, 160; gender 2, 60,
   160; gestures 72, 74, 77, 145, 148,
   150; identification with 73–4, 119;
   use in trolling 81, 163, 238

baptism, online 13, 37–40, 243
Barna, G. 17, 25–7
Barret, J. 41–2, 70
Becker, P.E. 105
Bennetson, H. 158
Bennett, J.M. 162
Bible: digital projects 65, 101, 179; in
   preaching 176; readings in church 66,

136, 245; study 98, 100, 163, 196; as
   topic of discussion 122–5, 186
bishop, as supporters of online churches
   5, 6, 17, 67, 80, 110–11, 145, 215,
   249–50; as critics of online churches
   15, 32, 39; *see also* Partenia
blogging 44–5, 61, 117, 125–8, 238
Boellstorff, T. 60, 62, 229–30
boundaries *see* privacy
Brown, M. 140, 144–9, 151–2, 155,
   205, 215–16

Campbell, H.: and authority 44;
   and community 12, 26, 32; and
   evangelism 28, 171; and the
   religious-social shaping of technology
   203–9, 215, 217; and research
   methods 59; and ritual 36, 221
Catholic: *The Church and Internet* 19,
   25, 32, 35, 44; examples of online
   initiatives 12, 14, 18–19, 20, 211,
   247; online impersonation 19, 160;
   Pope and social media 45–6
Cheong, P.H. 44–5
Church, definition of 2–3, 20, 99–100
Church, local: attendance statistics 68,
   97–9, 118, 146, 227; not attending
   local church 82, 92, 98–9, 103, 131,
   178; *see also* disability and ill-health
Church, online: acceptable alternative
   to local church 12, 15, 17, 25–6,
   30, 92; changes over time 8, 242–4,
   254–6; compared to local church
   by users 99, 178, 227–9, 236;
   dangerous rival to local church 25,
   33; early examples 10–11; early
   study of 4, 12, 14; eternal newness
   of 29, 244; supplement to local
   church 26–7, 31, 226–7; themes
   in study of 24, 52